MEDICINE AND THE BIBLE

MEDICINE
AND THE
BIBLE

Editor

Bernard Palmer

Published for the Christian Medical Fellowship by
THE PATERNOSTER PRESS
EXETER

AUSTRALIA
Bookhouse Australia Ltd.,
P.O. Box 115, Flemington Markets,
N.S.W. 2129.

SOUTH AFRICA
Oxford University Press,
P.O. Box 1141, Cape Town.

British Library Cataloguing in Publication Data

Medicine and the Bible.
1. Medicine in the Bible
I. Palmer, Bernard II. Christian Medical Fellowship
220.8'61 R135.5

ISBN 0-85364-423-3

Typeset by Photoprint, 9–11 Alexandra Lane, Torquay, Devon and Printed in Great Britain for The Paternoster Press, Paternoster House, 3 Mount Radford Crescent, Exeter, Devon by A. Wheaton & Co Ltd, Exeter, Devon.

Contents

Contributors

The Late Stanley G. Browne, C.M.G., O.B.E., M.D., F.R.C.P., F.R.C.S., D.T.M., F.K.C., K.L.J.

Past Secretary, International Leprosy Association; Past Consultant Adviser in Leprosy, Department of Health and Social Security

Averell S. Darling, M.B., B.Ch., D.P.H.

Specialist in Community Medicine, Stockport

Colin J. Hemer, M.A., Ph.D.

Research Fellow, Tyndale House, Cambridge

Roger F. Hurding, M.A., M.B., B.Chir.(Cantab.), D.R.C.O.G.

Counsellor, Psychotherapist and Author; Past Medical Officer, Student Health Service, University of Bristol

Douglas M. Jackson, M.A., M.D., F.R.C.S.

Formerly Consultant Surgeon, Birmingham Accident Hospital

David R. Millar, F.R.C.S.(Ed.), F.R.C.O.G.

Consultant Obstetrician and Gynaecologist, Jessop Hospital for Women, Sheffield

Bernard V. Palmer, M.A., M.B., M.Chir.(Cantab.), M.R.C.P., F.R.C.S.

Consultant Surgeon, Lister Hospital, Stevenage

Andrew C. P. Sims, M.A., M.D., F.R.C.Psych.

Professor of Psychiatry, University of Leeds

Richard Winter, M.B., B.S., M.R.C.Psych.

L'Abri Fellowship, Greatham, Liss, Hampshire

Donald J. Wiseman, OBE, D.Litt., FBA

Emeritus Professor of Assyriology in the University of London

Preface

The idea for this book was first put forward several years ago by the late Mr. C. G. Scorer and Dr. Douglas Johnson, who were concerned to establish the essential relationship between the Bible and Medicine.

Many people today assume that the 'age of science' has displaced the 'age of the Bible'. Modern man no longer regards the Bible as the authentic Word of God in the way that Jesus and his contemporaries viewed the Old Testament Scriptures, or as the Church has traditionally regarded the Bible as a whole. The concept that science is the only arbiter of truth is commonly held in medical circles, although there are insuperable problems with this view. For example, science can give no light on questions of purpose or morality, and while the achievements made possible through medical research have brought great benefits to mankind, we are in danger of losing a knowledge of the principles of behaviour that are set out for us in the Bible. The two disciplines need each other, for the ability to achieve an end does not necessarily make it right. Sir Herbert Bragg, the Cambridge scientist, wrote: 'From religion comes man's purpose; from science his power to achieve it. Sometimes people ask if science and religion are not opposed to one another. They are; in the sense that the thumb and fingers of my hand are opposed to one another. It is an opposition by means of which anything can be grasped.'

Following the untimely death of Jim Scorer in 1981 the original plan of the book had to be reconsidered. A new editor was appointed and new authors commissioned. The resulting work is an up-to-date survey of some of the most important issues facing the medical profession today as seen in the light of the teaching of the Bible.

The book is in two sections. In the opening chapters two eminent scholars describe medical practice in Old and New Testament times. They have included much new material which helps to increase our understanding of the context and meaning of many of the incidents recorded in the Bible. For example, to realize that Moses in all likelihood attended the Royal University at Heliopolis, where students learned to speak five languages and read eight texts (one of which was on medicine), does help our understanding of the Pentateuch. A chapter on the Levitical Code is included because of the popular misunderstanding that this is basically a code of rules for public health, and the one on Leprosy shows how biblical 'leprosy' differs from the disease we recognize today.

The second section contains articles written on a selection of current medical topics to show the relevance of biblical principles to modern medical practice. Each is written by a doctor with particular experience in the subject. Supernatural Healing and Demon Possession are included since they attract wide public interest and concern and seem to lie outside a strictly scientific view of a world which discounts the possibility of external influences on its workings. The chapter on the Value of Human Life deals with abortion, IVF, the care of the newborn and euthanasia. Homosexuality remains a live issue, and Dr Richard Winter contributes a wide ranging discussion on the historical, legal, medical and ethical aspects, and also considers the possibility of change in an individual's sexual orientation. The final chapter deals with the question of the conscience of the doctor in his practice of medicine.

This book will appeal to all who have an interest in the relationship between the Bible and Medicine—to Bible expositors, teachers and researchers who want to obtain a deeper understanding of medical practice in Bible times; to members of the medical and other caring professions who are concerned to apply biblical precepts to their work; and to all who see in the Bible a precept for living in the confused social climate of the 1980's.

The editor would like to pay tribute to the late Mr Jim Scorer and to Dr Douglas Johnson who originally planned this book and did much to ensure its production. Much editorial work and advice on the preparation of the mss. for publication has been given by the Rev. John Rivers, whose skill has been invaluable.

The publication of this book completes the original plan which was for a trilogy of books. The other two volumes have already been published. *Decision Making in Medicine* (1979) deals with a number of ethical issues that doctors and surgeons have to face in day-to-day practice. *The Influence of Christians in Medicine* (1984) is a historical work that traces the impact of the Christian faith in individuals who have influenced the development of medicine from the earliest times until now. Both are available from the Christian Medical Fellowship Office in London.

BERNARD PALMER

1

Medicine in the Old Testament World

DONALD J. WISEMAN

Medical references in the Bible always need to be examined in relation to similar information obtainable from the contemporary ancient Near East. Many aspects of the civilizations of ancient Egypt, Assyria, Babylonia and the Hittites (living in Anatolia/Turkey and Syria) can now be studied in detail from the thousands of papyri, clay tablets written in the cuneiform script, and other written and usually dateable inscriptions. Some knowledge became widely diffused by the interchange of scholars and messengers between the royal courts of these early kingdoms, and medicine was included for its obvious widespread demand and interest. In each country local practices and remedies are attested. This chapter is an attempt to bring together, mainly from Egyptian and Babylonian sources, a picture of the medical knowledge with which the scattered references and incidents recorded in the Old Testament may be readily compared.

Ancient Sources

With the advent of writing in Babylonia c.3000 BC and in Egypt soon thereafter, (and with the development of various alphabet scripts from c.1000 BC) recording and dissemination of texts, including medical data, is widespread. References are found in many types of literature, historical annals and chronicles, literary epics, poems and in letters and administrative documents, quite apart from those of primary medical intent. Most of these provide direct, contemporary and reliable data though interpretation is often difficult. They give us an insight into the medical practices in the ancient Near East which were known, sometimes through secondary and later sources, to classical writers such as Herodotus, Strabo, Diodorus Siculus and others on whom our understanding of these early steps in medicine once relied.

In *Egypt*, though medical traditions go back to the Vizier Imhotep c.2700 BC, the oldest surviving treatise (Edwin Smith Papyrus) dates from c.1600 BC and is mainly concerned with the treatment of wounds, injuries and fractures and describes the clinical examination and procedures to be carried out in forty-eight different cases described topographically from the head downwards. The level of knowledge revealed was not otherwise attained until later classical Greek times or in England in the sixteenth century AD. Other sixteenth century BC papyri include the lengthy text (20m long with 877 sections in 10 columns) of the Ebers Papyrus which was based on earlier originals. Following an introduction on 'magical' treatments it collects details of prescriptions of treatment to be used for digestive troubles, eyes, skin, gynaecological, heart and 'arterial' ailments, as well as of surgery of tumours and abscesses. This, with the almost contemporary Hearst and Berlin Papyri, a third of whose 269 sections duplicate the Ebers papyrus, is a major source for the study of the pathology and therapy practised at the Egyptian court at the time of the early Hebrews' stay in the land. Other Egyptian texts, while mixing magic and medicine, offer further valuable insights[1] as do paleopathological studies of disease in human remains based on the examination of more than 30,000 skulls, skeletons and mummies.[2]

In *Mesopotamia* (ancient Iraq-Syria, the home of the Babylonians and Assyrians) isolated medical texts in Sumerian go back to c.2100 BC,[3] while the major texts written down c.1680 BC already group together into a series of clay tablets their concern with medical traditions and treatments. One group of therapeutic texts with prescriptions (the Assyrian *Vademecum*)[4] remained unchanged in content from the fourteenth to the seventh centuries BC when many copies of medical texts were made for the royal library of King Ashurbanipal at Nineveh.[5] These were furnished with commentaries to explain archaic terms, more modern names of plants were added to their older equivalents, and the ancient origin of 'tried and tested' remedies noted. There are details of the contents of an apothecary's stock of the fourteenth century BC which consisted mainly of seeds and dried substances and special oils but no ready made-up prescriptions. This was the source from which others sought the ingredients for their pills, potions and poultices which were prepared with oils, milk and beer. The pharmacopoeia lists plants and sometimes the illness in which they were considered effective.

In Babylonia the most copied medical texts were a series of reference books (forty clay tablets) of a diagnostic series entitled: 'When the practitioner (*āšipu*) enters the house of a sick person'. This gives observations of the patient, physical and mental, followed by a brief and sometimes detailed prognosis. Some texts abstract diagnosis and prognosis according to a given part of the anatomy, disease or those ailments considered to have a fatal outcome. Prognosis ranges between 'he will live' and 'he will die', sometimes with forecasts, up to seven days, of how long the patient might linger. This was the basis of Babylonian medicine from the tenth to the fourth centuries BC when the increasing influence of consulting omens or astrological texts giving favourable or unfavourable days for medical treatment, or listing the winds ('humours') thought to bring disease, is found.

Medical Practitioners

The Old Testament makes only incidental references to the 'healer' (Heb. *rōpē'*) and most are to foreigners. A 'physician' embalmed Jacob in Egypt (Gen. 50:2), while those of Gilead were considered worthless (Jer. 8:22; cf. Job 13:4). Hosea implies that Ephraim turned for a cure to an Assyrian physician (5:13) and this is criticized as was Asa's reliance on 'idolatrous' physicians rather than on God himself (2 Chron. 16:12). God was the Healer above all others. The story of Naaman implies a knowledge in neighbouring countries of eminent healers in Israel and the interchange of letters between courts on medical matters is attested throughout the ancient Near East (2 Kgs. 5:3). That prophets, and priests, included the role of 'physician' is implied in several references (2 Sam. 12:14; 1 Kgs. 14:1–13; 17:18; 2 Kgs. 1:1–4; 4:22; 8:9–10; Isa. 38:1,21) and ordinary people probably had recourse to them when other local practitioners failed. The mention of rational remedies and the emphasis on preventive medicine and hygiene (as in *Leviticus*) implies a corpus of indigenous medical knowledge.

Later tradition ascribes to Noah the authorship of a medical textbook which was passed to Shem and down to Abraham.[6] To this Moses could have added knowledge gained in Egypt, as did Solomon and his heirs from contacts with Near Eastern traditions elsewhere. By 190 BC professional physicians were well respected in Israel and apparently included some Greeks. 'Honour the doctor for his services for the Lord has appointed him. His skill comes from the Most High and even kings reward him . . .' (Ecclus. 38:1–15).

EGYPT In Egypt two kind of doctors were recognized: the *hry-hзb*, 'carrier of the ritual book' of magical incantations, an 'exorcist', and the *synw* or 'physician doctor'. Both probably underwent a formal training based on traditions passed from father to son, of which it was said that 'the laws judged that few physicians would ever be wiser than the way of treatment followed so long and prescribed originally by the ablest physicians'.[7] The *synw* appear to have been state employees, or attached to the household of the king or noble. Some were appointed to work in the army, factories or in burial grounds. Promotion was from physician to physician inspector, chief physician, court physician to chief of palace physicians and ultimately chief physician of the king. Specialization, though never exclusive of general practice, is found in the Old Kingdom period (c.2700—2300 BC) with doctors known for their work on the abdomen, anus, eyes, teeth or 'inner liquids' and the like. Thereafter, specialization seems almost to have faded out and some have attributed this to increasing knowledge of anatomy and pathology with an emphasis on the unity of the human body. However, about 420 BC Herodotus claims that in Egypt 'every physician treats one disease not many; some are physicians for the eyes, others for the head, teeth, abdomen or for unknown diseases'.[8] Throughout all periods prominent medicals and their cases were depicted on the monuments and named in texts.[9] One shows a physician receiving gold from the king in fourteenth century BC Amarna, another being consulted by a Syrian prince. A few female physicians under a chief are named but their function is not given.

The physicians were supported by nurses and bandagers who had as their main text *The Book of Bandagists*. These were associated also with the art of embalming. It is not known whether they worked in groups, though the 'House of Life' (*per-ankh*) attached to temples may have housed sick-rooms as well as medical libraries and documentation centres. Some inscribed potsherds have been interpreted as 'bedside notes' with medical recipes, perhaps made by students.

ANCIENT MESOPOTAMIA From the earliest times respect was accorded to the physician (*asû*), one of whom is depicted with his forceps and an attendant deity on a carved cylinder seal dated c.2000 BC.[10] This class of therapeutic practitioner was skilled and experienced and was concerned also with the preparation and application of drugs, pills, potions, poultices, suppositories, purgatives and bandages. His precise relationship to the 'exorcist'-psychologist, magician-diviner (*āšipu*) is not yet known. The latter, from the mid-second millennium onwards, sought by incantations, rituals and laying on of hands to bring the patient into harmony with the gods. As such he has been considered a 'member of the clergy'. It is likely that each complemented the other in practice, as did their Egyptian counterparts. Both were learned and literate, shared many of the same reference books, and have been compared with the barber-surgeon and physician of medieval England.

BABYLONIA Here the tradition of medicine was long and unbroken according to extant text copies. Herodotus' allusion to the lack of physicians in Babylon in his day and to the practice of laying the sick out in a (temple[?]-) square for advice from passers-by may refer to sick quarters being assigned in temples as at Nippur (c.1350 BC) when a written request was sent from a temple area set aside for female patients for urgent advice from a superior official.[11]

The status of the physician was high, due mainly to the demands of the royal courts. A Babylonian king asks the Hittite ruler for the urgent return of a doctor who had been on loan to their court despite the fact that other Babylonian and Egyptian physicians had been in attendance there for some years. Other letters from the Mari court on the River Euphrates underline the demand for medical help. 'One of my boys is ill with an abscess below his ear discharging. Two physicians who are with me are bandaging him but his fever has not altered. Now let my lord send the physician Mardamanu who is a competent doctor so that he may examine the fever and rebandage him so that his sickness will not be prolonged.' 'Let the physician Merānu come quickly and save Rishiya's life lest she die. She is terribly ill and in danger of death.'[12] In some way the physician must have been an easily recognizable member of the community for in one old Babylonian humorous tale a poor man disguises himself as a physician in order to gain access to the mayor's private apartments and gain revenge by beating him up.[13] There is certainly no evidence to support the interpretation of a later account by Herodotus[14] that there were no physicians or medical texts in Babylon in the fifth century BC and so the sick were laid out in a square for passers-by to pronounce on them.[15]

Attitudes to Health, Disease and Medicine

In lands where disease was endemic much emphasis was placed

on healthiness, that is the absence of disease. In the ancient world the Egyptians had the reputation, next to the Libyans, of being the healthiest,[16] though they, like their neighbours, had no specific word for 'health' in the sense of 'being well'. For the Babylonians the ideal was to be 'one who is perfect in body and mind' and for them as for the Hebrews health was 'well-being, wholeness, peace' of body, mind and spirit in harmony with the environment and with god.[17] This is reflected also in personal names.[18] When health was lost, the concern was to regain it.[19]

Life was considered the gift of the god(s) and they, for reasons usually unknown or unknowable, could send or allow disease. Sickness was commonly considered to be the result of divine displeasure for some sin, wittingly or unwittingly committed. Thus disease might be classified as 'striking' or 'seizure' or 'the hand of god', usually of a deity known both as the inflicter and the healer. Similarly, some diseases were 'the hand of (evil) spirits' and amulets were frequently worn to ward them off. In Egypt the god Seth was a noted source of sickness. Other deities were particularly associated with healing, largely because their spheres included the incantation necessary to obtain a remedy. Among these were Thoth, the patron of science and magic, and Isis as patroness of medicine. Initially Amon, as healer of the common eye diseases, and later Horus, as representing both the sun and the moon, were thought to be the healers *par excellence*.

In Babylonia, though the sun deity Shamash and Ishtar, the goddess of love and war, were those who inflicted illness and healed, the god most frequently associated with healing was Gula, whose symbol was a dog.

It is noteworthy that these deities were not closely associated with the 'magic' or divinatory techniques which also play a part in healing. A sick ruler might consult both a physician and an 'exorcist', the latter to direct the prayers for healing and the appropriate rituals and incantations which occur for specific ailments, e.g. snake or scorpion bites. The rituals include washings, fumigations and actions based on the principle of similarity or homeopathy to lead to the transfer of evil by symbolic acts, charms or even dreams. Amulets or seals and other charms were worn to ward off the evil spirits or demons. Some plaques, perhaps hung up in a sick room, depict medical scenes illustrating the folk medicine of the time.[20]

In contrast to Egypt and Mesopotamia, the Hebrews with their strong monotheism viewed their God as the true healer. 'He forgives all my sins and heals all my diseases' (Ps. 103:3; cf. Acts 3:12–16). To him was attributed healing of men (Gen. 20:17) and women (Num. 12:13). The occurrence of personal names such as 'Asayâ (Yahweh heals) lends support to this, but similar names also occur in Egypt and Ugarit.[21] Their prayers for healing were directed to the Lord God (Yahweh) alone and resorting to divination, omens, exorcists or sorcerers was forbidden by law and was an abomination to the Lord (Lev. 18; 19:31; 20:6). Such techniques for ascertaining the divine will were foreign. The association of prayer with healing may have been universal for it occurs frequently in the Old Testament, e.g. Miriam (Num. 12:13), Hezekiah (Isa: 38.1) and Jeremiah (17:14). This was not dissimilar in intent to the letter-prayers, calling for healing from specific diseases or for a longer life, that were placed in Babylonian temples.[22]

In summary, throughout the ancient world of Old Testament times the sick sought for the practitioner of 'pure' medicine and for spiritual relief through prayer while at the same time making the fullest use of 'folk medicine'. It could be argued from the extant text that the Hebrews also laid special stress on physical 'wholeness', ritually acquired, as a necessary reflection of the desired spiritual well-being pictured in the social hygiene and sanitary regulations in *Leviticus*, which comprise 213 of the total of 613 biblical commands and prohibitions.[23]

Knowledge of Anatomy and Physiology

Throughout the area from the earliest times animals were slaughtered for meat or for sacrifice. The latter were scanned for divinatory purposes and this led to a detailed knowledge of the liver and lungs of sheep and to a developing veterinary science.[24] Egyptians and Babylonians used terms applied to animal anatomy for the corresponding human internal organs. Some additional observations were made on the wounded or corpses. Though the Egyptian embalming techniques rely on a high level of observation, there is no evidence that they, or the Babylonians, ever dissected human bodies.[25] Plinius, and first century AD rabbinic traditions, recount how Cleopatra brought before the king pregnant slaves who had been condemned to death so that they could be cut open to observe the development of the fetus.[26] But normally the reverence for life and for the dead would preclude such actions.

Observation of the external parts of the body was meticulous and detailed and always ran from the top of the head to the soles of the feet. The same applies to the Hebrews who employed early, mainly bi-consonantal, roots for naming the major parts of the body.[27] The terms, though used with their literal meaning, also became the basis of idiomatic expressions. For example the 'heart' (AV Heb. *leb(ab)*, cf. Akkadian *libbu*), though occurring 827 times in the OT, was never used of that physical organ, though for them it denoted the inside of the body,[28] the stomach, belly, entrails, or more frequently the mind or emotions. Idiomatically it was used of the heart failing, panting, and the mind sinking in fear or anguish, and most frequently to denote emotion.[29] Nevertheless, the palpitation of the heart, especially under stress, was recognized[30] and both Egyptians and Babylonians observed the pulse rate without counting it and recorded the points of the body at which it can best be felt.[31] The Babylonians seem not to have connected the heart with the supply of blood to various parts of the body but the Egyptians, who described the pulse as 'the heart speaks', did so.[32]

They conceived of the heart as connected with other vessels and receiving air and water through the 'receiver' (aorta)[33] and with the vessels connecting it with every limb named with its own god. The relation of the heart to the lungs was known.[34]

The liver, well known from the many sacrifices for divinatory purposes, was designated 'the heavy' organ of the viscera[35] and was regarded as the seat of the strong emotions of happiness and anger. The Ebers Papyrus (477–481) said that the liver had four 'canals' or channels leading from it to carry faecal matter. Diseases of the liver were usually treated by a diet of fruit.[36]

The Hebrews had other terms for the abdomen and intestines which in general denoted the belly or 'bowels'.[37] Since it made rumbling sounds (Isa. 63:15 AV. cf. 16:11) and stirred (Job 30:27 AV) in sympathy, this part became a synonym for that emotion.[38] The kidneys (AV 'reins') were primarily referred to as the seat of affection and joy (Ps. 139:13; Prov. 23:6) and, since they were the most used organ from sacrificial animals, were considered as always open to the divine scrutiny.[39] Compared with the detailed knowledge of the external body, contemporary knowledge of 'internal' anatomy was very general, though many individual items are named. The Hebrews, according to the Mishnah, name 248 bones against the Egyptian and Babylonian 200.[40]

Specific Ailments

WOUNDS of various types and causes are described, e.g. piercing (Isa. 53:5), crushed or bruised, infected, all the Hebrew terms for trauma following the same lexical pattern.[41] Or they were classified generally, as was any injury, as 'severe' (Jer. 10:19; Nah. 3:19) or 'incurable' (Jer. 15:18; Mic.1:9; Job 34:6). The Egyptians give one 'remedy for a wound: the first day (apply) meat (or grease?) of an ox until it suppurates; but if it suppurates too much then you will bandage it with mouldy barley bread until it is dried up . . . if it closes over its effluency then you will prepare grease and . . . bandage it until its mouth is opened and it suppurates.'[42] The application of the meat was presumably to prevent haemorrhaging and the mouldy bread may have served as an elementary antibiotic. The Babylonians siphoned off pus to prevent the fetid wound smelling (cf. Ps. 38:5).[43] The common dressings were oil, honey, and astringent herbs, especially cedar-resin. The lips of clean wounds were closed by an adhesive tape or by stitching. It was considered fatal when injuries from the sole of the foot to the top of the head included 'opened wounds and welts and opened sores not cleansed or bandaged or soothed with oil' (Isa. 1:6). The technical vocabulary for the different styles and types of bandage is extensive in Egyptian and Babylonian.[44]

FRACTURES and 'wound surgery' were the main subject of the Smith Papyrus and paleopathological studies attest fractures of skull, ribs, thorax, vertebrae and limbs. Open fractures were usually considered fatal. Egyptian monuments picture the setting of a dislocated shoulder, though they appear to have had no knowledge of traction. From predynastic times fractured long bones were set in splints. The Hebrews refer to this in the case of the broken arm of a Pharaoh 'not bound up, or put in a splint to become strong enough to hold a sword again' (Ezek. 30:21).

OPERATIVE SURGERY was practised in Egypt and Mesopotamia. This was most frequently employed to lance abscesses (variously described as 'tumours' or 'boils' in the texts) with a knife heated in a fire. Care was taken not to touch 'leprous' tumours, aneurysms or varicose veins, nor to pierce 'veins' to avoid haemorrhage. A blister was usually pierced with a thorn.[45] Drainage was assisted by inserting a reed. Many 'tumours' (perhaps benign or cysts) were left smeared with ointment until they ulcerated, then opened and cleared, especially if they contained a capsule.

Seventh century BC skulls from Lachish (Tell-ed-Duweir) and elsewhere, including Egypt, have been found with a hole at the top usually thought to have been caused by trepanning. This has recently been questioned, but an earlier Babylonian text seems to refer to the opening of the cranium to relieve pressure.[46] A liver abscess after dysentery was treated by incision 'between the third and fourth ribs' (=8–9th). In the second millennium BC in Babylonia a number of 'Caesarean sections' were performed when the mother died in labour and it was suspected that the child was still alive. Since all the patients were slave-girls, it is assumed that the motivation was economic rather than humanitarian.[47] There is the record of the lancing of a carbuncle in the eye with a bronze instrument leading to a loss of sight and the surgeon being penalized by having his hand off. This was a special case and since we do not know the precise circumstances behind this legal decision by King Hammurapi (c.1700 BC),[48] it indicates not so much a particular attitude to surgery as the fact that such operations were commonplace. Amputation of hands, noses or genitals was a punishment meted out to enemies and criminals alike and is alluded to frequently in ancient curses. There is one attested case of amputation in a mummy of the Egyptian IXth Dynasty.

Nothing is known of the method of castration of eunuchs. Indeed the number of these has probably been exaggerated. The evidence appears to be drawn from the presence of beardless youngsters pictured on the monuments. Some eunuchs were employed in the royal household and as singers. Circumcision seems not to have been practised in Mesopotamia, and in Egypt and Israel it was not usually performed by physicians.[49] Illustrations of the act are given on Egyptian reliefs. Surgical instruments are shown on reliefs and a knife was part of the Egyptian hieroglyphic writing of 'physician'. A number of small knives found in excavations have been interpreted as surgical instruments, but this is often questionable. There are no direct references to anaesthesia, though the 'deep sleep' into which God made Adam pass while a rib was removed (Gen. 2:21) has been so interpreted by some. Sedatives (opium and belladonna) were freely available and for local application on the skin an unidentified paste was used.[50]

DEFORMITIES Physical deformities and handicap were referred to in all ages and areas. Both the Hebrews and Babylonians employed technical terminology for them based on distinctive nominal forms.[51] Such persons were helped and not ostracized, nor were they the object of malice or superstition. In Israel they were, however, precluded from the priesthood or from participating in the ritual of the tabernacle and temple, for 'no man with any defect (may come near to offer food to his God); no man who is blind or lame, disfigured or deformed; no man with a crippled foot or hand, or who is hunchbacked or dwarfed, or who has any eye defect, or who has festering or running sores or damaged testicles' (Lev. 21:18–20). The principle was that such defective persons, like any defective offerings (Deut. 15:21) would detract from the wholeness (holiness) of God. Respected individuals bear a name denoting their deformity, probably incurred at birth. Paseah was presumably 'lame' (Neh. 3:6; 7:51) and 'the limper' was a figure used of God's erring people (Mic. 4:6,7; Zeph. 3:19). The care of the lame, as of the blind, widows and fatherless, was a bench-mark in all societies of the way the rulers exercised social justice in response to the divine call.[52] The lame were a picture of helplessness (2 Sam. 5:6–8) and it is significant that, in Israel at least, the penalty of eye for eye and tooth for tooth was never exacted literally but was probably transmuted to the payment of an appropriate fine. The Babylonians and Assyrians exacted such penalties regularly for those who broke interstate covenant-treaties made with them.[53]

Lameness was readily recognized, for 'the legs of the lame are not equal' (Prov. 26:7 AV) and two cases are cited in the Old Testament. Mephibosheth was dropped by his nurse at the age of five and 'became lame in both his feet' (2 Sam. 4:4; 9:3, 13). He was thus unable to act for himself when a servant failed to saddle a donkey for him in an emergency (2 Sam. 19:26), though he was later specially cared for by King David. Though no detail is given, various diagnoses have been proposed such as a fracture of both legs with gross displacement, but this is unlikely in one so young. Poliomyelitis has been suggested[54] or a damaged spinal cord secondary to a partial dislocation of the vertebral column.[55] Jacob was 'a limper' (literally 'bent on one side, curved') when a sinew shrank 'in the hollow of his thigh' during a wrestling match (Gen. 32:24–32). This is unlikely to have been a mere dislocation of the hip joint which, as in Egypt, was reset, for Jacob would not have been able to stand or walk. He might have suffered a ruptured or prolapsed intervertebral disc producing a severe and intractable sciatica from pressure on the nerve roots. This could explain the Hebrew regulation forbidding the eating of the sciatic nerve of any animal, out of respect for their forefather.[56] The baked clay plaque with the impression of a child's foot with a large lump on the ball of the foot, found at Gezer in Palestine, could have been made as a support or used in a healing rite or be merely a local curiosity.

Giantism could have been known to the Hebrews if the traditional identification of the Anakim (Gen. 6:4; Num. 13:33) in the Hebron area is upheld.[57] Certainly the size of these people was emphasized (Deut. 1:28; LXX *gigantes*) as was that of the Rephaim. Although King Og of Bashan, a Rephaite, had a bed measuring 4 metres long and 1.8 metres wide preserved as a curiosity(?) at Rabbah (Deut. 3:11), there is no indication that the occupant was necessarily a giant. Moreover Goliath at 3.2 m. tall is never designated a giant (1 Sam. 17:4). Indeed such a height is not an impossible phenomenon and skeletons of large size have been excavated in Palestine.[58]

Dwarfs are depicted in the ancient Near East on cylinder seals but no sure reference to them occurs in the Old Testament. The 'dwarfed' in Leviticus 21:20 may well be an inexact translation in that the Hebrew word *daq* is elsewhere used of cattle shrunken through starvation (Gen. 41:3) and of day-old manna which became withered (Exod. 16:24). Rickets is not mentioned in Egyptian papyri and most dwarfs there were achondroplastics.

INFECTIOUS DISEASES. The Hebrew word for 'infectious disease' (*ng'*), often translated 'stroke, disease, plague or pestilence,' basically pertains to physical contact or touch between two persons or objects.[59] It was commonly used of divine punishment (Exod. 9:14; Num. 11:33) as it was by David (2 Sam. 7:14) and his successors (Ps. 89:23) and of a 'mortal blow' inflicted by God (1 Sam. 4:8,17; Isa. 9:13). The word could also be used literally of a severe beating (Deut. 17:8; 21:5; Ps. 89:23) and of heavy slaughter and casualties in battle (1 Sam. 4:17; 2 Sam. 17:9; 18:7). In *Leviticus* the word is most frequently used of contagious skin diseases (Lev. 13:13, 44 and see p. 103). The Hebrews were aware that some diseases could be communicated to others through garments (Lev. 13:47), utensils or another person.

The Old Testament includes an instance of an epidemic following the eating of what might have been stale quails (Num. 11:31–33); another of striking down Israelites who were spreading bad reports about the promised land (Num. 14:37) and yet another after an earthquake when 250 Korahites died, if their deaths were not the direct result of it. If it was an epidemic it has been suggested that Moses stayed the infection with disinfectant smoke, separating the living from the contaminated zone (Num. 16:30–35). The plague that killed 24, or 24,000, following the association of Hebrews with Moabite women at Baal-Peor is unlikely to have been venereal disease, as has been suggested, since this was unknown in ancient Egypt and there is scant evidence for it so early. Rather, like so many of the biblical incidents taken as the direct action of God, the means is not now ascertainable. Epidemics were usually associated with large numbers of people (Lev. 26:25; Ezek. 7:15). But the death of 70,000 in Israel following David's census must have been a special 'act of God' over ten days. It is unlikely that the enumerators brought some infection back to Jerusalem.[60] As well as a 'plague' the event is described as a 'destruction'. A similar plague was threatened at the time of Jehoram's sin (2 Chron. 21:14). Certainly infectious diseases were known to the Hebrews, for Deuteronomy 28:21 refers to '*the* pestilence', but for this, as for the cattle plagues (Exod. 9:3) and the 'destructive plague',[61] no precise definition is possible.

The same ambiguity remains in defining the cause of two outstanding infectious diseases recounted at some length and both long popularly identified with bubonic plague. The first struck down the Philistines at Gath and later at Ekron and the Levites who took over the ark of the Covenant from them to move it to Beth-Shemesh where 70 (NIV), 50,070 (AV), people died (1 Sam. 5:6; 6:19). The disease is described as an affliction of both young and old with an 'outbreak of tumours'.[62] The swellings were symbolically reproduced in the votive offering of golden mice (or rats) which the Philistines made in an attempt to stave off the 'hand of Yahweh' to which they and the Israelites attributed the attack. However, bubonic plague is attested only many centuries later in Syria and Libya[63] and the disease has a three-day incubation period and is a disease of the lymphatic system. Shrewsbury proposes a tropical form of bacillary dysentery.[64] This identification would also be well suited to the case of the 185(000) men of Sennacherib's Assyrian army struck down in one night by the 'Angel (messenger) of the Lord'. The interpretation of bubonic plague follows the later relation of this incident by Herodotus[65] in which, according to a local temple tradition, the disease followed an invasion of mice (or rats) which ate through the soldiers' quivers, bowstrings and leather shield handles, rendering them unprotected. On the other hand, the biblical account—while ascribing the deaths to the same divine source—states either that 'when the people got up the next morning . . . there were all the dead bodies. So Sennacherib broke camp and withdrew' (2 Kgs. 19:35-36), or, since the Angel of the Lord is said only to have 'smitten' the 185(000) some could have recovered by the next morning to observe the dead and then withdrawn to Assyria rendered weak through this dysentery, which can be transmitted through food contaminated by mice and with little delay in incubation. Adamson suggests that the plague which afflicted the inhabitants who resettled Jericho following its destruction by Joshua can be best explained as bilharzia (schistosomiasis), and the one that struck down some Hittites as typhus. He considers that most of the ancient epidemics recorded from the second millennium BC onwards are related to warfare and are thus associated with mass migrations and the breakdown of public health in areas subject to devastation.[66]

In Babylonia the advantage of isolation in treating some infectious diseases was known. The King of Mari, c.1680 BC, gave instructions concerning a woman in his household who was ill with a fever. 'Take strong measures. No one is to use her drinking cup, chair or bed. She is to be set apart and kept in isolation. It is better for one woman to die than for all the palace-women to become sick. Her illness is contagious.' Another letter from the same court says, 'The city of Terqa is well but in Kulhitu the god has chosen to devour both men and cattle. Today two or three men have died', and later, 'The family of Bahlu-gâyim has completely perished in the "devouring of the god". All his children have died and there is no one left to take charge of that house.'[67]

In Egypt, according to the examination of the mummy of a priest of the XXIst Dynasty, there is evidence of spinal tuberculosis, or Potts' caries. The mummy of Rameses V appears to show that he died of smallpox.[68] Tuberculosis and schistosomiasis are well documented in Egypt, the former being prevalent among children when the Hebrews were there.[69] It could perhaps have been the 'wasting disease' recorded by the Hebrews soon thereafter (Lev. 26:16; Deut. 28:22). There is no sure evidence for the existence of malaria.[70]

MENTAL AND NEUROLOGICAL DISORDERS. The Hebrews were aware of a wide range of mental and emotional disorders for which they had a specific and descriptive terminology (Deut. 28:28).[71] A number of incidents are also cited. Saul suffered from 'madness' shown in recurrent attacks of homicidal and suicidal mania followed by melancholia (1 Sam. 16:14–16; 18:11; 20:30,33). When David feigned the same to win the attention of Achish of Gath it is noticeable that such persons were not separated from the community (1 Sam. 21:13).[72] Elijah, though 'a man of God', exhibited symptoms of manic depression, wishing for death, with loss of appetite and an inability to manage and with excessive self-pity. He was unmoved by visitors, even by God or visions, but was restored when given a new and demanding task to fulfil (1 Kgs. 19:4–15). Attempts have been made to show that Job was a schizophrenic but this is contradicted by the wide range of the symptoms described.[73]

Nebuchadnezzar's illness, predicted by Daniel, was described in these words: 'Let him be drenched with the dew of heaven, and let him live with the animals among the plants of the earth. Let his mind be changed from that of a man and let him be given the mind of an animal till seven times pass by for him' (4:15–17). In interpreting the dream which led to this prediction Daniel added that the king 'will be driven away from his people' (i.e. isolated), 'he would eat grass like cattle (4:25). This came to pass a year later when he lived thus roughly sufficiently long for his hair to grow 'like the feathers of an eagle and his nails like the claws of a bird'. At the end of the stated time, and after prayer, his 'sanity was restored' and he resumed his royal position (4:33–34, 36). Those who do not regard this as merely symbolic see here a rare mental disease reported with great accuracy. It is commonly assumed that this was similar to the later lycanthropy which gave rise to the 'werewolf' legends of the Middle Ages. However, there is no agreement on any classification on the basis of the biblical evidence. Harrison thinks 'this ailment was a form of monomania, in which the psychosis is restricted to a single concept or subject, as here where the subject imagines himself, and behaves, like cattle (boanthropy)'. He reports a case known to him where the subject ate grass.[74]

Short, who cites the case of a man who thought he was a cock-pheasant (avianthropy) took Nebuchadnezzar to be suffering from a fixed delusion (paranoia) as did Preuss, since a melancholic would simply have died from hunger.[75] The view that this incident is a confusion with the illness suffered by a later Babylonian king, Nabonidus, does not sufficiently take into account the diverse symptoms.[76]

The Babylonians were also aware of mental states like 'depression', morbid anxiety and hysterical reactions and described among other symptoms 'wasting flesh, limp limbs; he forgets the words he is trying to say'.[77] Kinnier Wilson believes that a series of incantations provided the main textbook on Babylonian psychiatry carried out by *āšipu*-priests.[78]

It is not easy to identify neurological disorders in the ancient texts since so many were described as 'demon possession'. Nonetheless, the Midianite Balaam who describes himself as 'one who fell down with his eyes open' (Num. 24:4), has been taken to be an epileptic (myoclonus). Similarly, Saul who 'fell down every day and every night' (1 Sam. 19:24) could represent a case of frequent epileptic seizures.[79] The Egyptians and Babylonians certainly knew of epilepsy, the latter described the symptoms as 'falls with eyes wide open, head turned to right (or left), clenched fist, averted eyes, a cry of *'uai* (an 'epileptic cry'), foaming at the mouth', also certain types of 'aura' which presaged an attack, a 'cold' numbness in the tips of fingers and toes and a pricking sensation in the trunk or limbs. Epilepsy among babies was also noted.[80] The brain—the Hebrew 'golden bowl' as the spinal cord was 'the silver cord' (Eccles. 12:6)—was well explored by Egyptians and Babylonians. They observed the effects of brain damage including cervical trauma leading to quadriplegia, incontinence and seminal emission after fractures affecting the mid-cervical area, hemiplegia, squint following a fractured skull, facial distortion and other symptoms.[81]

A number of Old Testament happenings have been ascribed to

neurological disorders. Nabal, whose 'heart failed and became like a stone' when he was confronted by Abigail, and who died in a coma ten days later when 'the Lord struck him' (1 Sam. 25:36–38), has been taken to have died following a brain lesion. There is not so much evidence of 'heart failure' (i.e. coronary artery disease) as for a 'seizure' (NEB) in popular parlance.[82] Preuss cites another case of apoplexy: 'the mouth became closed and he was paralysed and could no longer utter a word or give orders about his household. So Alcimus died at that time in great agony' (1 Macc. 9:55,56). Philopater's death is described in similar terms for 'God jolted him hither and thither like reeds in the wind so that he lay on the ground motionless with paralysed limbs and, justly punished, he was unable to make any sound' (3 Macc. 3:27).[83]

Jeroboam I's reaction against the prophet in a burst of frenzy resulted in his hand being 'shrivelled up so that he could not pull it back', though it was restored after prayer to its former condition (1 Kgs. 13:4–6). If not purely functional, this might have been due to a sudden blocking of the main (axillary) artery of the limb or the result of a cerebral haemorrhage or embolism of which the clot dispersed. Others have thought the cause to be a chronic cerebral abscess or the result of cataplexy. Such a paralysis would be interpreted as a sign of divine disfavour (Zech. 11:17).

Similarly, some have seen a case of cerebral haemorrhage in the death of the young son of the Shunammite woman who complained of headache after being out with the reapers at noon and died after a few hours (2 Kgs. 4:18–20). It has more commonly been taken as an instance of sunstroke (insolation/siriasis) marked by acute headache. However, though the plain of Esdraelon can be hot at harvest time, children there are only very rarely affected by sunstroke.[84] Others have therefore suggested that death was due to cerebral malaria,[85] or an ultra-severe attack of meningitis, but that seldom kills so quickly. A more identifiable case of sunstroke is that told of Judith's husband who died during the barley harvest. He had stood overseeing the men who were binding the sheaves in the field and was overcome by the burning heat. He threw himself on his bed and died in his town Bethulia (Judith 8:2–3). Similarly, Jonah was overcome by the hot sun and dry sirocco wind East of Nineveh and may have suffered from syncope, an early symptom of insolation, and the headache in these conditions may have contributed to the physical and spiritual causes of his misery (Jonah 4:5–8).

Headaches, next to dysentery, were and are the most prevalent ailment in the Near East and the Hebrews often mentioned them[86] as did the Babylonians[87] and the Egyptians. Many popular remedies were prescribed to gain relief including laudanum, natron, pine-seeds, fruit, burnt fish bones and goose fat.[88] Incantations against headaches are found and some have interpreted the prayer of Jabez (1 Chron. 4:10) as a request for freedom from headaches.[89]

Other Ailments

EYES

Eye diseases, including blindness, were common in biblical times so far as can be judged from contemporary texts and illustrations. In the Old Testament the eye (*'ayin*) is, next to the hand and heart (mind), the most frequently named part of the body (577 times). The eye was created by God (Ps. 94:9) as a distinctive organ as that which 'flowed' with tears (Gen. 3:6). It was used metaphorically for sight or perception as of God himself (Ps. 33:18). The eye was thought to show emotion, pride, pleasure and pity, or the lack of it.[90]

Sight was known to be impaired by sorrow and weeping (Job 17:7; Ps. 88:9) or old age (Gen. 48:10; 1 Sam. 4:15). It might be partial—'right eye darkened' (Zech. 11:17; cf. Isa. 29:18), or the 'weak eyes' of Leah (Gen. 29:17)—if not attributable to some more specific cause.[91] The 'eye defect' of Leviticus 21:20 (NIV) might be a general description or specifically a squint. Eye injury or loss of sight, if not congenital, might be caused by external action such as a blow on the head, and was a matter for compensation at law.[92] The blind wandered or groped in darkness, felt their way along walls and were the subject of charity.[93] Blindness in humans and animals may have been distinguished.[94] It was thought to have been a defect inflicted by God, as on the men of Sodom (Gen. 19:11) or the Syrian army (2 Kgs. 6:18). Rarely it was inflicted as a judgment by an enemy on prominent prisoners, as the Philistines on Samson (Judg. 16:21) and the Babylonians on the sons of Zedekiah (2 Kgs. 25:7). For the Hebrews the Lord God alone could 'give sight to the blind'.[95]

The Egyptians had a good working knowledge of the external anatomy of the eye, calling the pupil the 'handmaid' of the eye, with which the Hebrew 'little man' of the eye can be compared.[96] They listed and described many eye diseases[97] as did the Babylonians[98] who described the eye as 'becomes dry' in time of famine (xerophthalmia or xerotic keratitis), the 'fixed eye' (ophthalmophagia), discoloration of the eye with opaque spot and attendant ulcers, cysts, squint (exophthalmos), 'filaments moving about in the eye' and the defective sight of a 'man who can recognise another only at a distance of about six metres'.[99] The unsuccessful eye operation quoted in the laws of Hammurapi was less likely to have been for cataract or scarification than for an abscess of the lacrimal sac.[100] Therapeutic treatment of eye diseases was normally with ointments and drops made with verdigris, dust, yellow sulphide of arsenic, malachite or lead sulphate, and with bandaging. In all areas the blind were employed as musicians and singers and in certain types of manufacture, such as reed mat making.

EAR

The Hebrews thought it was God who made a person deaf and dumb, and spoke of the unstopped ear as an act of blessing. However, the phrase 'to open the ear', as with the eye, was the idiomatic way of expressing revelation.[101] An abnormal ear disqualified a man from the Hebrew priesthood (Lev. 21:18). Since this occurs in a list of physical disabilities, later Judaism sought to interpret this specifically either as an abnormally large ('cauliflower') or small ear. A 'deaf ear' was also described as a 'heavy ear'.[102] They knew that mutism was associated with deafness—'I am as a deaf and dumb man' for 'when a man is deaf he cannot speak'.[103] The Egyptians thought that the right ear was the channel of the breath of life and that vessels from the ears led to the temple and eyes and affected them. The Babylonians listed diseases of the ear.[104]

NOSE

The nose and nostrils were considered the channel of the breath of life.[105] Man was a 'pneumatic creature' for breath was in his nostrils (Isa. 2:22). The eruption of breath through the nose (a sneeze) was a sign of life (2 Kgs. 4:35), while 'the nose (or nostrils)' came to be used for 'anger'.[106] Abnormality of the nose as a disqualification of a person from the Hebrew priesthood was based on a later interpretation of Leviticus 21:18.[107] Lack of the sense of smell was attributed to disease.

The Egytians who defined life as 'having breath in the nose', and death as the absence of it, thought that air entered the heart, lungs and belly through the nose. The nasal blood vessels were known and thought to be separate from those producing mucus.[108] In Babylonian medicine, with its many prescriptions for catarrh and coughs of all kinds, the nose figures prominently in diagnosis.

They checked whether it was hot or cold, was persistently rubbed while the patient talked, hurt on the right side, or whether the patient breathed through his mouth but not his nose.[109] Nosebleed (epistaxis) was well known, the Babylonians curing it by pouring cold water over the head or applying tampons, taking care not to press upon the cartilage unduly. Other injuries, including a broken septum, were treated by inserting grease-smeared plugs in the nose while swollen, substituting these later with two firm rolls of linen. A case relating to a nose bitten off is cited in a Babylonian law c.1700 BC. These peoples cut off the noses of certain prisoners of war, as was done for erring wives and slaves.[110] Cuts in noses were stitched.

THROAT

The throat, to the ancients the organ for swallowing and the voice box (Ps. 115:7), was by the Babylonians also termed 'the life'.[111] When dry through sobbing or thirst the remedy was a lubricant, our English word 'gargle' coming ultimately from the ancient Semitic word for it.[112] There is evidence that the Egyptians and Babylonians identified the larynx and tonsils and common throat conditions.[113]

Speech deformities included the lisp and stutter and a continuous stammerer often bit his lips. Isaiah looked forward to the day when the stammerer would be able to speak fluently and clearly (32:4).[114]

TEETH

The ancient Hebrews prized fine teeth, especially those 'whiter than milk' (Gen. 49:12) and well paired 'like a flock of sheep coming up from the washing' with none missing (Cant. 4:2; 6:6). A loose or broken tooth was troublesome and to have one was 'like having confidence in an unfaithful man in a time of trouble' (Prov. 25:19). Teeth could be broken by biting gravel stones or set on edge by sour things like the harmful irritant, vinegar.[115]

'Tooth for a tooth', though prescribed in the law, does not seem to have been enforced literally, for the knocking out of a tooth involved the injurer in paying recompense.[116] In old age 'the grinders' became fewer (Eccl. 12:3). The interpretation that Job escaped 'by the skin of his teeth' is doubtful, though it has entered into our idiom (Job 14:20).[117]

Archaeological evidence indicates that caries was rare in early times though in later periods, perhaps due to a change of diet, erosion was prevalent. Analysis generally shows a sufficient intake of calcium and an adequate vitamin D metabolism.[118] Egyptians and Babylonians thought that caries was caused by a worm which dwelt in the gums and chewed the marrow of bones, so destroying the blood supply. This may have been symbolic language, for both recorded numerous proved cures for toothache and the profession of dentistry was active in ancient Egypt.[119] Apart from extraction, there were at least ten prescriptions for toothache available in the times of the Patriarchs, including chewing anemone roots or narcotic plants, and taking solutions and mouth washes for weak teeth.[120] There is a unique case in one non-royal mummy of a healthy tooth tied to an artificial bone or ivory tooth with gold wire to form an artificial bridge.

SKIN

Skin diseases were common throughout the ancient Near East and many are described. The most discussed are, however, the chronic skin diseases grouped by the Hebrews under the word *ṣarāʿaṯ*, formerly translated 'leprosy' (AV) but now more reasonably as 'malignant skin disease' (NEB) or 'infectious skin disease (NIV). The reason for this is that the word covers various skin conditions marked by swellings, scab, bright spots or dark patches, raw or flaking skin. It was also used of mildew on wool, linen or objects of skin or leather or of a pigmented fungus on house walls.[121] Browne and others have shown that it does not accord with leprosy (Hansen's bacillus) as it is known today, and cautiously offer a wide variety of medical interpretations.[122] (For details see chapter 4.)

The Babylonians describe similar conditions, e.g. 'If the skin of a man exhibits white *pūṣu*-areas and is dotted with *nuqdu*-spots, such a man has been rejected by his god and is to be rejected by mankind.'[123] As with the Hebrews, visible blemishes were thought to render a person 'unclean'. There are insufficient details to identify the 'skin disease' which afflicted Naaman and Gehazi (2 Kgs. 5). Both continued in service after the attack, which could have been scabies. True leprosy was unknown to Hippocrates (c.400 BC) and first surely attested in India c.600 BC. In Egypt no skeletal remains have been identified as having it before the Ptolemaic period (second century BC).[124]

The Egyptian boil, tumours or swellings and festering sores and itch are threatened in the curse of Deuteronomy 28:27. Among the identifications proposed are psoriasis, eczema, scurvy and scabies.[125]

Job was smitten with 'painful sores' all over his body which he tried to relieve by scratching himself with a broken potsherd as he sat outside the town on an ash-heap (2:7–8). His skin was broken and festering and he described himself as worm- and scab-ridden, with a blackened and peeling skin, burning with fever and 'nothing but skin and bones' (7:5; 19:20; 30:28–30). Some symptoms may have been complications following a severe malady which started suddenly and was long drawn out but not incapacitating or fatal. Preuss suggested it was universal eczema and Short smallpox.[126]

Hezekiah's boil or carbuncle was cured by the application of a lump of figs, presumably in the form of a heated poultice (Isa. 38:21; 2 Chron. 32:24). The use of figs to draw an abscess is recorded by Pliny and in two veterinary texts from Ugarit in the thirteenth century BC.[127]

HAIR

The Hebrews viewed baldness as a curse, especially when it occurred in women (Isa. 3:24; Jer. 48:37). Unlike their neighbours, some of whose priestly classes were bald, the Hebrews prohibited a bald man from assuming priestly office (Lev. 21:5). This may have been due, at least in part, to the shaven head, or one with hair torn out, that was, with the cut-off beard, a sign of mourning.[128] There is no evidence that a prophet was distinguished by a bald pate for Elisha, mocked by the children who said, 'Go up, you baldy', may have suffered from alopecia. The curse on the children may have resulted from their disrespect for his office.[129] On the other hand, Esau's excessive hairiness was noted.[130]

Some Egyptians similarly suffered baldness, to judge from mummified remains. The kings Amanophis III, Seti I and Rameses II were bald. Queen Nefertiti wore artificial pigtails.[131] Baldness was treated with castor oil by them and by the Babylonians, who considered baldness as due to a weakness for which prescriptions and incantations were prepared.[132]

Other diseases

Other descriptions of diseases in the Old Testament include the account of King Asa of Judah (c.911–870 BC) of whom it is reported that 'in his old age his feet became diseased' (1 Kgs. 15:23). This has been long and widely attributed to gout which is, however, uncommon in Palestine and the ancient Near East and only vaguely indicated in Egyptian texts.[133] It has, therefore, more recently been interpreted as a circulatory dysfunction of the extremities culminating in gangrene.[134] Since the 'feet' are sometimes said to have been used euphemistically for sexual organs, it has been suggested that his was a venereal disease. This also is unlikely since such diseases are not definitely identified in the Old Testament period.[135] The 'bodily discharge' (Lev. 15:25–33) has been thought to be a reference to an infectious urinary bilharziasis for which there is contemporary evidence in the Egyptian 'Aaa-disease' and in the parasite *Schistosoma* found in shells of the *Bulinus truncatus* snails in the mudbrick walls of ancient Babylon and elsewhere.[136]

A later king of Judah, Jehoram, was afflicted by God with a lingering disease of the bowels. 'In the course of time, at the end of the second year, his bowels came out because of the disease, and he died in great pain' (2 Chron. 21:15, 18–19). This has been interpreted as a massive rectal prolapse following chronic diarrhoea or bacillary dysentery.[137]

Pregnancy and Childbirth

There is insufficient evidence to assess the rate of infant mortality which may be presumed to have been high. The ideal was 'to be fruitful and multiply' (Gen. 1:27) and children were regarded as a blessing from the Lord. The need to maintain the family and its name, to provide labour in a largely agricultural environment and for support in old age, led to large families. Families of more than ten children by one wife were not uncommon. Infertility, also attributable to God (Gen. 16:2), was offset initially by polygamy and by marriage contracts entitling the husband to take another wife or concubine to get children after seven years, if there were no offspring by the first.[138] Both Egyptians and Babylonians noted the aphrodisiacal and the contraceptive powers of various substances.[139] Overpopulation, however, was a known problem and the earliest Babylonian traditions were that the gods sent famine and plague, lions and wolves, and finally the great Flood to curb mankind's expansion.[140]

Early pregnancy was diagnosed by Egyptians and Babylonians, as with the early Greeks, by traditional means—the appearance of the skin, eyes and breasts, and by urine tests made on vegetables and cereals.[141] There was much folk-lore also directed towards the determination of the sex of the unborn child.[142] The Babylonians recognized recurring bouts of vomiting in pregnancy (toxaemia) and the swelling of the ankles caused by pressure by the enlarging uterus on the veins. The growth of the bones within the womb was a marvel (Eccles. 11:5) as was the amniotic membrane protecting the fetus—'the house of the unborn child.'[143] False pregnancy ('wind egg') was a picture of futile efforts (Is. 26:18) just as labour pains were taken as a common picture for all writhing and pain from whatever cause.[144] There is no evidence that the prohibition of alcohol on the mother of the yet unborn Samson related to any supposed medical benefits so much as to the future child's role as an abstemious Nazarite.[145] Phineas' wife's miscarriage was attributed to sudden fright on hearing the news of her husband's death (1 Sam. 4:19–21) and other cases to impure water (2 Kgs. 2:19) or to a blow.[146] Difficulties in childbirth, treated by the Babylonians with antispasmodics,[147] were well known. Rachel's difficulties and subsequent death in labour are described (Gen. 35:16—19) and, according to Jewish tradition, Michal, David's wife, and Queen Esther died in giving birth.[148]

The Hebrews, like the Egyptians, employed 'those who help to give birth' (midwives) and used birthstools consisting of two stones; birth was customarily 'on the knees'. This is illustrated in the Egyptian hieroglyph for 'birth' of a woman kneeling or squatting above such stones.[149]

A diagnosis of twins to Rebekah had been made before delivery when the initial presentation of one arm of the child born second was noted, and the firstborn marked by a tied thread because of the legal importance of primogeniture.[150] Breastfeeding, thought to have a contraceptive effect, was given for at least eighteen months and sometimes up to three years.[151] If this was not possible, a wet-nurse was provided, as for Deborah and the mother of King Ahaziah, or a mixture of honey, water and diluted goat's milk used.

Preventive Medicine

'The chief glory of biblical medicine lies in the institution of social hygiene as a science.'[152]

In the Book of *Leviticus* the Hebrews collected regulations in which the terms 'pure, clean' or 'impure, unclean' stressed the theological as well as the practical concept of 'holiness, healthfulness, separateness'. These included physical and mental hygiene as applied to the individual, family, tribe and society in general. Here is to be found a distinctive Hebrew regimen typified by unique dietary laws (Lev. 11; Deut. 14:3–21) and their concern to diagnose and treat infectious diseases and so prevent the spread of epidemics.[153] To assist this they prescribed a period of 'quarantine' which varied from a day to a week or as long as the case required.[154] Thus, all soldiers at war carried a small instrument for burying excreta to prevent any spread of intestinal infection or air pollution (Deut. 23:13–14). On return from battle they had to disinfect all clothing and all gear including that made of leather or wood. Everything, including the metal loot, which could withstand fire was so treated. Articles which could not were immersed in boiling water and nothing could enter the camp until after seven days (Num. 31:21–24). Similar regulations applied to those in contact with the dead, infested housing or polluted clothing, and may reflect a general attitude and personal habits.

Personal and communal health was aided by a strict enforcement of rest for every Hebrew and his household, livestock and land once in every seven days (Sabbath), with periodic intermissions for longer periods (Jubilee). When they entered into urban life, domestic sewerage was removed down gullies (some covered) in the centre of the streets, such as have been excavated in towns in contemporary Egypt and Babylonia. Larger houses and buildings had built-in latrines. Such sanitation was of a higher standard than that prevailing in Europe in the Middle Ages.[155] The importance of an uncontaminated water supply is attested both by concern at its pollution by a dead animal and by the elders of Jericho in their anxiety for the purification of their only water spring at a time of epidemic (Lev. 11:29–36; 2 Kgs. 2:19–22).

Bathplaces and bath tubs have been excavated in large houses but in most places the Hebrews, like their neighbours, poured water over their bodies and washed themselves and their clothes.[156] Cleaners (fullers) were an old attested profession using soap made of lye, a fossil carbonate of soda dissolved with olive or sesame oil or an alkali of salt-wort or similar plant.[157] In all cultures the washing of hands and feet, the body and head, and dishes, and delousing were important.[158] Men and women anointed themselves with perfumed oils and some women applied cosmetics. Analysis of the latter has shown that the compounds, including lead, were a cause of poisoning.[159] Organized sport or exercise, though described and illustrated in Egyptian, Babylonian and Hebrew texts and remains, played little part compared with the strenuous daily routine of the largely agricultural communities of the region.

Diet

Physical wellbeing promoted by a balanced diet may have been part of the essential purpose of its many references in the Hebrew laws. Like their neighbours, their staple diet was grain, vegetables and fruit and there was no restriction on these (Gen. 1:29–30; 2:16). Meat was consumed rarely and restricted to that killed for the purpose with the life blood drained from it. No suet (AV 'fat') from around the kidneys or viscera, or flesh from an animal found dead or killed, was allowed.[160] Vegetarianism appears to have been practised only rarely.[161] Ordinary folk ate two or three meals daily, the Hebrews having an abundance of milk products and honey. The latter, like nuts, was a luxury food found only at royal feasts in Egypt and Assyria.

Drunkenness and alcoholism appear to have been commonly described. In a Babylonian case a man drank *šikaru* (grain) beer, his head is affected, he has some amnesia, is incoherent in speech, his attention cannot be held and his eyes remain motionless.[162] It occurred at all levels of society, including the gods of Egypt and Babylonia, so that it is interesting to read the words of an ancient Egyptian moralist: 'Take not upon yourself to drink a jug of beer. You speak and unintelligible utterances issue from your mouth. If you fall and break a limb, there is no one to hold a hand to you. Your companions in drink stand up and say: "Away with this sot!". If someone comes to seek you out and to question you, you are found lying on the ground and are like a little child.'[163] Herodotus follows his account of health and diet in Egypt with the observation that 'in social meetings among the rich, when the banquet is ended, a servant carries round to the several guests a coffin, in which there is a wooden image of a corpse, carved and painted to resemble nature as nearly as possible, about a cubit or two cubits in length. As he shows it to each guest in turn, the servant says, "Gaze here, as thou dost drink and be merry; for when thou diest, such shalt thou be"'.[164] The Book of Proverbs and other Old Testament passages warn of the dangers of excessive drinking.[165]

Some taboos were local, because a given animal was dedicated to a god, or by reason of class distinction as in the case of Egyptian priests who ate no beans or lentils, or were confined to a specific period in the prohibition of eating pork at the time of the full moon. In general the average person ate only when hungry and never to satiety.[166]

Nutrition was generally adequate through a rich variety of easily obtainable foods: barley and wheat, vegetables, fruits (but not citrus fruits in Babylonia), dairy products, figs, dates, and some meat, fish and fowl. The essential nutriments and energy intake calculated from the ancient documents compare well with modern records and the vitamin intake recommended by UNFAO today.[167] Nevertheless, for a people dependent upon an agricultural system subject to variation through drought, flood or pest-disease, famines were inevitable and are recorded.[168] Scurvy was known in Egypt and Babylonia and Kinnier-Wilson identifies it with the 'evil-smelling disease' causing the loosening of teeth, swelling of the gums and with the black haemorrhages beneath the skin described in the account of the siege of Jerusalem in 588/7 BC. He also finds evidence for blindness following vitamin A deficiency.[169]

Therapy

In matters of therapy the Hebrews did not differ substantially from their neighbours with whom, through local traditions, many common remedies were known. These included washings, ointments and herbal remedies. The Egyptians listed more than five hundred, mostly made from vegetable products, compounded from mineral drugs or from the products of thirty different animals.[170] There, as in Palestine and Babylonia, some remedies were prepared by perfumers working either in a temple or private establishment.

Though exorcism was common throughout the areas and the centuries surrounding the establishment of the Hebrew kingdom, it is first attested in Israel only during the intertestamental period. The therapeutic effect of music and of prayer were known.[171] Moses' prayer for Miriam's recovery—'O God, heal her, please'—is the shortest recorded prayer in the Bible (Num. 12:13). Later Jews considered prayer for healing 'to be efficacious if offered by the proper person at the proper time with proper intent under the proper circumstances'![172] The practice is derived from Abraham's prayer for the recovery of Abimelech whom God healed, as he did the Shunammite boy but not David's son (Gen. 20:17; 2 Kgs. 4:33; 2 Sam. 12:16).

Life Expectancy

In antiquity specific records of the date of birth were not kept before the fifth century BC with the introduction of horoscopy in Egypt and Babylonia. The dates of the death of a king were recorded. Demographic data are, however, too scanty for any judgment to be made on such matters as infant mortality or longevity.

For the Hebrews the normal 'length of our days is seventy years—or eighty if we have the strength' (Ps. 90:10) and the ideal was to live to a hundred years old.[173] All the patriarchs lived longer.[174] That this was given as genealogical evidence for the continuity of the ancestral line does not diminish the validity of the evidence. The theory has been put forward that the reduction to a lifespan of 120 years marks the effect of sin on the human body when compared with the recorded figures of 130–969 years for Adam's antediluvian successors. The Babylonian pre-flood ancestors are given even greater ages. Jehoiada at 130 was later considered 'very old with a glut of years' (2 Chron. 24:15), while Barzillai at 80 was 'very old' with a diminished sense of taste and hearing (2 Sam. 19:31–35). Though Ecclesiastes 12:1–7 has been variously interpreted, it has been commonly accepted as a picture of old age:

'The sun and the light and the moon and the stars grow dark'
  (diminished sight).
'the clouds return after rain'
  (mental and emotional changes with depression).
'the keepers of the house tremble'
  (trembling hands).
'the strong men stoop'
  (degeneration of bones, bowed legs, stooping shoulders).
'the grinders cease because they are few'
  (possible loss of teeth).
'those looking through the windows grow dim'
  (loss of sight).
'the doors to the street are closed and the sound of grinding fades'
  (loss of hearing).
'Men rise up at the sound of birds but all their songs grow faint'
  (increased nervous response to small sounds or the tendency of the aged to wake and rise early).
'Men are afraid of heights and of dangers in streets'
  (anxieties due to ageing).
'the almond tree blossoms'
  (whitening of the hair).
'the grasshopper drags himself along'
  (faltering steps).
'desire is no longer stirred'
  (diminishing sexual desire).
'the silver cord is severed'
  (spinal cord weakened).
'the golden bowl is broken'
  (deterioration of the brain).
'the pitcher is shattered at the spring'
  (urinary incontinence—and troublesome prostate gland in the male).

'the wheel broken at the well'
(a metaphor for cardiac failure).
'the dust returns to the ground it came from and the spirit returns to God who gave it'
(death).[175]

Old age was respected, and a consolation to the Hebrew family where the elderly were nurtured, and so becomes a picture of the ideal future.[176] The early Rabbinic tradition was of attaining 'old age' at sixty, 'the hoary head' at seventy, 'special strength' at eighty, 'bending' at ninety and 'as though already dead' at a hundred.[177] The Babylonians considered the time span of a generation to be 'forty years', taken to be 'the prime of life', while fifty was a short life ('few days'), sixty 'maturity', seventy 'long life', eighty 'old age' and ninety 'extreme old age'.[178] Adad-Guppi', the mother of Nabonidus, died in Babylon aged 104. Many were the prayers of the Babylonians and Assyrians to the gods 'for the lengthening of my days and the multiplying of my years', sometimes associated with requests for health of body and mind and cheerfulness of spirit. Hezekiah's prayer for extra years after illness may be compared with this (2 Kgs. 20:1–6). A study of life expectancy in Babylonia c.650–400 BC based on personal names in dated texts shows that several scribes there lived at least to seventy to ninety years of age and some slaves to eighty years.

Death

Throughout the ancient Near East the attitude to death was one of sober realism regarding the inescapable destiny of mankind. The Hebrews were unique in considering it also as a result of man's original sin (Gen. 2:17; 3:3), Yet God has no pleasure in anyone's death for it is his will that man should live (Ezek. 18:32).[179] Premature death, especially in the prime of life, was a matter for lament.

The Egyptians had no word for 'death' which was for them but a step in the soul's journey through life and eventually the entering into new life. Death was a protracted sleep in which the diseased followed their normal lives. 'This is convalescence after sickness . . . like a man who goes out to catch birds and suddenly finds himself in an unknown country. Such is death.[180] The Babylonians had one word, and ideograph, for 'death', but carefully distinguished between the death that came naturally to a man at the end of his days ('death from god, destiny') and violent death.[181]

None of these peoples made a medical assessment of the point of death, which was taken to be when breathing had obviously ceased finally. It was a great outrage to inflict on a corpse any mutilation or to leave it unburied and to decay. Egyptian embalmers sometimes restored parts to bodies deficient of major limbs. Cremation was rare among Semitic peoples though the bodies of those who died in epidemics may have been burned (Amos 6:10). Those who touched the dead were thought to have thus been rendered unclean, but only the Hebrews prescribed ritual washing of the person and clothes before the return to community life (Num. 5:3–4; 19:11–22).

The cause of violent death was often noted. In the Old Testament, Goliath was rendered unconscious by concussion from a sling-stone striking his forehead and then decapitated (1 Sam. 17:50); Abimelech was fatally wounded by a blow from a millstone thrown down on him from the gate-tower at Thebez (Judg. 9:53) and blinded Samson was crushed to death by the collapse of a temple roof on him (Judg. 16:30). Ahaziah's death followed a fall from a window (2 Kgs. 1:2) as did that of Jezebel who was subsequently crushed under chariot wheels (2 Kgs. 9:33). Deaths in war or by murder or assassination are described by Babylonians and Hebrews.[182]

Suicide

Suicides reported in the Old Testament are all of prominent people. Saul, having seen his own three sons killed by the Philistines, and since defeat was inevitable, took his own sword and thrust himself through (1 Sam. 31:4). Ahitophel, seeing that his plan for the crown-prince Absalom to attack King David was not followed, went to his house, put his household in order, and then hanged himself (2 Sam. 17:23). The rebel Zimri, besieged in Tirzah, saw the town about to fall, so went into an inner room of the royal palace and set the palace on fire over him and so died (1 Kgs 16:18). When Ragesh (Razis) saw he could not escape from the soldiers sent by King Demetrius Soter to arrest him, he fell on his sword unsuccessfully, tried to throw himself off a wall and finally disembowelled himself (2 Macc. 14:41–46). The traitor Ptolemy poisoned himself (2 Macc. 10:13).

It has been argued that Samson's efforts to pull down the temple of Dagon upon himself and his mockers with the cry, 'Let me die with the Philistines', was a case of suicide which in Judaism was regarded as a criminal act forbidden by the sixth commandment—'You shall not murder'—even though all the recorded examples evidence extenuating circumstances and are all psychologically understandable. This attitude is quite different from that of the later Greeks. It should be noted that Job refused the suggestion of strangulation by his own hands and viewed his wife's plan for him to 'curse God and die' as a sinful folly.[183]

Artificial resuscitation

Much attention has been paid to the two incidents of apparent resurrection from death in the Old Testament. In one Elijah laid the young son of the widow of Zarephath on a bed in the roof chamber after he had died from a severe illness. He then stretched himself over the child three times 'and the soul ("life and breath") of the child came back into him and he revived' (1 Kgs. 17:17–22). His condition had been described as 'no breath left in him' (AV v.17; NIV 'stopped breathing') and his mother assumed her son to be really dead. Some interpret this to mean that the boy only appeared to be dead[184] although most biblical commentators think that the boy had actually died. It is assumed that in the other instance Elisha followed his predecessor's practice when he placed his mouth to the Shunammite child's mouth and eyes to eyes to breathe into the boy and to warm him with the natural warmth of his own body. While this could be an instance of mouth to mouth resuscitation, the time interval between death and revival makes this questionable. The emphasis in the narrative seems to be on the answer to prayer.

This partial survey of the state of medical knowledge and practice among the peoples of Old Testament times would seem to show that the Hebrews in Palestine were abreast of, and probably aware of, work being undertaken by contemporary physicians in Syria, Egypt and Babylonia. The most striking features of the biblical records are the absence of the use of magical and omen practices in prognosis, diagnosis and therapy, the close integration of Hebrew religious and medical thought, especially in the application of social and preventive medicine, and the part frequently played by prayer by, and on behalf of, the patient.

2

Medicine in the New Testament World

COLIN J. HEMER

The Greek Background

The cultural world of the New Testament was extraordinarily complex, and diverse concepts of medicine and of the nature of disease coexisted within it. Even within the Greek perspective popular superstition and magic persisted in a civilization which developed a scientific and rationalistic approach to medicine, and there was a continuing link between the rational and the religious in a relationship which is not easy for us to enter into. Some account of Greek medicine at its best is clearly of major importance for understanding the knowledge available to people of New Testament times.

Greek medicine had a long history. The term *iatros* (physician) and its cognates are in general use as early as the *Iliad* (c.800BC), where there are references to simple surgery, like cutting out arrow-points, and washing and dressing wounds with pain-killing roots (e.g. Homer, *Iliad* 4. 844–848), though at one point in the *Odyssey* a similar case is treated with incantations (Homer, *Odyssey* 19.457). It is said that 149 wounds are mentioned in the two poems, over 75% of them mortal, and their descriptions constitute a notable body of anatomical data.[1]

Herodotus is the first to give some account of the professional career of a doctor, Democedes of Croton, a Greek city of southern

Italy, who was hired successively by Aegina, Athens and Polycrates of Samos at large annual fees to act as public physician, and finally achieved high honour, at the cost of freedom, as personal doctor to King Darius of Persia (522–486 BC). His Greek gentleness in handling the king's injury is contrasted with the violent methods of his Egyptian doctors (Herodotus 3.130–133).

In early Greek thought deities had healing powers, and conversely cults developed of famous healers.[2] The temples of Asclepius (Latin Aesculapius), notably at Epidaurus, Cos and Pergamum, also became major centres of scientific medicine. Hippocrates, the reputed 'Father of Medicine', was a native of Cos, and the great Galen (second century AD) a native of Pergamum. The practices of *incubatio* (oracular vision to the patient sleeping overnight in a shrine), and of votive offerings representing diseased organs, were characteristic of Asclepian cult, but the temples were also the custodians of much sound medical knowledge, especially in dietetics. And the psychological element in Asclepian cult may have been important. The god's sacred serpent has actually persisted as the emblem of medicine.

Hippocrates, according to the Roman Celsus (*de Medicina*, Prooem. 8), was the first who separated medicine 'from the study of philosophy'. Of the historical Hippocrates (? c.460–370 BC) remarkably little is known. Of the so-called 'Hippocratic Corpus' of surviving medical writings, none can confidently be pronounced authentic. They may include material transmitted through his school, but they comprise diversities of doctrine, including much at odds with teachings attributed to the master. In particular the date and provenance of the original form of the so-called 'Hippocratic Oath' are keenly debated. It may never have been more than the ethical statement of one medical sect; Edelstein assigns it to a Pythagorean group of the fourth century BC.[3] But in any case the ethics of Greek medicine will be an important aspect of our inquiry, and we shall return to the subject below.

This separation from 'philosophy' reads strangely today. But the close (and persisting) relationship of medicine to philosophy is a facet of the emphatic rationality of Greek medicine, over against popular superstition and magic. The various schools of Hellenistic medicine corresponded closely to the contemporary philosophical parties, Dogmatists to Stoics, Empirics to Epicureans, and the like. The treatment of disease seemed indissolubly linked with an understanding of the nature of man and his world. It has indeed been suggested that a cardinal weakness of Greek medicine resided here, that its scientific empiricism never excluded the controlling influence of deduction from axiomatic philosophical systems.[4] The strength of presupposition is a factor to be recognized, for good or ill.

The religious language of Greek antiquity also seems disconcerting today. Separate technical terminologies had not been developed, and 'God-language' was often used to express thought which we should do well to transpose into secular terms. The relationship of medicine with religion goes deeper than this. Gods were interpreted as natural powers within the uniformity of nature, or natural powers conceived as divine, without the underlying rationality of thought seeming to be at stake. There was a general rejection of demons as the cause of disease,[5] whereas Asclepius was seen as representing a 'rational theology'.[6] Doctors were not hostile to religious cures. When the physician's art failed, people resorted to prayers and incantations.[7] Indeed, doctors felt absolved from the responsibility of treating hopeless cases; it was part of their art to exercise *pronoia* ('prescience', wider than 'prognosis'), not least to escape blame where chronic or terminal conditions were involved. Such could be referred to the temple, and the doctor's responsibility ceased.

The social status of doctors increased progressively. If at first they were like higher craftsmen, the development of a rational philosophy and science raised their standing. Already in Plato Hippocrates is the type of the man of reason who understands the whole nature of man (*Phaedrus 270* C—D), and in the *Symposium* the pedantic Eryximachus contributes as the spokesman of science. But ethical and professional standards were subject to no public control, and there were doubtless many charlatans at work, especially as the physician was often an itinerant practitioner, plying his trade for hire. Later a more regular programme of training developed with the establishment of medical schools. In Roman times there were 'public' doctors paid by the state, acting in Egypt in mummification, or as coroners or forensic scientists (*POxy* 1.40; 1.51.4). Though the standing of medicine had originally been low in Rome itself, Greek culture came to exercise a great influence there, especially through the residence of eminent figures in Rome, Asclepiades (40 BC) and later Galen himself. In inscriptions of the Empire there were *archiatroi* (chief doctors), often paid by the state and enjoying special privileges.[8] An interesting example of honours paid to a once eminent physician is recorded on an inscription of Rhodiapolis, in Lycia, Asia Minor (*IGRR* 3.733). He was a priest of Asclepius and Hygieia (goddess of health), while also in the first rank as a physician and as medical and philosophical writer and poet ('the Homer of medical poetry'),[9] the recipient of honours from various cities and other bodies, including the council of the Areopagus and the Epicurean philosophers of Athens. His native city further awarded him exemption from public burdens (*aleitourgēsia*) and precedence in seating on public occasions (*proedria*; cf. Mark 12:39 and parallels). The breadth of his achievement, and the conjunction of materialist philosophy not only with medicine but with religious office, are characteristic.

Such an ethical programme as the 'Hippocratic Oath' needs to be understood in its likely social context. It was evidently not of general application, for extant writings include teachings which violate some of its provisions. Before medicine became institutionalized, there was no public guarantee of the competence or ethical standards of independent practitioners, until a school or its leader voluntarily accepted a code of obligation to raise and maintain standards and exclude abuses. Whatever the precise provenance of the Oath, it displays features of this kind. A very close bond unites teacher and pupil in the science, in a relationship of parent to child. The pupil undertakes an obligation to transmit medical knowledge free of charge to his children or the children of his teacher, but to no unauthorized person. Then follow the summary statements of medical ethics, to apply dietary treatment for the benefit of the sick, to refuse to prescribe deadly drugs even if asked, to refuse abortion, to guard life and act in purity and holiness. In visiting a house he must come for the benefit of the sick, to do no intentional injustice, and in particular to have no sexual relations with any person. He must on no account divulge anything he hears or sees in professional confidence, in his treatment or outside it. The most problematic injunction is that he abjures surgery, even on sufferers from stone, but will leave this to those who do it: this may perhaps be the clearest indication that the Oath is a sectarian ideal.[10] But in its totality the Oath sheds evident light on the kinds of abuse to which medicine was prone, and also on the exacting standards demanded of the worthy practitioner.

Medicine was distinctively the 'philanthropic' profession. Where the 'love of man' (*philanthrōpiē*) is present, there is also love of the art (of medicine) (Hippocr., *Praecepta* 6; cf. *de Medico* 1). The Greek concept of 'philanthropy' was not quite ours. It was essentially an outward ethic of public behaviour, of etiquette, and 'bedside manner', of charitableness in accommodating fees to the ability of the poor to pay, for all this redounds to the good name of the doctor's profession and his practice of it, as well as easing the distress of the sick and aiding his recovery. And there is no tension between the ethics of the profession and making a living from it (cf. Plato, *Republic* 340C ff.).

The briefest outline of the principles of Greek medicine would not be complete without some account of its crowning achievement in the work and influence of Galen (c. AD 129–?199). Though later than the NT he sums up much of the thought of preceding periods and his influence pervaded early Christian, and indeed medieval, times. After training in philosophy he travelled and studied widely before his first appointment as surgeon to the gladiators in his native Pergamum. He visited Rome, became a prolific writer and a virulent critic and controversialist, and was later recalled to the capital as personal physician to the Emperor Marcus Aurelius. His own approach was broadly eclectic in theory and practice. His acknowledged master was Hippocrates. He stood with him on the same side of a persisting controversy, that 'nature is the healer of diseases', that the healthy body holds its 'humours' in harmony, and that the doctor's task is basically to assist nature in restoring the proper equilibrium. The focus is upon the organic health of the person, not upon diseases as self-subsisting entities to be matched mechanically to fixed remedies. But Galen's vast range of observation and experience, his grasp of anatomy and clinical practice, enabled him to sum up and extend the whole essence of Greek medical thought in a form adapted for the use of posterity, with the beginnings of a terminology which looks very modern.

Apart from the Hippocratic and Galenic Corpora, neither of them yet completely available in critical editions nor exhaustively studied, a considerable body of ancient medical literature survives. Great figures of the Hellenistic period, like Herophilus and Erasistratus, are represented only in fragments and secondarily in the first-century Roman encyclopaedists Celsus and Scribonius Largus. There is also the *Materia Medica* of Dioscorides (c. AD 60). These sources are supplemented by an interesting variety of archaeological finds, and it is then possible to build up some picture of the practice of Greek medicine in the NT age. Famous temples of Asclepius have been excavated at Epidaurus, Cos, Pergamum and elsewhere, and the island-temple in Rome was the resort of the poor and of sick slaves from an early date. At Pompeii a nursing-home and surgeon's house have been found, and at the latter over two hundred surgical instruments were preserved, identifiable from the descriptions in Celsus. There were military hospitals (*valetudinaria*) on the Roman frontiers, forerunners of medieval and later hospitals. Many inscribed stone stamps have also been found, used for impressing ointments, especially for the eyes, with the maker's name and instructions.

The Romans themselves made little direct contribution to medicine, but their public hygiene, fostered through unequalled arrangements for water-supply and sanitation, marked a great advance. They often scorned clinical practice as fit only for slaves and foreigners, but theoretical medical knowledge was an accepted part of the education of a gentleman.[11] Educated Greeks sometimes served as doctors in Roman households, either as slaves or freedmen, compatible with highly responsible and specialized employment.

Popular attitudes to health and medicine are more widely documented. There are extant many inscribed stones bearing votive inscriptions and thanksgivings to Asclepius and other healing gods. There is much information to be gleaned from the papyri and inscriptions, both about medicine proper and about miraculous temple healings.[12] There are also non-medical literary sources: the literary hypochondriac Aelius Aristides recounts his travels from temple to temple in western Asia Minor. The satirist Lucian (*Philopseudēs* 6–26) gives a typically sarcastic story of superstition undermining science. His spokesman, the sceptical Tychiades, pours scorn on superstitious remedies for a case of rheumatism. A doctor prescribes drugs and dietary treatment, and declares how the gods restore health through doctoring. Then he tells, to Tychiades' disgust, his own accounts of his bronze statue of Hippocrates which walks and mixes drugs, and of a resurrection he had witnessed.

In practice Greek medicine seems to have relied extensively on dietetics, and its principles there were substantially those of the present day. The doctor prescribed rest, baths, clysters, cupping and bleeding, but made less use of drugs, though those used sometimes became very complex compounds in the later periods. There were also notable developments in surgery. Though the surgical part of the Hippocratic Corpus is in confusion, there is an impressive picture to be gleaned from it. Preparation of the operating room, scrupulous cleanliness, arrangement of lighting, dressing of wounds, and some actual surgical procedures, all suggest skilled experience and even resemble modern usage. Anatomical knowledge came into surgery through the Alexandrians after 300 BC, and a standard account of first century surgery is contained in the seventh book of Celsus.[13]

It has been said that the general line of treatment, apart from surgery, was 'not very unlike that of an intelligent and rather conservative English country practitioner of about a century and a half ago'.[14]

The Jewish Background

The cultural world of rural Palestine in the first century was probably more diverse and complex than appears from our limited evidence. The OT tradition of God's sovereignty over health and disease, of the spiritual and moral dimensions of life, of obedience to divinely ordained ritual and dietary laws, was separate from the Greek influence we have been considering. The medical and hygienic importance of the OT laws impresses modern writers; their emphasis is preventive rather than therapeutic (but see also chapter 3).[15]

In first-century Judaism the Essenes, with whom the Qumran community which produced the Dead Sea Scrolls is usually identified, were noted for their medical studies: 'They display an extraordinary interest in the writings of the ancients, singling out in particular those which make for the welfare of soul and body; with the help of these, and with a view to the treatment of diseases, they make investigations into medicinal roots and the properties of stones.'[16] J. B. Lightfoot, however, argued in the light of another passage in Josephus, that these studies related to charms for exorcizing demons rather than to medicine proper.[17] In any case this sect laid great stress on purification by water.[18]

Contemporary with the Essenes and akin to them were the Therapeutae in Alexandria, described at length by Philo (*de Vita Contemplativa, passim*), their name bearing the double sense of 'worshippers' and 'healers' (*de Vit. Cont.* 1–2). They were apparently an ascetic group who professed the skill to heal bodily, psychological and spiritual ills alike.

Whereas these sects seem to have represented strong religious and ascetic tendencies within Judaism, it is likely that most Jewish life had already been strongly pervaded with Greek influences and that country people in Galilee were open to many unsophisticated superstitions and misunderstandings. The Gospels sometimes reveal popular beliefs, that sickness was the consequence of sin, and its penalty might work out in later generations (e.g. John 9: 2–3).[19] Such views might, of course, claim Old Testament support, in the sense that they moralize disease as divine punishment under the rule of a holy God, but they reduce the profound ethical wrestling and theodicy of the Scripture to a popular notion of offence and retribution. Even if mind and body interact, even though *some* human disease is traceable, directly or indirectly, to human sin, this is not a sufficient or normative explanation of sickness and suffering, as Jesus himself pointed out.

Early Jewish literary sources are not easily found. A passage in Ecclesiasticus 38:1–15, of the second century BC, reflects the honour due to the doctor. The main sources for ancient Judaism are contained in the Rabbinic writings, which as they stand are of considerably later date, but include compilations of much earlier traditions. There is always a certain danger in using their evidence retrospectively; until the discovery of the Dead Sea Scrolls our picture of first century Judaism, and of Pharisaism in particular, was inevitably a reading back of partly later material.[20] Subject to this necessary caution, we may obtain a lively picture of Jewish medicine from Rosner's account of references in the Talmud, especially the sections dealing with physicians.[21] There is a curious recurring phrase that 'the best of physicians are destined for Gehenna'. The point may be that such are tempted to conceit before God and may be responsible for their patient's death, or else refuse to attend the poor—though a physician who heals for nothing is worth nothing. The full account of the renowned physician and sage Mar Samuel (c. 2–3 AD) shows his great versatility as a polymath, as well as his range of pronouncements in all areas of medicine, notably in ophthalmology and bloodletting. Many of his sayings read quaintly, and many of the remedies are based on folk medicine and have no modern medical counterpart (p. 164). He seems, however, to have had a vast knowledge of anatomy.

The Talmud enters into refined debates about the rights and wrongs of permitting a heathen to treat a Jew, or whether he may do so without payment, or circumcise a Jewish boy, or offer treatment which might involve profanation of the Sabbath.[22] The relationship between Judaism and Greek culture was a very difficult and sensitive question, and many stereotyped traditional impressions are probably open to debate. This is specially true of the Judaism of the Dispersion, where Jews were living in a predominantly Greek context.[23]

Diseases in the New Testament World

Evidences for the incidence of diseases and their identification are not so easily found for the NT period, as we depend largely on the uncertain terminology of literary sources, and there are few bodily remains, like the Egyptian mummies of earlier date. Nevertheless, some fascinating glimpses have been unexpectedly preserved. Occasionally coin-portraiture preserves identifiable physical blemishes even of kings, where their heads have been depicted realistically without idealization.[24] Lesions on the forehead or beneath the eyes of Parthian kings have been diagnosed from their coins as cases of *epithelioma adenoides cysticum* or *trichoepithelioma*, a tumour originating in a hair follicle, often hereditary, and sometimes bilateral, and so seen in some full-face portraits. Goitre, endemic today in mountainous areas of Greece, Sicily and Asia Minor, has been observed on coin-heads of rulers from these areas, notably of Philetaerus and Eumenes II of Pergamum and Nicomedes II of Bithynia, and probably also of the famous Cleopatra. As even gods and goddesses are represented with goitre in this area, the condition may have been so prevalent as to be acceptable even in idealization. The features of Ptolemy I of Egypt typify acromegaly, an overgrowth of bone and soft tissue and a backward-slanting forehead.

Occasionally there have been finds of skeletal remains well enough preserved to permit some anatomical examination shedding light on deformities or causes of death. A remarkable group of finds from Jerusalem will be considered later from the point of view of the discovery of a victim of crucifixion.[25] The tombs concerned are of first century BC to first century AD, containing the secondary burial in ossuaries of family groups. Apparent causes of death include crucifixion, violence, fire, childbirth, and in two children starvation, indicated by a type of cribrosis of temporal bones and the orbital roofs, and probably also in one case osteomyelitis consequent upon a brutal molar extraction. There are traces also of arthritis and of osteoporosis in older subjects. The remains of the crucified man were of special interest. His facial skeleton was asymmetrical with a palatal cleft, features explained as denoting critical stresses in his mother's pregnancy and a most difficult birth, but his life showed no signs of physical damage or hard labour before its violent end, in striking contrast with the remains of women who showed physical development suggesting hard labour or constant hill climbing.

Such finds are exceptional. Whatever their intrinsic interest, they give us no sufficient basis for generalizing about the incidence of medical conditions in first-century Palestine. We may get a slightly more representative idea from the comparative statistics offered by Prof. A. Rendle Short for Transjordan in 1936 and Bristol in 1951.[26] The incidence of a group of infectious diseases differs sharply between the two lists, and their fatality more so. Measles was far more prevalent in Bristol, but was the dominant killer of the group in Transjordan. Almost all the Bristol deaths were caused by tuberculosis, a lesser factor in Transjordan. Malaria far outnumbered all other notified cases in Transjordan, but scarcely occurred in Bristol. Typhoid, typhus and cerebro-spinal meningitis were all much commoner and more dangerous in Transjordan, whereas dysentery (of a mild type) had almost double the incidence in Bristol, though frequent in both. Of other diseases, trachoma, a potent source of blindness, was a major problem in Transjordan, and in the 1932 census 8 per thousand of the population of Palestine were blind.

Figures of this kind are not of course a sufficient guide. They can be no more than suggestive of continuities where climate and conditions remain relatively unchanged, but the position is hugely complicated by the spread of epidemic diseases and even the onset of new illnesses, no less than by the conquest of former scourges by medical advances. There is indeed the contention that leprosy itself was rare or unknown in the Middle East in early times, a point of focal biblical interest to which we must return below.

Thus far we have considered the possibility of inferring or diagnosing ancient conditions externally from modern survivals. The central problem of this study will be the identification of the diseases named or described in our biblical texts. This is a far more difficult and doubtful matter. Many of the ancient lexical terms are flexible and unsystematic. They are commonly applied to symptoms rather than to the technical discrimination of the diseases causing those symptoms. As, for instance, with the naming of plants in Theophrastus or Pliny, superficial resemblance is not consistently separated from deeper relationship. And there are no detailed technical descriptions of medical conditions in the Gospels to justify overconfidence in diagnosis. It may be questioned whether some of the identifications commonly offered are sufficiently established linguistically or contextually.

The 'leprosy' word-group is the classic case. The lexica render *lepra* as 'leprosy', *lepros* as a 'leper'. The words have been much debated, and the OT Hebrew words they render in the Septuagint. It is now quite widely agreed that the Hebrew and Greek words do not refer to any type of 'leprosy' (Hansen's disease) now so called, but to a variety of skin conditions which brought temporary or permanent defilement, among which Hansen's disease was probably not even included (see chapter 4).

The New Testament Language of Healing and Disease

Three Greek words are used for 'heal' in the New Testament: *iasthai, therapeuein* and *sōzein*. It is important to see words in terms of usage, not to argue from theoretical studies of etymologies, and so to realize the inherent flexibility of language, whose nuances are not to be hardened into subtly rigid distinctions of general application. Subject to this caution, *therapeuein* is commonly the word used of medical treatment. It may, however, be a quite general word for 'heal', and is freely used of Jesus' healing miracles, occurring forty-five times altogether, almost all in the Gospels and Acts, and applied either to healing diseases or people 'from' diseases. The cognate noun is *therapeia* (3 times). The root meaning is of 'service', often of 'worship' of a god (cf. Acts 17:25). The word-group can be used of unsuccessful medical treatment, as in the papyrus where patients complain of 'bad' *therapeia* (POxy 1.40.8, 2nd—3rd cent. AD.

Iasthai is also a general word for 'heal' (twenty-six times in the NT), often apparently interchangeably synonymous with *therapeuein*. Sometimes, however, it occurs in the context of an immediate healing at a definite time (Matt. 8:13, 15:28; Luke 8:47) or of the patient's realization that healing has already taken place (Mark 5:29; cf. again Luke 8:47). Unlike *therapeuein* it is also used metaphorically of spiritual regeneration or restoration (Matt. 13:15; John 12:40; both reflecting Isa. 6:10 *LXX*; 1 Pet. 2:24).

Sōzein is the verb commonly rendered 'save', cognate with *sōtēr* (saviour) and *sōtēria* (salvation). In Hellenistic culture of the first century the concept of 'salvation' was very prevalent, as may be seen for instance in Paul's encounters with Gentile paganism at Philippi (Acts 16:17,30). The word-group is very common in the inscriptions in several senses, notably where 'saviour' is a formal title accorded to emperors or public benefactors are referred to. The god Asclepius is 'Soter' in his capacity as healer. At a more mundane level, 'salvation' is the constant prayer of the ordinary man, in a sense comprehending health and prosperity and deliverance from all ills of life and eternity. It is a comprehensive word, in which the material, the spiritual and the physical are not necessarily conceptually separated, a vogue-word with something of the emotive flavour of 'security' today. The verb *sōzein* (but not its cognates) is used sometimes in the NT of physical healing (Mark 5:28,34 = Matt. 9:21–22; Mark 6:56) or of the healing of a demoniac (Luke 8:36). In some of these cases an explicit link is made with the 'faith' to be healed (cf. also Acts 14:9). Of Lazarus in John 11:12 the implication is: 'If he is asleep he will recover (be saved).' The taunt to Jesus on the cross is 'save yourself' (Mark 15:30–31 = Matt. 27:40,42,49). 'To save one's life' (from shipwreck) in Acts 27:20,31, or in the saying of Jesus, 'whosoever will save his life (*psychē*) shall lose it' (Mark 8:35 = Matt. 16:25 = Luke 9:24) is similar. 'To save from danger' may in fact be expressed by a compound *diasōzein* or *eksōzein*. But even the explicit thought of physical healing passes over very easily into the spiritual (Jas. 5:15,20), and the medical image, whatever the actual words used, provides a ready metaphor for the spiritual (Matt. 9:12 = Luke 5:31; Luke 4:23, 'Physician, heal yourself', using the ordinary *therapeúein*).

The noun *iatrós* (doctor, physician) occurs only seven times in the NT, and the corresponding abstract noun *íasis* three times. Four of the references to *iatrós* are in the figurative expressions just mentioned. In Mark 5:23 we are told that the woman with the haemorrhage had suffered many things at the hands of many doctors and had spent all her substance, and the parallel in Luke 8:43 stresses that none could cure her.[27] There is no indication whether we should think of Greek or Jewish practitioners, or whether perhaps a sufferer sought help in whatever quarter she might, reputable or otherwise. The point is that Jesus possessed authority over disease and suffering where every human resource, scientific or religious, had failed. The only other passage is the allusion to 'Luke the beloved physician' in Col. 4:14. The noun *íasis* is found only in the Lukan writings (Luke 13:32; Acts 4:22,30), referring to miraculous healings by Jesus and the apostles.

The identification of particular diseases in their biblical contexts must be held over for further consideration below, but something must be said on the general terms used for sickness. Again, it is good to register a caution against making refined distinctions on grounds of etymology.[28] The ordinary Greek word for 'disease' is *nósos*' (eleven times in the NT): the verb *noseîn* is used only once, and then figuratively (1 Tim 6:4). The commoner word in the NT is *asthéneia*; in Paul's writings mostly in its etymological sense of 'weakness', or in the plural 'infirmities', but sometimes, especially in the Gospels, of sickness generally. There are twenty-four occurrences altogether. The word is freely used in a spiritual sense, but the line between the literal and metaphorical is not always easy to draw. The corresponding verb *astheneîn* is the regular NT term for 'to be sick' (35 times), and the adjective *asthenēs* is freely used both for 'sick' and 'weak' (23 times). Other occasional words are *malahía* (literally 'softness'), *mastix* (literally 'whip', 'scourge') and *básanos* (literally 'trial', 'torment'). Matt. 8:17 cites Isa. 53:4, with *nósoi* and *asthéneiai* (plurals) in Hebraic synonymous parallelism. Elsewhere Matthew couples *nósos* both with *malakía* (4:23, 9:35, 10:1) and with *básanos* (4:24). Other general terms include *árrhōstos* ('sick', 'powerless'), almost an exact synonym of the common *asthenēs*, and *pyretós* ('fever') with the corresponding verb *pyréssein*. *Kámnein* ('to be weary', 'to be sick') is used literally only in the important passage Jas. 5:15 (but cf. Heb. 12:3); it should probably not be pressed to denote 'be hopelessly sick', 'waste away', for the word, though so rare in the NT, is a common and relatively colourless one.[29] There is also the idiomatic *kakōs echein* ('to be bad', literally 'to have badly').

Luke the Physician

Early tradition is unanimous in ascribing the authorship of the Third Gospel and Acts to Luke 'the beloved physician'. The supposition that the two longest books in the New Testament, together amounting to some two-sevenths of its total bulk, were written by a doctor, trained in some kind of the cultural background we have described, would be of wider interest and implication. As the two books are anonymous as they stand, this traditional identification demands some discussion.

The first-person narrative sections in Acts (the so-called 'we-passages', 16:10–17; 20:5–21:17; chaps. 27–28) have been most naturally understood as indicating unobtrusively the presence of the author as eye-witness and companion of Paul on those occasions, a view corroborated by the wealth of precise, incidental detail in these passages. Luke is named in the New Testament only at Colossians 4:14, 2 Timothy 4:11 and Philemon 24.[30] Only Colossians characterizes him as the 'beloved physician', and its context (vs. 10–11) implies also that he was a Gentile. There is no apparent reason why the early church should have chosen to ascribe the writings unanimously to this person unless it preserved sound tradition. The ascription has been almost universally accepted until nineteenth-century criticism began to question more radically authorship by a companion (or contemporary) of Paul. The late dating of Acts in the Tübingen School's reconstruction of early Christian history automatically involved discarding the tradition.

In 1882 W. F. Hobart published a classic study, *The Medical Language of St. Luke*,[31] which argued impressively with extensive documentation that the medical vocabulary of Luke-Acts, as paralleled with the language of the Greek medical writers, showed the author's medical background. This long seemed a powerful corroboration of the tradition, until Hobart's work was trenchantly criticized by H. J. Cadbury, who exposed the perils of arguing from uncontrolled parallels.[32] Many of Hobart's examples are indecisive or inappropriate. Where a word might seem distinctively medical, it is not necessarily found in Luke: *haimorrhoein* (to have haemorrhage), for instance, is found only at Matthew 9:20. We have also seen that Greek medicine, having its roots in philosophy, was slow to develop a narrowly technical vocabulary. Most of the words in

Hobart had a much wider currency. So his case can no longer be accepted, though his work remains valuable as a compendium of lexical evidence.

Yet, while we concede that Hobart has not proved his case, the fact remains that the richer vocabulary of Luke's writings is fully consistent with the traditional view, as the work of a man of some considerable Greek culture. If, like the present writer, one is firmly convinced on other grounds that the book must be the authentic work of a companion of Paul, the tradition is persuasive. There is no alternative candidate in the field.

A first question then arising is whether the writer's profession has otherwise left its stamp on his writing. It is an old speculation, held in differing forms by Hobart and by Ramsay,[33] that Luke attended Paul in his professional capacity. If Paul's 'thorn in the flesh' was a chronic or recurring disease, this possibility might seem the more plausible. It will not, however, be profitable here to read too much into even the first-person narratives of Acts. It may be too easy to find what one is predisposed to seek.

A further question is whether a scientific temper appears in the quality of Luke's reporting. Current biblical scholarship is apt to discount this line of thought in favour of stressing Luke's importance as a creative theologian. There is of course no doubt that he writes as a theological advocate, but to assent to that does not answer the different question of his reliability as a reporter. He ostensibly follows the style of Greek historical writing, with a formal preface (Luke 1:1–3) and a shorter resumptive preface and address in the sequel (Acts 1:1).[34] However, his real qualities are not to be assessed by the facile application of comparative literary studies, but by his performance, where many details can be confirmed, especially from the evidence of inscriptions. This in its turn is not a simplistic formula for proving his reliability, though it does serve to dispose of errors in some incautious attacks upon it. I have argued elsewhere that Luke actually stands in the tradition of a very exacting school of Greek historiography, stressing autopsy and the critical interviewing of eye-witnesses, and that his theology is intimately linked to his history, as the interpretation of that history, the truth of which is assured by rigorous standards of evidence.[35]

This has become a somewhat unconventional view, contrary to over-simplified assumptions about the pre-critical and pre-scientific character of classical antiquity. It may also seem for a moment to have been a digression from our medical theme. But ancient learning was less specialized or compartmentalized. We have noted the instance of a doctor who was also an historian, and a classic description of the symptoms of the plague in Periclean Athens is given by a historian who practised an exacting standard of critical observation (Thucydides 2.48–50). Again we must insist on caution, not to draw a simplistic direct link between medicine and historiography, especially as some historians stood in a very different rhetorical tradition. But the stress in Luke's preface on the part of the eye-witness (*autoptēs*) and participant is closely paralleled in the language of the best Greek historiography (e.g. Polybius 3.4.13), as well as in the observational basis of the best Greek medicine: Hobart cites eleven instructive cases of *autoptēs* from Galen.

We shall refrain from building on unverifiable inferences about the qualities of 'Luke the physician', and rest content with posing some of the questions implicit in the identification. (a) There is much discussion today of the social status of Paul. That of Luke is no less debatable. If a doctor, and a highly educated Greek Gentile, was he also a slave, or perhaps a freedman dependant who stood legally in a socially formalized 'client' relationship with his 'patron' Paul? We can only speculate, while recognizing that Luke's Christian devotion transcended any such unknown status-pattern.[36] (b) The development of a Christian culture and ethic and its relation to Greek culture is an evident problem of the early church.[37] We find here (if only from the Pauline reference in Colossians) that a doctor was a prominent figure in the earliest Christian movement, and the practice of his art evidently fully accepted. (c) The double work Luke-Acts is a storm-centre of critical debate today, and a view of the writer as a later theological editor of traditions, remote from the historical Paul and even uninterested in him except as a vehicle of Lukan theology, is widespread, even prevalent. Of course this debate raises hugely complex questions, on which opinion tends to be polarized. In this context it is unfashionable to defend 'Luke the physician', a notion tied inevitably to a traditional view dismissed as naive. But I am firmly convinced of the traditional view, upon what I take to be compelling evidence. And then it is legitimate to explore the implications of Luke the 'historian', the 'man of science'. To do that is not to deny for a moment that he is also a theological advocate, but a balanced view must ask all the relevant questions. This, however, is not the place to pursue the critical implications, and I shall not attempt here to draw further conclusions.

Miracles

The survey of the New Testament evidence cannot altogether

avoid the issue of miracle in its bearing on the exegesis of passages of medical importance. The concept of miracle itself raises acute difficulty for secular modern man, whereas in some other cultures miracle actually authenticates belief.[38]

The central crux for our present purpose focuses on the healing miracles ascribed to Jesus in the Gospels. The intrinsic difficulty of the subject is greatly compounded here by prior critical doubts of the authenticity of the incidents presented. The techniques of 'form criticism' (particularly as extended in 'tradition criticism') and of 'redaction criticism' have often been used to suggest that the narratives were created or elaborated in the post-resurrection church. It may be objected that the valid perceptions on which these methods rest have been over-extended and built into a structure of cumulatively sceptical hidden presuppositions, themselves deriving ultimately from the rationalistic principles of the German Enlightenment. These methods must then be handled with discrimination. The state of Gospel criticism today is fluid, even confused, and the mechanical outworking of over-rigid techniques of criticism has led some into an unbalanced hypercriticism. This is no place to pursue the debate. I would argue strongly for an early essential date of the Gospel materials, a point at once circumscribing the time-lapse on which elaborate tradition-history theories depend. I want to defend the essential authenticity of the material, and so to argue that the question of miracle must be faced as posed by the ostensible texts, where some current views actually miss the issue by dismissing the textual witness too easily.

At another level modern medicine has sometimes been enlisted in defence of the miracles, in its fresh understanding of the psychosomatic dimensions of sickness. But attempts to see Jesus as anticipating modern techniques of psychotherapy, or as treating only a narrow range of diseases of hysterical origin, seem ill conceived.[39] These rationalizations will clearly not explain the nature miracles, if we take them seriously. Jesus is presented as wielding a spiritual authority, not a technique. Further, there is the crucial case of the resurrection. Despite modern scepticism, we have to reckon here with physical phenomena, the empty tomb (whose rejection by some is arbitrary), the evidences of death (notably the 'blood' and the 'water', John 19:34),[40] the testimony of the eyewitnesses and of the appearances of the risen Christ. In the assessment of some of these evidences the medical aspect is clearly relevant, and the issue transcends the psychosomatic dimension.

The attempt now sometimes made to dismiss miracle as rooted in a pre-scientific world-view is itself presuppositional.[41] It may involve a radical oversimplification of the processes of intellectual history. The ancient world had its own varieties both of popular superstition and of materialistic rationalism. Paul faced the scorn of Epicurean philosophers at Athens (Acts 17); and the concept of demon possession was alien to scientific Greek medicine. Yet the New Testament distinguishes physical disease from possession. Jesus is presented as recognizing the differences between the physical and the spiritual roots of illness. He corrects popular belief that suffering or disease is divine punishment for sin, though it may be the raw material of redemption to God's glory.

The NT never indulges in tales of the marvellous, in the manner of apocryphal writings. Its writers are restrained in their accounts. The 'we-passages' in Acts, which we assign to a doctor and eye-witness, are almost devoid of miraculous healings, and where one such case, the raising of Eutychus, occurs within their general limits, the author himself was briefly absent, and writes with an almost ambiguous reserve. The implication seems to be that Eutychus was dead, but he cannot vouch personally for clinical death. We see the same reserve in the snake incident on Malta (Acts 28:3–6), which may in any case have involved a harmless species. There is no attempt to magnify the event; indeed Luke turns his irony upon the superstitions of the local people.[42]

The NT miracles are never wonders for their own sake. Those of Jesus are in some respects unique. (1) The incarnation of God in human life in a unique personality involved the manifestation of that divinity to those who had eyes to see. (2) The love of Jesus for people in need overflowed in the application of his personality and power to them where doctors and other human resources could not help. (3) In his miracles, as in his spoken discourse Jesus was teaching people as they were ready and able to understand, against a background of misunderstanding. (4) The miracles were, in John's term, 'signs', specifically to challenge faith and point to the great events of Jesus' death and resurrection where the purpose of his life was supremely manifested. These facets are not, I think, really separable, but illustrative of Jesus' unique person in its unity and integrity. In the Gospel accounts he displays a reserve, almost a secrecy, where people were moved only by curiosity or misunderstanding, or wanted to use him for ends of their own. Yet his miracles focus on his own personality, and bear their testimony to it, whereas those of his disciples focus also on him, and the human channel is unimportant.

In such a context a medical approach to the miracles of Jesus must, I think content itself with seeking to glean what we may about the diseases, and recognize where Jesus' dealing with people displays spiritual, pastoral and psychological insight integral to his unique personality and perhaps describable with relation to modern understanding of psychosomatic medicine and the like, but not explained by it. The actual healings are evidently not amenable to medical explanation.

The range of the question may be conveniently demarcated by citing statistics from Rendle Short (p. 102): 'There are twenty-four stories of the healings of individuals, usually one, sometimes two, once ten. From seven of these a demon was cast out. On eleven occasions friends brought the sufferer; in six, the patient himself made an appeal. In seven cases, Christ healed without any request being recorded. On three occasions, He healed at a distance without meeting the patient. Eight sick persons He healed by a touch; in seven He just spoke the word. On three occasions He spat, and touched the one who was to be cured'. These computations may of course be questioned, even if only because it is not always quite clear where we are dealing with separate incidents. But this listing will suffice for our present purpose. It is good to observe their variety. Only in a minority of cases did Jesus heal in direct response to the expressed faith of the sufferer. We may too easily extrapolate from a few familiar passages to an oversimplified spiritualizing, of physical healing as a picture of spiritual salvation from sin through faith. To register this caution does not deny that Jesus could not do many mighty works because of the unbelief of his own people (Matt. 13:58). It suggests merely that faith is not invariably the central lesson to learn. The healing miracles are profound and varied in their testimony to Jesus' own person and to his dealings with the complex variety of human need. The means and circumstances are very varied, but where Jesus uses or commands any physical means the point lies not in medical efficacy but in personal dealing and obedient response. It is true that the physical and spiritual here cannot ultimately be divorced, but the relationships are not conformed to a simple pattern. A further point is the strong emphasis upon testimony to the truth: in John's perspective the miracles are 'signs' (*sēmeia*) pointing to the person of Christ. The tendency of much modern scholarship is to discount the particularities in John in favour of seeing it as a reflective, 'spiritual' Gospel, but this separation of the historical from the spiritual seems quite misconceived in view of the writer's expressed intention (John 20:30–31).

The Virgin Birth

It is a very debatable question whether modern biological science has any contribution to make to the problem of the virgin birth.

The point has sometimes been made that instances of parthenogenesis are known, and even widespread, among the lower animals. It is also very doubtful whether that fact may credibly be seen as a kind of stepping-stone to ease the sceptic's difficulty in accepting the miraculous birth of Jesus. The classic study of the virgin birth by J. Gresham Machen deals very fully with the textual evidences and objections, but wisely cautions against inadequate apologetic: 'If the virgin birth is reduced to the level of a biological triviality, it becomes quite unbelievable; the weight of presumption against it is too powerful to be overcome.'[43] Again, 'It still remains true in general that the question of the virgin birth brings us sharply before the question of the supernatural, and the man who accepts the virgin birth has taken his stand squarely upon supernaturalistic ground.'[44] A medical writer, A. Rendle Short, gives an interesting account of biological parthenogenesis, but repeats a similar caution. There is nothing grotesquely impossible in the idea of inducing artificial parthenogenesis, and in fact it is not certainly known why fertilization is necessary. Such an affirmation of course counters the dogmatic denial of parthenogenesis, but does nothing to support the claims for the birth of Jesus, which was in its essence unique and not amenable to an inadequate naturalistic explanation.[45]

Undeterred by these warnings, some have continued to seek biological interpretations. Most recently an interesting and (apparently) biologically authoritative article attempts to unravel the mechanics of virgin birth; concluding that Jesus was unique in the consequence of being 'chromosomally female and phenotypically male at the same time', and thus the perfect human being, androgynous in a unique sense.[46] The writer gives a most impressive array of evidence for parthenogenesis in nature, but he leaves the layman with the persisting impression that he is offering, with all his up-to-date sophistication, the wrong kind of explanation.

The Crucifixion

Three problems here claim at least brief discussion: (1) the mode of crucifixion; (2) the actual cause of Jesus' death; (3) the medical significance of the blood and water flowing from the body (John 19:34). The three topics are closely related and will be considered together.

The aim of crucifixion was to prolong agony, often for several days. The Romans had refined the process by driving the nails through the flesh of the ankles and wrists to avoid the bone, and supporting the body sufficiently to prevent rapid death through collapse due to the total weight dragging on the arms. Scholars of differing viewpoints concur in the belief that none of the wounds inflicted on Jesus in the scourging and crucifixion would normally be quickly fatal to a man of his age in good health.[47] The early onset of Jesus' death was evidently unusual, and surprising to Pilate.

Some new light has been thrown on the mode of crucifixion by the first discovery of actual skeletal remains of a victim from a tomb-ossuary found in 1968 at Giv'at ha-Mivtar in the northern suburbs of Jerusalem.[48] There has been some debate here about the position of the legs. The man may have been crucified in an abnormal position, whether with the legs spread apart or with the knees bent together to one side. In either case it may be problematic to argue from an exceptional instance. It is, however, worth observing at this stage that recent study has stressed the great variety of practice in the forms of crucifixion, even in the Roman period.[49]

First, then, let us seek to clarify some points in the text of John 19. The soldiers did not break Jesus' legs because he was already dead (v.33), but one of them thrust his spear into Jesus' side, and blood and water came out. The writer makes a very solemn asseveration of the truth of the eye-witness testimony on this point (v. 35). This happened, then, *after* Jesus' death, and the soldier's intention is not explained.[50]

The breaking of a prisoner's legs (Latin *crurifragium*) was occasionally a punishment in itself, but was not necessarily a part of crucifixion. In the present case we are told it was prompted by the Jewish desire to have the business finished before the Passover Sabbath (v.31). John's point is to stress the fulfilment of Scripture (Ps. 34:20; Zech. 12:10) in the particular circumstances of Jesus' death, which were distinct not so much from usual practice as from those of his fellow-sufferers, whose deaths were otherwise induced and bore none of the same unique significance.

It seems likely that the spear-thrust was not gratuitous abuse of the body but to verify death. Roman soldiers were not experts in human physiology, but they were certainly trained to know beyond question when a crucified man was dead, and where precisely to strike to expose the accumulation of fluids in the newly dead. The ancient difficulty that corpses do not bleed is clearly beside the point: the problem is to identify the precise conditions under which unclotted blood and colourless fluid would have been separately discernible by a witness. The circumstances have occasioned much debate.

The normal immediate cause of death in crucifixion was asphyxia,[51] where the weight of the arms fixed in a position of inspiration would impair oxygenation and produce gradual asphyxiation, a process which might be greatly prolonged if a wooden peg gave some support to the victim in his continual reaching to ease his weight and breathing. But the death of Jesus was unusual in its rapidity, and the question persists whether a different physical cause operated earlier in his case.

The layman approaches this question with diffidence and bewilderment in the face of the diverse medical suggestions. In a most interesting study[52] Dr. J. Wilkinson argues that none of the proximate sufferings, the spiritual agony, exposure, hunger, thirst, infection or loss of blood would in themselves cause death so rapidly, though any or all, singly or in combination, were mortal in the long run. There was also the imperfectly understood factor of shock, to which several of the preceding conditions could have contributed. But 'shock involves a depression of all the body's faculties and functions, and a gradual ebbing away of life as the state of shock becomes irreversible and then fatal' (p 105). According to the Gospels Jesus did not lose consciousness before he died (cf. Mark 15:34; Luke 23:46). Wilkinson argues further against four main theories of the cause of death: rupture of the heart (Stroud 1847), embolism (Vincent Taylor 1957), asphyxia (Le Bec 1925, Barbet 1950), and acute dilatation of the stomach (J. L. Cameron 1947, Rendle Short 1953), as for various reasons none of these could naturally explain the rapid and sudden death of a man not suffering from previous disease of the coronary arteries or some other relevant condition. Wilkinson himself believes that Jesus voluntarily surrendered his life on the cross before the merely physical causes of death by crucifixion could operate.

There is certainly a truth in the idea that Jesus held the initiative and surrendered himself to death. But a theological difficulty arises if this idea is pressed to give an alternative explanation of the physical causes of death. If Jesus could choose the moment of his death, he did not experience death as men know it, and his full humanity is called in question.[53] Alternative views of the physical cause of death are still vigorously urged as live options.

Dr. K. Leese argues that medical knowledge of the effect of stress on the organs of the body is still so uncertain that lethal psychosomatic effects cannot be excluded. Bleeding from laceration of the hand could be very serious,[54] and shock could have been rapid in onset. In particular, coronary thrombosis is not necessarily associated with previous heart disease. 'Much experimental knowledge is available nowadays, which suggests that the cause of such heart attacks is really linked to a cascade of biochemical events initiated by the stress-stimulated production of noradrenaline. If this is so, mental agony, associated with the oligaemic shock produced by injury, could have been a lethal combination producing the sudden death of Christ by cardiac syncope.'[55]

I am indebted to the editor for much assistance here. He assures me that the majority of medical opinion still favours cardiac tamponade (though most of the classic statements of this position are now old) as fulfilling the requirements of the two basic clues, the suddenness of death, and the blood and the water. If the left side is pierced after death by a large knife (or a Roman spear), three well-recorded or two very rare conditions may ensue. Death by crucifixion would normally occasion one of the commoner cases, where a copious flow of blood only follows the wound, from a condition of the lungs similar to that caused by drowning or strychnine poisoning. But if a victim died from rupture of the heart, this would produce the rare case where a copious flow of blood was succeeded by a copious flow of water. In experiments with animals Dr. John Hunter found that the presence of fear and pain before death prevented clotting of the blood, a phenomenon now explained by the presence of fibrinolysins in the blood in such cases. Fear and pain would certainly have been present at the crucifixion. The only real possibilities for the source of the blood and the water are the pleural and pericardial cavities, for the heart itself contains too little. A large collection of pleural fluid could be explained only by broken ribs from the flogging, but then Jesus could never have cried aloud just before death. On the contrary, his death has all the characteristics of a cardiac death, with a few seconds' premonition and sudden collapse. The leaking of arterial blood under pressure into the pericardial sac would rapidly cause cardiac tamponade. This leaking could be due to rupture of the heart itself, or more probably at the join between the arch of the aorta and the left ventricle. The effect of circulating fibrinolysins in preventing blood-clotting would be that the blood would settle within thirty minutes, with the red cells falling to the bottom and leaving the clear plasma at the top.

This amounts to an updating of Dr. W. Stroud's classic theory of heart-rupture, which is criticized by Wilkinson as untenable today.[56] The matter cannot be clarified without some further discussion of the origin of the blood and the water, of which Wilkinson again offers the fullest consideration of alternative explanations. He finally favours one of those explanations which derive the two fluids from separate but adjacent locations penetrated by the spear, the blood either from the lung (Houghton, before 1881) or the heart cavity (Barbet 1963), the watery fluid coming in either case from the pericardial sac, Houghton being preferred if the order 'blood and water' be taken as significant, but needing modification to be acceptable to modern medical knowledge.[57] To these possibilities we must add the above suggestion that both blood and water came from the pericardial sac, for Wilkinson rejects this in the dated form held by Stroud, who supposed that the blood would have clotted and separated into clot and serum. The newer knowledge shows that the conditions would have prevented clotting. In any case, then, there is significant agreement that the 'water' came from the pericardial sac, though the source of the blood remains in dispute. There might be significant further light if we knew the height of the cross and the type of spear and blade, for these factors could have made significant differences to the nature and angle of the wound. On Wilkinson's suggested diagnosis Jesus was but newly dead, and postmortem changes had barely begun to occur: on the editor's view a short lapse of time after death is required for the settling of the components of the blood. In either case it seems that the collected fluids flowed out when exposed to the force of gravity—there is no evidence here for circulation. Probably more water emerged than blood, for thus they would have remained more distinctly visible to the observer.

We come back to the various causes of death which have been canvassed recently. The part played by asphyxia in prolonged deaths by crucifixion will not explain Jesus' rapid and sudden death. Wilkinson objects, also, that the *sedile*, a peg on which to sit and take much of the weight, was necessary, or the nails would tear out if inserted through the palms of the hands. Barbet 'is obliged' to suggest that they were driven through the wrists[58]—but this is precisely the case in the Jerusalem find. Acute dilatation of the stomach is a condition occurring as a complication of surgical shock, and has the attraction of providing a possible explanation of the blood and water,[59] the 'water' in this case being a brownish-black liquid and the wound being on the left side to involve the stomach. But again a crucial objection is that this complication usually takes a few days to develop. Embolism is not explicable as a consequence of spiritual suffering, but again implies preceding disease or injury which cannot be postulated here. Wilkinson makes similar objections to the classic theory of heart rupture, but Leese (above) denies that coronary thrombosis is necessarily associated with previous heart disease, and the editor explains the case as characteristic of a cardiac death.

That is as far as a layman dare venture to collate the differing perspectives of others. The difficulty may, of course, be due simply to the incompleteness of the clinical data for a firm diagnosis. But the case is discussable in principle; its unusual features are very precisely recorded as faithful testimony; they put the fact of death beyond dispute and seem to point to a cardiac cause. It is wise to be cautious, but Wilkinson may be unduly pessimistic about the prospects of identifying a physical cause or combination of causes.[60] Jesus was already dead at the time of the spear-wound, and that in turn, whether intended merely to verify or to ensure death, was itself a mortal blow to the heart or its vicinity.

Despite these considerations, variants of the classic 'swoon' theory of H. E. G. Paulus are occasionally revived. W. B. Primrose, the Senior Anaesthetist in a Scottish hospital, has argued from the blood and the water that Jesus was not really dead.[61] After discussing the effects of the scourging and nailing he explains the fluids as a pale, straw-coloured serum with a staining of red, accumulated in the abdomen, and released from it by a penetrating, but unimportant, wound there. He draws attention to the carefully recorded eye-witness testimony to the fluids, and regards it as providing evidence that some circulation was still present. He supposes that Jesus revived under the influence of the rapid drop of temperature in the tomb at night, 'a definite interval of time separating the two phenomena of "death" and revival, the somatic activities having been maintained at a very low level from which recovery took place as soon as conditions came to favour this' (p.388).

This reconstruction bristles with problems. Wilkinson points out that Primrose's account of the scourging is contrary to what we know of Roman practice. Primrose has to insist on the application of scourging to the *front* of the body, for it is thus that he explains the fluids in the abdomen. The spear-thrust in the abdomen was unimportant and would have healed quickly: it is taken to be a different wound from that shown to Thomas (John 20:27) in Jesus' side, and which was due, not to the spear-thrust, but to the splitting of the skin by the scourge. But both John 19:34 and 20:27 speak of a wound in the 'side' (Gk. *pleura*): it is scarcely conceivable that they were not meant to refer to the same. Primrose, however, denies that this obvious wound could have been that produced by the spear, for a penetrating wound in the side, piercing the lung, would give 'every chance of a fatal outcome'. He has thus to discount the straightforward reading of the text where it contradicts his theory. Yet more strangely, in his doubtful expedient of invoking the Turin Shroud (see below), he has to explain that the hypothetical abdominal wound left no mark on that either.

If there is a medical problem over Jesus' death, it is to explain the cause of its relatively rapid onset. There is no serious doubt that some or most of Jesus' wounds were eventually mortal, singly or in combination, directly or through the consequent operation of shock, infection and loss of blood. Primrose admits that a man in Jesus' supposed state of 'incipient revival' could not have survived 'much more than one hour' in his condition in the tomb, certainly not a night. But even if there had been the slightest doubt that he was already dead on the cross, the spear-thrust must have put the issue beyond dispute. Roman soldiers knew when a man was dead, and they knew how to make doubly sure. It is unnecessary to pursue the supposition that Jesus had expert medical attention at a crucial time early that sabbath night in the tomb, and was able to impress his followers as conqueror over death on the basis of a freak escape from absurdly incompetent executioners.[62]

Scepticism of this order has to depend on an inadequate or a wildly speculative handling of the texts. I append a note of an example of such speculation. Professor J. D. M. Derrett (in the book mentioned below) has taken up the significance of two ossuary inscriptions from Talpioth, a southern suburb of Jerusalem, found by E. L. Sukenik and interpreted by him as invocations or laments for Jesus. For Derrett the fragment *Iēsous iou*, and its companion piece *Iēsous alōth*, are invocations to Jesus, who revived in the tomb, to raise his followers at the last day. But Derrett should here have noted the improved reading of the former, based on reexamination of the actual stone.[63] It reads *Iēsous Ioudou* ('Jesus son of Judas'), and the other is to be read 'Jesus Aloth' or 'Jesus son of Aloth', Jesus (Joshua) being a common name, and these brief identifications being precisely of the pattern of dozens of parallels. There is no reference to Christianity here, far less support for any theory about the crucifixion and resurrection. This should serve as a caution against some of the sensational hypotheses sometimes based on the demonstrable misreading of evidence.

Apart from rejecting inadequate explanations, we are wise to be cautious in our conclusions. It would not be unreasonable to my mind to speculate that Jesus' initiative in self-giving fell together with the natural outworking of physical causes of death. The contributory causes are not now clinically accessible or quantifiable; the unique spiritual agony of Gethsemane, involving the almost unparalleled bloody sweat (Luke 22:44) strikes the layman as likely to have been a powerful factor. Whether this contributed to cardiac tamponade, or how the physical, spiritual and psychological equation may be assessed in the attempt to explain the hastening of death, I must leave to others to consider. The point to emphasize is that Jesus was really dead, and the fact is in principle amenable to the application of evidence, and that two days later he was alive, a fact abundantly attested by testimony and circumstantial corroboration, but not amenable to natural explanation.[64]

The Burial and Resurrection

Both burial and cremation were widely practised at different times and places in the ancient world. In the New Testament period cremation was almost universal among the Romans, but inhumation again became prevalent from the second century AD.[65] In the Semitic East, however, burial had always been predominant, and was the universal practice among the Jews. The Jewish Law required burial of the executed criminal the same day (Deut. 21:23), and care was taken to bury enemies slain in battle. To be denied burial was a shameful indignity. Tombs were usually the communal possession of a family. In the New Testament period it was common to practise secondary burial, placing the bones in ossuaries which were stored in rock-cut family sepulchres, often in niches called *kôkhîm* in Hebrew (Latin *loculi*), radiating from the main chambers of the tomb. The Gospel accounts of the tomb of Jesus mention features, like the rolled stone, which are paralleled in surviving contemporary examples, but there is no certain agreement on the actual site, and after the resurrection it ceased to be of focal importance to the primitive church.[66]

According to the Talmud (Semaḥoth 47a) it was the custom for mourners to visit the tomb within the first three days after death. After that the progress of decomposition was thought to be irreversible. So the case of Lazarus is highly significant here. Jesus' delay in coming meant that Lazarus had already been four days in the tomb (John 11:17). Jesus' raising of Lazarus thus displayed his absolute mastery over death. It polarized reactions and pointed forward to his own resurrection. It stresses Jesus' unique authority where resuscitation lay indisputably beyond all medical science and human resource.

Jesus' burial was hurried and imperfectly complete before the Sabbath began at sunset. Among the physical details we may note the enormous quantity of myrrh and aloes brought by Nicodemus, according to John 19:39. The use of spices was a usual practice (cf. John 11:44), but in this case their sheer quantity represented a costly act of devotion, like that of Mary (John 12:2–11). The Jews did not embalm like the Egyptians, but myrrh and the other aromatic spices represented the preservation of the body, which was seen as a prerequisite of resurrection. We may compare the significant gift of myrrh to the baby Jesus (Matt. 2:11). Thus the words of Ps. 16:10 ('nor will you let your Holy One see decay') were significant in the earliest Christian preaching, as applicable to the risen Christ, but not to his ancestor David, whose body had seen decay.[67]

Two well-known controversies of recent years concern physical remains purporting to confirm the resurrection. I set aside here the so-called Nazareth Decree, an inscribed stone of debated date and credentials, ostensibly an imperial edict against tomb-robbery, which some have taken speculatively to reflect official reaction to the problem of the empty tomb.[68] The second case is that of the celebrated Turin Shroud, which is widely believed to be the actual burial-cloth bearing impressions of the body and wounds of Jesus, imprinted there by a scientifically inexplicable burst of energy representing the resurrection.[69] This raises the startling question whether the death and resurrection of Jesus are actually in this bizarre way accessible to some degree of medical diagnosis. Our theme demands at least a brief reaction to such a claim. The shroud is evidently an artefact of high antiquity, which merits rigorous assessment from every relevant discipline. It is difficult for anyone to pass instant judgement on a relic which touches so many specialities, so I venture only a comment of general method and principle. In such an interdisciplinary study there is a real danger that each expert who is impressed with the application of its claim in his own field will be the more suggestible to the force of circumstantial support from other directions. Then rigorous controls and the force of objections may become submerged under a growing bandwagon. So I am doubtful. My instinct is against it. I should be pleased to be proved wrong. It would seem to be too good to be true to have such a spectacular confirmation of the resurrection. But I am sure the problem of the shroud is far more complex. The danger is if some come to rest their faith on a doubtful base, which could be instantly shattered by a carbon-14 dating showing the material to be not quite old enough. There is thus the possibility of disillusionment over an object which would merely then be shown to be irrelevant. We are better advised to rest our assurance of the truth of the event on the physical details recorded in the Gospels, notably the empty tomb, and the testimony preserved in 1 Corinthians 15. Conversely, I shall not use the impressions on the shroud as retrospective evidence for Jesus' wounds and death.[70]

Medical Conditions in the New Testament

1. BLINDNESS (Gk. *typhlos,* blind) There is no semantic problem

here, but there are points of unusual interest in two of the Gospel healings, in Mark 8:22–26 and John 9, both of them cases of men born blind.

We have already noted the probability of a very high incidence of blindness in ancient Palestine, and the prominence of ophthalmology as a specialization of Greek medicine. In both Mark 8 and John 9, Jesus applied a physical means (spittle, mud) and the healing was in two stages or delayed. An article by R. E. D. Clark offers a fascinating explanation, in particular of the fuller detail in Mark 8.[71] Congenital blindness, if due to cataract, may be remedied by surgery, but until recent times such cures were extremely rare, and there are very few documented cases of adults who could describe their sensations at receiving sight for the first time. From these few cases it is clear that the congenitally blind have no spatial sense and that the gift of sight produces confusion and bewilderment unimaginable to the sighted. The man in Mark 8 saw 'men as trees walking': an impression fully in accord with documented cases. The two stages of the healing then represent a double miracle, the second enabling the man to control and use his new faculty. Clark points out the implicit testimony this bears to the authenticity of the event, for such healings could not have been known to contemporary medicine, and the peculiar difficulties were undocumented and unappreciated, and so not amenable to invention by the tradition of the primitive church. The case in John 9 may perhaps be seen in similar terms, where the second stage is achieved at the washing at Siloam, without experience of the intervening confusion as the eyes were sealed with mud. Perhaps this kind of explanation is very speculative, and I should not press it. I would see the second stage as essentially enabling the subject to cope with the consequences of being healed, by telescoping a hazardous process of bewildered reorientation and re-education into a brief space, an act of Jesus' continuing compassion for the further needs of the person, comparable with his command to give food to Jairus' daughter (Mark 5:43).

Other cases of blindness were probably due to trachoma and other diseases.

2. MALARIA It has been convincingly argued that the general word for 'fever', *pyretos* (Matt. 8:15, = Mark 1:31; cf. Luke 4:38–39; John 4:52; Acts 28:8), was used specifically of malaria. The classic, but now dated, work of W. H. S. Jones[72] shows that the Hippocratic Corpus consistently links *pyretos* with marshy localities and with repetitive, periodic onset. Jones supposed that its first coming to Greece in the fifth century BC marked the decline of classical civilization, but later studies have challenged these ideas.

Even if less prevalent at some periods, it seems to have been endemic in the Eastern Mediterranean in the Roman period.[73] The medical writers freely use the terms *amphēmerinos, tritaios, tetartaios* to distinguish quotidian, tertian and quartan fevers. The NT cases are located in Capernaum or in Malta. Hippocrates classifies many forms of the disease by name (*Epidemics* 1:24).

3. DYSENTERY (Gk. *dysenterion*, Acts 28:8; elsewhere also *dysenteria*) 'Dysentery' is distinguished as a dangerous disease from the mild *diarrhoia*, being accompanied by fever (cf. Acts), ulceration of the bowel and the passing of blood (Hippocrates, *Regimen* 2.74). It may have included any severe intestinal trouble and perhaps typhoid and paratyphoid, if these were then prevalent, as well as dysentery proper (Jones in Loeb ed. of Hippocrates, Vol. 1, lviii–lix).

4. EPILEPSY A whole Hippocratic treatise is devoted to the 'sacred disease',[74] never otherwise named in the text and usually referred to there simply as 'this disease', the word *epilēpsis* occurring only once (chap. 13) in the sense of 'seizure'. While there is no serious doubt that this treatise deals essentially with epilepsy, other forms of seizure and even of insanity may be included, classification being by similarity of symptoms rather than causes. The writer is concerned to deny that this disease is due to possession or divine visitation.

Epilepsy is never named in the NT, but it is widely agreed that the boy whose symptoms are described in Mark 9:14–29 (cf. Matt. 17:14–20; Luke 9:37–43) was suffering from this disease. Both Mark and Luke ascribe the trouble explicitly to demon-possession, and in Matthew the boy's father describes him as 'moonstruck' (*selēniazetai*, Matt. 17:15). An important discussion by Wilkinson[75] examines the case carefully, noting that the earliest Markan account suggests its derivation from the eye-witness Peter and that Luke gives a masterly compressed clinical description. The sudden loss of consciousness, endangering the boy's life, is a strong pointer, and conclusive against the explanation as a case of mere hysteria, for a hysteric never throws a fit in a dangerous place. Wilkinson stresses that epilepsy is a symptom and not a disease, and may have many causes, among which possession, despite the Hippocratic writer,[76] cannot be excluded. The larger number of cases are, in fact, 'idiopathic': the cause cannot then be determined, and modern medicine knows no cure. Jesus' instant and final cure of the boy is thus particularly striking in medical terms.

5. DEFORMITY A notable case is that of the bent woman, recorded only in Luke 13:10–17. Again Wilkinson has offered a helpful study.[77] She had had a 'spirit of weakness' for eighteen

years and was 'bent together' (*synkyptein*), unable to straighten herself up (*anakyptein*) completely (or at all).[78] Wilkinson inclines to believe that she suffered from an infective disease rather than a degenerative disease like osteoarthritis or osteoporosis of the spine, for she was likely to have been comparatively young when it began so long before.[79] He concludes from Luke's description that her kyphosis was more probably caused by *spondylitis ankylopoietica* than by tuberculosis of the spine, which might have produced rather an acute local angulation of the spine than a rigidity of its whole length. Despite the language of v.11 and the phrase 'whom Satan bound' (v.16), there is no implication of demon-possession here, but rather a reference to 'the activity of Satan as the primary cause of sin and disease' (p.204). Again he stresses that no theory of a 'hysterical paraplegia'[80] will suffice, for the atrophy caused by eighteen years' disuse was irreversible by natural means.

6. PARALYSIS This is another general term describing a type of condition which may have many medical causes, and the Greek words are not necessarily of much help in diagnosis. The usual New Testament word is *paralytikos* (paralytic), or the verb *paraly-esthai* is used in its perfect passive participle *paralelymenos* (being in a state of paralysis, paralytic). These are the terms used of the man described in the traditional rendering as 'sick of the palsy' (Matt.9:2–8; Mark 2:2–11; Luke 5:18–26). Other cases include the man at the pool of Bethesda, crippled for thirty-eight years (John 5:2–9), and the man Aeneas, healed by Peter at Lydda after eight years of paralysis (Acts 9:32–35). We may note also the case of the man with a 'withered' hand (*xēros*, dry, *exērammenos*, being in a dried state; Matt. 12:10–13; Mark 3:1–5; Luke 6:6–10), and in John 5:3 the *xēroi* (dry people) are absolutely the paralysed, withered, atrophied.

It is suggested that anterior poliomyelitis (infantile paralysis) may have been the cause of some at least of the cases mentioned. This is described as inflammation of the anterior grey matter of the spinal cord, an infectious epidemic disease attacking children. Localized forms of paralysis are mentioned under the heads of hemiplegia and paraplegia, and are said to be due in some cases to injury during labour or at birth. Such may have been widely prevalent, and these explanations are evidently possible in cases where adults have been subject to paralytic conditions for many years, as in John 5. Shepherd attributes the paralytic agonies of the centurion's servant (Matt. 8:6) to spinal meningitis.

7. DROPSY (Gk. *hydrōps*, from *hydōr*, water). Mention of this condition is made only in Luke 14:2, where the man is described as *hydrōpikos* (full of water = suffering from *hydrōps*). Though there is

nothing in the context to specify his symptoms further, the literal meaning of the word, reinforced by independent allusions in medical and non-medical writings, is sufficiently diagnostic (cf. e.g. Polybius 13.2.2). The accumulation of fluid in body cavities is again a symptom, which might be a sign of a more serious disease of heart, kidneys or liver. Jesus' healing evidently dealt with the underlying disease.

8. MENORRHAGIA/METRORRHAGIA The woman with the 'issue of blood' (Mark 5:25; Luke 8:43) or 'haemorrhaging' (Matt. 9:20) for twelve years is taken to have suffered from an abnormally prolonged menstrual flow.

9. MADNESS New Testament references use popular language about unusual or unbalanced behaviour, and perhaps the instances do not merit separate mention here, except as they show the popular recognition of mental disorder apart from the attribution to demon-possession. Festus cried out to Paul, 'Much learning drives you to madness' (*mania*) (Acts 26:25). Paul himself, when provoked into boasting of his sufferings and humiliations, offers a disclaimer; he speaks as a madman (*paraphronōn*, being mentally beside himself) (2 Cor. 11:23; cf. the noun *paraphronia* in 2 Pet. 2:16). Many said of Jesus that he had a demon and was mad (*mainesthai*, to be mad, John 10:20), a case where the two ideas are associated. For *mainesthai* cf. also 1 Corinthians 14:23; Acts 12:15; and again Acts 26:24–25. Another word is *anoia* (mindlessness), whether used of 'ignorant folly' (2 Tim. 3:9) or of 'mindless fury' (Luke 6:11). Plato once describes *mania* as a kind of *anoia* (*Timaeus* 86B), and elsewhere associates the two terms (*Republic* 382C,E): 'folly is a disease of the soul' (*Timaeus*).

10. DUMBNESS (Gk. *kōphos*, blunt, dull; dumb; deaf; also *alalos*, Mark 7:37; 9:17, 25 and *aphōnos*, Acts 8:32; 1 Cor. 12:2; 14:10; 2 Pet. 2:16, both meaning 'without speech', the latter figuratively). Most of the dumb mentioned in the Gospels were presumably deaf-mutes, and their problem, if congenital, basically due to malformation or lesions in the inner ear, dumbness being a secondary consequence of the inability to learn speech by hearing and imitation. In Matthew 9:32–33 Jesus healed a dumb demoniac and he spoke when the demon was cast out (cf. Luke 11:14). In Matthew 11:5 the deaf and dumb (*kōphoi*) 'hear' and in Mark 7:37 Jesus makes the *kōphoi* to hear, and the *alaloi* to speak, the two functions here being distinguished. In Mark 7:32 they bring to Jesus a deaf man who 'had an impediment in his speech' (RSV, Gk. *mogilalos*, scarcely speaking). Perhaps the implication is that this man's deafness was not congenital, since he apparently had some ability to speak and had presumably once had hearing enough to

acquire the faculty. Perhaps again he had partial hearing, or a physiological speech-problem separate from his deafness. Jesus' treatment of him is striking, with touch of ears and tongue and anointing of the tongue with saliva. This procedure perhaps draws attention to the completeness of the cure, where both faculties had to be restored and are treated separately with physical signs to assure the man of the confidence to control his new abilities.

Very different is the case of Zacharias (Luke 1:20–22, 62–64). Shepherd explains it as temporary aphasia (without agraphia), possibly due to a lesion of the brain or a functional consequence of the vision.

11. RAISING THE DEAD The three significant cases in Jesus' ministry are those of Jairus's daughter (Mark 5:22–24, 35–43; = Matt. 9:18, 23–25 = Luke 8: 41–42, 49–56), the son of the widow of Nain (Luke 7:11–17) and Lazarus (John 11:1–44). There is no mention in any of these cases of the nature of the fatal disease, and in two of them Jesus emphatically insists that the persons are not dead but asleep. In these cases also Jesus receives information prior to death, but for different reasons arrives after death.

All three passages are very instructive, but the Lazarus incident is uniquely important in its demonstration of Jesus' mastery over death. The sceptic might question the clinical death of a girl newly deceased or a young man not yet buried, especially when Jesus himself rejects the sensational, but with Lazarus every mark of irreversible death and decay is specified: he has been in the tomb over three days (John 11:39), beyond the limit of the Rabbinic injunction to visit the dead (Semaḥoth 47a).

The first two cases illustrate Jesus' practical compassion. It is the sceptics themselves who scornfully attest the girl's death against Jesus' own reserve: death is but a sleep if one wakes from it. And he is careful to instruct the parents to give her food, a practical need of restored young life. The incident of the widow's son must be seen against the background of the terrible plight of a widow deprived of her only support. But Lazarus' raising points forward to that of Jesus himself. Its focus of interest is not medical, except as the story insists so powerfully upon the fact of death, and the processes of decomposition in a hot climate put that fact beyond doubt for those who accept the good faith of the report. The incident further polarizes the opposition to Jesus, and in John's account leads directly to the determination to kill him (John 11: 47–53).

The case of Eutychus (Acts 20:8–12) has been mentioned above. While Luke's reserve is striking, there is little doubt that he intends the reader to understand that Eutychus was dead, of concussion at the shock of impact. Paul himself experienced the effects of concussion after stoning at Lystra (Acts 14:19; cf. Acts 7:58–59).

12. PERFORATION BY WORMS According to Acts 14:23 Herod Agrippa I was 'eaten of worms' (*skōlēkobrōtos*). Another account is given in Josephus, *Antiquities* 19.8.2. 346–350, mentioning violent and persistent cardiac and abdominal pain terminating in death after five days, but not the worms. While Josephus' version is characteristically lurid and melodramatic, the two accounts are basically in striking accord, and it is suggested that the cause of death was peritonitis following some such primary disease as appendicitis. E. M. Merrins[81] draws attention to the repulsive deaths involving worm-infestation ascribed in the ancient sources to Antiochus Epiphanes and to Herod the Great, as well as to Agrippa. All three kings were guilty of blasphemous impiety. Merrins draws attention to different diagnoses in the three cases: Antiochus (2 Macc. 9:5–12; cf. Josephus, *Antiq*. 12.9.1.357) died of acute and chronic dysentery; Herod of chronic Bright's disease of the kidneys, perhaps complicated by cardiac trouble (Jos. *Antiq*. 17.6.5.168–171; *Jewish War* 1.33.5.656), and perhaps helping to explain his outrageous violence and mental imbalance, and so the slaughter at Bethlehem. In all three cases the putrefaction of wounds or organs caused the spread of infestations which may themselves have caused or hastened death.

13. PLAGUE There is no specific and identifiable NT reference to plague, as there is in the OT.[82] The various words which may be so translated are of more general application, shading off into general words for disease or denoting future apocalyptic woes. The most usual Greek word *loimos*, the word used by Thucydides (2.47,54) in connexion with his precise description of the plague at Athens in 430 BC (2.48–53), occurs at Luke 21:11 in an apocalyptic context, with a word-play on *limos* (famine). It is also used metaphorically of Paul in the prosecuting speech of Tertullus in Acts 24:5, denouncing him as a 'pestilential' troublemaker. Much commoner in the NT is *plēgē*, literally a 'blow', 'wound', literally of the victim of bandits (Luke 10:30) and elsewhere, but used fifteen times in Revelation of the 'plagues' of the last days. It is a word sometimes used, even in pagan sources, of divine 'visitation'. While 'plague' as such was known and dreaded in the ancient world, the NT allusions are metaphorical or future and not medically specific.

14. RESTORATION OF MALCHUS' EAR One healing miracle of Jesus is in some respects unique. The incident is among the few mentioned in all four Gospels (Matt. 26:51; Mark 14:47; Luke 22:50–51; John 18:10), but only John identifies Peter as the attacker and names the victim, and only Luke mentions Jesus' healing of the

ear. The occasion was clearly significant in its marking of Jesus' determination to yield himself to his enemies without bloodshed, and unique in his exerting his power to heal to restore a severed organ in a representative of declared opponents, a physical act not open to any psychosomatic explanation, and evidently deeply embedded in all strands of the earliest tradition and linked to Jesus' rejection of physical resistance in Gethsemane.

15. MEDICAL MATERIALS: HEALING, ANTISEPTIC AND OTHER PRACTICES There is very little reference in the New Testament to the actual practice of medicine, for which we are largely dependent on secular sources. I shall merely append here a few references. The Good Samaritan bandaged the traveller's wounds, pouring olive-oil and wine on them, substances evidently in common use as antiseptics (Luke 10:34). We may compare the oil of James 5:14 on the assumption that that was an almost universally used anointing material, and not merely symbolic. Apart from its use in cooking food, olive oil played a large part in ancient Mediterranean culture, notably as an unguent or cosmetic to protect the skin from the hot sun. In Mark 6:13 the Twelve use anointing oil in their healing mission.

Jesus on the cross refused wine mixed with gall (Matt. 27:34) or myrrh (Mark 15:23), substances apparently offered as a narcotic to ease the pain of crucifixion, but refused by one who chose to bear the whole burden of sin and suffering. This is evidently to be distinguished from the offering of vinegar in mockery (Luke 23:56). In John 19:29 the mention of 'hyssop' recalls Old Testament references to a plant representing purification: here however the identification of *hyssōpos* is problematic, and it functions as the 'reed' of Matthew 27:48; Mark 15:36 to bring a sponge soaked in vinegar to Jesus' mouth. It has been suggested that it was the 'reed' of the stalk of the tall cereal plant durra or sorghum.[83]

Paul's advice to Timothy in 1 Timothy 5:23 is evidently set against a background where Timothy was drinking exclusively water which may sometimes have been contaminated and a cause of illness to his weak constitution. Cf. the bad water of Laodicea, discussed below. Paul recommends wine as a medicinal safeguard, with perhaps a caution that Timothy may be over-scrupulous where his health and work are at stake.

The effects of climate and travel on health were clearly recognized. The Roman governor Gallio (Acts 18:12) is known from his brother's writings to have left his province of Achaia to go on a cruise for his health (Seneca, *Moral Epistles* 104.1). It has been suggested that Paul's journey to Pisidian Antioch was forced by the effects of the enervating and malarial lowlands of Pamphylia (see below on the 'thorn in the flesh'; Acts 13:14).

16. BIRTH, BARRENNESS, ETC The bearing of children, and especially male children, was of great importance, and barrenness was a shame. The principal NT references to pregnancy and childbirth are in the Nativity stories, especially the record in Luke, which may plausibly be explained as derived from Mary herself. The story of Elisabeth, whose barrenness until God's special blessing at an advanced age (Luke 1:7) recalls the Old Testament instances of Sarah and Hannah, is closely followed by Mary's pregnancy.

17. LEPROSY (See chapter 4). I refrain from further discussion here, except to reiterate the difficulty of identification of Hebrew *ṣarāʿaṯ*, Greek *lepra*, that 'leprosy' in the biblical sense may not even have included Hansen's disease, and that the status of this disease in the ancient world is unclear. It may even have been denoted on occasion by such other terms as *elephantiasis*, found in Celsus and Dioscorides, both first century writers.

Medical Imagery and Special Topics

Ancient languages are often relatively concrete in their forms of expression, more restrained than English in their freedom in the use of metaphor. Yet there is quite a rich array of medical imagery in the New Testament. We have noticed some of it already in discussing the basic healing words. In the word-group *sōtēr, sōzein, sōtēria* (saviour, to save, salvation) we may say that the notion of healing is included in a wider concept. These words are characteristic of the language of pagans, like the demoniac girl (Acts 16:17) and the gaoler (Acts 16:30), both at Philippi. The multiple connotations of these words are alive in the NT, but their application to each context is to be limited to what is proper and necessary in that context.[84]

The noun *hygieia* (health) is not found in the NT,[85] but the adjective *hygiēs* occurs twelve times and the verb *hygiainein* also twelve times. The adjective is normally used literally, but in Titus 2:8 of 'sound words'. The verb is mostly used metaphorically in the participial form *hygiainōn* (being healthy), applied again to 'words' or 'teachings' (1 Tim. 1:10; 6:3; 2 Tim. 1:13; 4:3; Tit. 1:9; 2:1). The word is also used of 'being sound in faith' (Tit. 1:13; 2:2). In fact it is a sustained metaphor, found exclusively in the so-called Pastoral Epistles. Its force is not to be overstressed, as this is quite common Greek usage, if not as trite as in the English phrase 'sound teaching'.

The metaphor of the body is commonly used, especially in Paul, with varying significances, of the parts played by the different members in the whole, or of the dedication of the whole being to God (1 Cor. 12:12–27; Rom. 6:13–19; 7:23; 12:4–5; 1 Cor. 6:13–15). In contrast with modern idiom the 'heart' (*kardia*) was seen as the seat of the will, the 'bowels', 'inward parts' (*splanchna*) as the seat of the emotions (literal only at Acts 1:18, of Judas), and the 'kidneys' (*nephroi*) of the mind or inner life (Rev. 2:23). The tongue (*glōssa*) is a small member with great power for evil (Jas. 3:5–6). Jesus, too, used a parable of the body: that which defiles is what comes from the heart, not what is passed through the 'bowel' (*koilia*, also used as 'womb', Matt. 15:11–18; cf. Mark 7:19).

'Circumcision' (*peritomē*) was physically the mark of the Jew, as opposed to the 'uncircumcision' (*akrobustia*) of the Gentile, but the real, inward mark of the people of God is a 'circumcision of the heart' (cf. Rom. 2:25–29; Col. 2:11). Heresy is likened in 2 Timothy 2:17 to 'gangrene' (*gangraina*), a 'cancer of spreading ulcers' (Arndt-Gingrich), a Hippocratic word used by Plutarch of the vicious effects of slander.

The 'drug' word-group is always used in the New Testament in a pejorative sense, of the evils of sorcery or the like, nearly always in the Revelation. The *pharmakos* is a 'sorcerer' (Rev. 21:8; 22:15), and *pharmakia* is 'sorcery' (Gal. 5:20; Rev. 9:21; 18:23), and in all but the last case the words are set in lists of vices defying the goodness of God. No conclusions should, however, be drawn from these few cases in one type of context. Early Christianity elsewhere uses *pharmakon* (drug) in a favourable sense.[86]

In 1 Corinthians 15:8 Paul records that the risen Christ appeared last of all to him 'as to one untimely born' (RSV), Greek *ektrōma* (untimely birth, miscarriage), a word used elsewhere as a term of insult or contempt.

'The Thorn in the Flesh' (2 Cor. 12:7)

There have been many theories, both medical and other, of the meaning of Paul's 'thorn in the flesh'. It has been said that a list of the theories 'reads like the index of a textbook of medicine'.[87] The word *skolops* is properly 'thorn' in Greek of this period, rather than 'stake', a meaning it bore in classical Greek. It is important to be as clear as possible about the evidence of the text itself. The text and context tell against explanations of the kind which were often current in earlier centuries. Many of these were non-physical: religious opposition or persecution, mental oppression, including excessive grief or remorse, neurotic or psychotic states, or spiritual temptation to pride, doubt, sensuality, violent anger or the like. Things of this kind seem for various reasons inadequate to explain the case; Paul accepted opposition as his lot, and the other suggestions are either inapposite to his known character or amenable to his striving in prayer. This disability began at a time in the past, associated with his ecstatic spiritual experiences of fourteen years before (v.2). It was chronic and recurring, an embarrassment to his work, but not debarring him from it. It was an individual and personal problem, not such suffering as was the common lot of Christians.

There are many places in the epistles where possible references to Paul's infirmities have suggested links with this passage and prompted more precise identification of a physical condition. But these links are hazardous unless we have more specific reasons to connect them. Several theories have made much of the physical impact and temporary blindness of his Damascus road experience. But if 2 Corinthians was written about AD 56, the first onset of the *skolops* was about 42–3: the date of Paul's conversion is uncertain, but was in any case much earlier than this,[88] long before this 'messenger of Satan' was given to him. The one very probable and specific correlation of the 'thorn' is with the infirmity which occasioned Paul's first coming to Galatia (Gal. 4:13–15). If this link is correct, Paul's disability is seen as one which was humiliating and apt to subject him to abhorrence and rejection. It also confirms its essentially physical character.

This still allows a vast range of possibilities, and there is no room for dogmatism or finality.[89] Probably the three most persistent and widely-held suggestions are eye-trouble, epilepsy and malaria. The Damascus road experience is often invoked in support of the two former, but we have seen that that is not relevant here. Galatians 4:15 might seem to give support to an ophthalmic problem, but the idiom is not necessarily related to Paul's sickness. Apart from its other difficulties, epilepsy does not usually first attack a man of mature years. Malaria is a very attractive possibility. It was first proposed by Sir William M. Ramsay in 1893, in the light of his own first-hand knowledge of the endemic malaria in the enervating coastal plain of Pamphylia.[90] If Paul sought relief from a reinfection of his recurring fever by ascent to the mountains, this helps to explain his journey through very difficult country from Perga to Pisidian Antioch (Acts 13:14), and that was the first place he reached in provincial Galatia. While recognizing that I am here skirting one of the most notorious cruxes of NT history,[91] I am clear that the occasion of Galatians 4:13–15 coincides with that of Acts

13:14, and confirms that Paul was suffering from a humiliating ailment which had been the reason for that first coming to Galatia (Gal.4:13). It is notable that Ramsay wrote four years before Ross demonstrated the transmission of malaria by the bite of anophelene mosquitoes.

Malaria probably fulfils the necessary requirements of the case as well as anything. The first infection will have been some five years earlier than the recurrence in Pamphylia. The chronic and intermittent character of malaria, the weakness, pain and humiliation of its attacks, are all suitable. That is probably as far as we can now take the question.

Eyesalve (Rev. 3:18)

The imagery of the letters to the Seven Churches is often derived from the OT, but applied very pointedly to the needs of Christians in the individual churches addressed. There is however relatively little OT background in the Laodicean letter, and its message is set very directly against a background of allusion to the sources of wealth in this 'affluent society'. 'Eyesalve' must be understood with relation to the standing of Laodicea as a medical centre. It had a celebrated medical school which is known to have specialized in ophthalmology. Its founder, Zeuxis Philalethes ('lover of truth'), a follower of Herophilus (third century BC), is named on Laodicean coinage: and his successors were Alexander and Demosthenes, both of whom bore the same cognomen. Demosthenes Philalethes was a renowned first-century ophthalmologist, who wrote a standard work of great influence which was still extant in translation in medieval times. He probably lived in the time of Nero (AD 54–68).[92]

The connection of 'eyesalve' with this institution at Laodicea is not explicitly attested, but is an inference from two passages which do not actually name the city (Pseudo-Aristotle, *de Mir. Auscult.* 58/834b; Galen, *de San. Tuend.* 6.12).[93] Both actually speak of Phrygia, a land in which Laodicea was the one famous medical centre, and the city is actually mentioned in a related matter in the immediate context of the Galen passage. So there is at least good circumstantial corroboration of the suggestion that eye-ointments, together with black woollen clothing and banking (contrast Rev. 3:17) were among the principal sources of local prosperity.

There are many surviving examples of '*collyrium* stamps' from the Roman period, nearly all from the provinces west of the Rhine, and including Britain.[94] *Collyrium* (Gk. *kollyrion*) is the word used here for 'eyesalve'. In the typical case, the 'stamp' is a flat square tablet of stone, bearing on each edge Latin words engraved in reverse, for imprinting proprietary name, purpose and directions for use, with the oculist's name, on a moist surface which hardened as a dry ointment-stick. The patient broke off a piece, and mixed it to a paste with water or other liquid as directed. This was evidently not the style of prescription in use in Laodicea, for the more eastern practice was to inscribe more perishable containers, and the evidence is rarely preserved. But an example will illustrate. The composition of some of the salves known from the stamps corresponds to some of those described in the medical writers. My instance is from Augusta Treverorum, now Trier in West Germany.[95] The oculist has his label for a separate ointment on each edge of the square stone:

Eugenius' Diarhodon for festering sores, with egg-white.
Eugenius' Diamisus for roughness (trachoma).
Eugenius' Chloron for aches, with egg-white.
Eugenius' Penicille, after an attack.

We cannot linger to attempt comment on this fascinating text. The name 'Penicille' is obscure. It is not to be taken as indicating knowledge of the medical properties of a fungus or blue mould. The root-word strictly means 'brush' or 'sponge', and this ointment may be named from its mode of application by smearing with a soft brush or pad. We cannot suppose that these concoctions were always successful in their claims. There are bitter satirical epigrams in the Greek Anthology against ophthalmologists whose ointments destroyed the sight they claimed to assist (*Gk. Anth.* 11.112,117,126).

Prayer for Healing (Jas. 5:14–16)

This passage in James is both difficult and very important. Indeed it may give a unique glimpse into the primitive Christian perspective on medicine and healing, where theological debate has sometimes focused upon secondary issues which rose to prominence only later. Dr. Wilkinson's study is again very helpful and thought-provoking, and I am much indebted to him in this section.[96] The key phrase is in James 5:16b: 'The prayer of a righteous man has great power in its effects' (RSV).[97] In three conditions of life mentioned in 5:13 ff, the troubled, the joyful, the sick, all are exhorted to the appropriate practice of prayer and praise. The last group is a special case, dealt with more fully than the others, for this alone specifically involves the church. The elders are involved, not as having some special gifts of healing, but as representatives of the church and perhaps as men of prayer and mature wisdom. The anointing with oil has been explained as medical, as a visual and tangible aid to faith (Tasker), or as sacramental. The reference is grammatically subordinate, and reads like an incidental mention of a current practice which James does not need to explain. The best parallel seems to be in the mission of the twelve in Mark 6:13. It may reflect the remarkably widespread medicinal use of olive oil (cf. Luke 10:34; Celsus 2.14.4). In this case we should perhaps see the care of the church as expressed in believing prayer conjoined with the use of appropriate medical means. If, however, the anointing is meant as an encouragement to the patient's faith, we may compare rather the various applications of touch or laying hands on the sick, by Jesus and the disciples (Matt. 8:3,15; 9:18,25; etc.). Perhaps the two cases are not mutually exclusive. In any case it is important to observe that the purpose of this prayer and action is the recovery of the sick, not consolation for the dying. Disease is not necessarily the consequence of specific sin, but if it is, forgiveness is comprehended in the ministry of prayer and healing described (5:15b).

Wilkinson draws out several positive teachings from James: that the church has communal concern and responsibility for the sick, and that this ministry is part of the normal work of the church; that healing is based within the Christian community—before the growth of an organized medical or nursing profession; that its ministry includes all appropriate methods of healing; and that sickness and healing always have more than a physical dimension. Some of these points may of course be queried, and there remains a hermeneutical problem in applying the practices of an embattled church in its first impact on pagan society to the conditions of a modern world with a long heritage of Christianization and secondary secularization behind its extreme specialization of function.

James should not be taken to refer to the elders or others as possessing special gifts of healing, though the occurrence of such gifts is attested in 1 Corinthians 12:9.

Conclusions and Implications

A discussion like the present aims first to do something to clarify the New Testament passages which refer to medical matters. It is only incidental that the discussion engendered illustrates the essential integrity of the documents. Yet some of the issues raised, like miracle, and the crucifixion and resurrection, are so fundamental that I must say something of them, while recognizing that this is not the place for the fuller discussion on a wider front which alone could do justice to them. There is, however, a special value in the attempt to set the text representatively in its fullest possible contemporary and cultural context. This can help to bring its reality alive. It also poses fundamental questions about the nature of primitive Christianity's relation to its contemporary world, Jewish and Gentile, and, in the present case, how far secular medicine was accepted or rejected or remodelled by Christian thinking.

The crucial further question is the implication of the biblical evidence for medical ethics today. This is a task for others to pursue. It strikes me that our texts give us relatively little material amenable to direct and prescriptive application to our very different society. The focus of our thinking should be on biblical hermeneutics, rather than the attempt to make of the Bible a repository of case-histories or proof-texts to buttress unanchored thoughts about modern problems.

An evident issue is the value of human life (see chapter 5). We see this affirmed in the Hippocratic injunctions against abortion and euthanasia. Yet it is evident that both abortion and infanticide were current practices in the ancient world, however abhorrent to Jews and Christians, and however difficult it may be to quantify their prevalence.[98] A famous papyrus letter of the Egyptian labourer Hilarion to his wife Alis, dated precisely 17th June, 1 BC, instructs her bluntly about their expected child: 'If it is a boy, let it be; if it is a girl, throw it out'.[99]

That is a glimpse of what was at least possible in the world of the early church. Yet we meet no explicit answer to such a view in the New Testament. It is perhaps rather that the documents contain such transforming teaching about the nature of God and man that Hilarion's outlook becomes unthinkable for the man who has become gripped by them. A fundamental need of our day is for the Christian mind rooted in a biblical way of thinking.

3

The Levitical Code: Hygiene or Holiness

AVERELL S. DARLING

When the children of Israel left Egypt at the time of the Exodus they were moving into a new era. The days of slavery were at an end and now they were free. From their past as a nomadic people they were in future to take on the status of a nation. They were God's chosen people, and he would eventually lead them into the Promised Land. God dwelt among them, he provided for their needs, and he spoke directly to their leader Moses. He was a holy God and they were to be a holy people. This was a new relationship, but they had yet to learn all that was involved in having such a God among them.

Through Moses God revealed to them the code that was to govern their hearts and lives. At its centre were the Ten Commandments which laid down their duties and obligations first towards God and then towards one another. Then, in the books of Leviticus and Deuteronomy, we find an amplification of this code, spelling out in more detail the ways in which the Ten Commandments were to be applied to the various aspects of daily life. Again, the first section of this code deals with their relationship towards God and how, both as individuals and as a nation, they are to approach him in his holiness and offer sacrifices for their sins. The second section concerns itself with personal conduct and behaviour, but again the basis for this is man's relationship with his God. In particular this section of what is generally called the Levitical Code concerns itself with matters which render a person 'defiled' and therefore 'unclean', and it prescribes the procedures to be carried out to restore the individual to a condition acceptable for worship. Certain animals, fish and birds are to be regarded as 'unclean'; they may not be eaten and even contact with their carcases brings 'defilement'. Certain sexual relationships are forbidden, such as incest, homosexuality and bestiality, while sexual activity outside of marriage is likewise proscribed. Even sex within marriage defiles. Contact with disease and death makes a man unclean, and so on. We shall discuss some of these issues in more detail later.

The question we have to ask ourselves is this. Was the code designed purely for ceremonial purposes, or was it a programme of health and hygiene? Or could it possibly have been intended as a combination of the two? For even if one adopts the ceremonial viewpoint, it cannot be denied that the practical advantages to the Israelites were considerable. The sexual and marriage prohibitions of the code would, if adhered to, ensure freedom from sexually-transmitted disease and from some of the heritable disorders. Other elements in the personal and public hygiene of the Hebrew encampment—clean food, a clean water supply, clean air, clean clothing, clean dwellings, the disposal of sewage, the burial of the dead, and quarantine regulations for some forms of infectious disease—meant that Israel was in these respects well ahead of the neighbouring nations of the day. It is interesting to recall that the word quarantine itself is derived from the Mosaic Code. During the fourteenth century, at a time of severe plagues in Italy, it was noted that the Jews were less often afflicted. It was suspected that this might be due to their ceremonial washings and their rules concerning the touching of bodies and early burial. Hence the regulations of Leviticus 12:1–4 were adopted into the public law, with the Italian *quaranta* (forty) as the designation of the prescribed number of days for isolation of the patient, or those who were contacts of an infected person.

Let us first consider the view that the Levitical Code provides a prescription for healthy living.

Is it a Sanitary Code?

For a hundred years readers of the Bible have tended to see in the Mosaic Code of 'uncleanness' a scheme designed to promote physical health and hygiene. Some have believed this to be the code's primary purpose. In the past even the medical profession has given support to this view, maintaining that strict observance of the code would lead to real gain in individual and community health.

For example, in a large two-volume work published at the beginning of this century, Dr Alexander Rattray[1] of Edinburgh asserted that the code was a divinely given and universal 'Sanitary Science', designed 'for the prevention of disease, prolongation of life and improvement of health'. He went further: 'In this preventive treatment of leprosy, and inferentially of all infectious diseases, the maxims of Moses thus ante-date all mediaeval and indeed modern theory of practice.' He was even prepared to state that, 'In fact, at Sinai, God enunciated the great base facts of hygiene for man as a race for all time. The Mosaic hygiene is one of nature's biological laws.'

Many others since Rattray's day have supported him wholly or in part. Venzmer[2] as recently as 1972 wrote that, 'It was the priest who took action in the realm of hygiene, the battle against infectious diseases, with disinfection and isolation. Practical regulations are abundant in Leviticus chapters 11–20.' Similarly, Rosner[3] writes, 'Although the Bible is not a medical text, its historical accounts, laws and precepts, and even its wording, yield an abundant harvest of information concerning the structure of the human body, diseases, injuries, cures and, above all, preventive and sanitary procedures. The material contained in some portions of the Pentateuch (such as chapter 13 of the Book of Leviticus) is so factual that even the sophisticated present-day student cannot help but be amazed at what he reads there. Especially the sanitary regulations of cleanliness and purity, such as the prohibition against consumption of blood and quarantines for infectious diseases, are unique and do not occur in the codes of the civilized nations of antiquity that surrounded the Land of Israel.' In the same connection the American medical historian F. H. Garrison[4] quotes the German Max Neuburger's comment, 'The chief glory of Biblical medicine lies in the institution of social hygiene as a science.'

Two factors may have helped to foster this view:

(1) Early in the life of the new nation God promised the children of Israel immunity from the diseases that had afflicted the Egyptians. 'I will put none of these diseases upon you which I brought upon the Egyptians, for I am the Lord who heals' (Exod. 15:26). But this immunity was to be conditional on their constant obedience to his laws and they are warned (Deut. 28:58–61) that continued disobedience would, among other forms of judgment, bring a veritable epidemic of various diseases. This association between obedience and health, and disobedience and disease, has

led some to think in terms of cause and effect—that infringement of the code leads not only to ceremonial defilement but also to a state of physical disease. The converse should then be true and therefore the code could be regarded as a rule of health.

Against this assumption lie the facts that a great deal of illness would not be affected by the most rigorous application of the code, and that the immunity provided by God as part of his covenant went far beyond any possible benefits provided by the code. When disobedience was punished by a major epidemic, the disease swept through the community without any apparent hindrance. It is true that some sickness is the result of our own behaviour, e.g. venereal disease and sexual promiscuity, lung cancer and smoking, but the protection provided by God applied to diseases that were not necessarily self-inflicted.

(2) The unfortunate translation of the Hebrew word *Tsarāˇath* or *sāraˇat* by the word 'leprosy' in English translations has caused many generations of Bible students to believe that the skin lesions detailed in Leviticus 13 are indeed manifestations of modern leprosy. This belief has been reinforced by the way in which the disease was handled, from the early days of suspicion with its periods of quarantine and observation, through the long period of exclusion from the community wth unkempt hair and face half-masked and the wailing cry of 'unclean, unclean', to the final elaborate and costly cleansing ritual. In all this the priest appeared to play the role of the Medical Officer of Health, doing his utmost to prevent the spread of a highly infectious disease.

Although we now know that this scaly form of dermatitis was not the leprosy of today or indeed the leprosy of the past two thousand years, but a deep-seated skin affliction which was probably non-infectious, certainly non-fatal, and self-limiting, this knowledge has only recently been accepted and is still not fully realized by some Bible students. The subject is fully dealt with in chapter 4.

The Ceremonial View

When we study the first five books of the Old Testament we find that the concept of 'cleanness' and 'uncleanness' is mentioned many times over, but always with a religious or ceremonial significance. It is in relation to a holy God that the necessity of 'cleanness' is emphasized as many passages of scripture indicate, for example: 'I am the Lord your God; consecrate yourselves and be holy because I am holy. Do not make yourselves unclean . . .

I am the Lord your God who brought you up out of Egypt to be your God; therefore be holy because I am holy' (Lev. 11: 44,45). It would seem, therefore, that the instructions given in Exodus, Leviticus, Numbers and Deuteronomy concerning the problem of 'uncleanness' are meant to have a mainly spiritual significance and should be regarded today as practical Old Testament illustrations of New Testament teaching concerning holiness, for during the state of ceremonial uncleanness, which lasted for varying periods of time, the individual was excluded from worship and from contact with others.

We therefore need to look at the code in some detail so as to compare its purpose in furthering religious fellowship with one another and unbroken communion with God with its potential as a code of hygiene. We shall do this by considering the five main ways in which defilement can occur, making use of the following alliterative headings:

1. *Diet*. Eating any unclean beast, or even touching its dead body, led to uncleanness and exclusion for the day.
2. *Delivery*. Giving birth to a child rendered the mother unclean and excluded her from the Temple for thirty-three days for a son and sixty-six days for a daughter.
3. *Discharges*. Any discharge, normal or abnormal, from the genital tract of male or female led to exclusion, which in some cases was maintained until symptoms had been absent for seven days.
4. *Death*. Contact with any human body, bone or grave led to seven days' exclusion.
5. *Dermatitis*. A chronic, scaly, form of skin disease, which for many years has been wrongly confused with modern leprosy, led to exclusion which lasted until either the disease was healed, or it had covered the whole body and apparently burned itself out.

Looking at the causes of defilement in more detail may enable us to come to a fairly firm conclusion concerning the primary significance of the code. We shall try to find if there is a practical health benefit from each prohibition and at the same time look critically at the cleansing ritual laid down for each case, asking the question, 'If microbial infection has occurred as a result of the defilement, will the remedy effect a cure?'

DIET: LEVITICUS 11

As the laws concerning diet seem to cause the most obvious distinction between the Jew and his Gentile neighbour, we shall consider them first. In the book of Genesis, when Noah received instructions concerning the living creatures that he was to take into the ark, God made a distinction between the 'clean' and the 'unclean', but we are not told how they were to be distinguished. When Noah was offering sacrifices as a thanksgiving to God for his deliverance from the flood, the animals and birds sacrificed were chosen from the 'clean' category. God said to Noah and his sons, 'The fear and dread of you will fall upon all the beasts of the earth and all the birds of the air, upon every creature that moves along the ground and upon all the fish of the sea; they are given into your hands. Every thing that lives and moves will be food for you. Just as I gave you the green plants, I now give you everything. But you must not eat meat that has its lifeblood still in it' (Gen. 9:2–4). Thus, many generations before the advent of Moses, a distinction was drawn between creatures that were clean and those that were unclean. This distinction was apparently for ritual purposes only, as all were freely available for food. The only prohibition was on the consumption of blood, not because it was a hazard to health but because of its typical connection with the life of the creature. In Mark 7:19 our Lord is recorded as declaring, 'All food is clean'. In the Christian era, as described in the book of Acts, the early church decreed that the distinction between 'clean' and 'unclean' creatures need no longer be observed, though for reasons of expediency the members of the Jerusalem Council maintained their prohibition against the consumption of blood. This prompts the question: had there been any major hazard to the consumer in meat from an 'unclean' creature compared with a lack of hazard in meat from a 'clean' creature, would this not have been brought out in the days of Noah and perpetuated in the Christian era?

When, at Sinai, God told Moses to divide all living creatures into 'clean' and 'unclean' categories, he also told him how the distinction was to be made. The details can be found in Leviticus 11. Broadly speaking, the division was linked to their feeding habits and, if they were earth-borne, to their manner of progression over the earth. Herbivores that chewed the cud and also walked on divided hooves were 'clean'. All others, whether herbivores or carnivores, were 'unclean'. Among the birds the division was clear-cut. The grain eaters were 'clean' while the predators were 'unclean'. In the marine world all creatures with both fins and scales were 'clean' while all others were 'unclean'. Possibly the distinction may be linked with feeding habits. Thus we have all predators, scavengers and 'bottom-feeders' excluded. The creatures that feed on death and decay were 'unclean', while the creatures that fed on living material such as grass, leaves, grain, etc., and were ruminants and walked on divided hooves, were accepted as clean. Other herbivores that made closer contact with the earth either by walking on paws or by creeping over it were 'unclean'.

Many have seen in these dietary distinctions the parallel between the feeding of the body and the feeding of the mind. Much of the material provided for the feeding of our minds today certainly seems to come from the 'earthy', the 'scavengers' and the 'bottom-feeders'. For those who would accept this line of teaching the primary significance of the dietary laws would appear to be ceremonial or typical.

But did these dietary prohibitions have a hygienic benefit? Was the flesh of the predator and scavenger more likely to be infected with parasites and other harmful organisms? The answer must be a qualified 'yes'. Some of the forbidden creatures such as the pig would have been more likely in those days to be infected, but it is very unlikely that any infestation present could not have been eliminated by adequate cooking. Even the 'clean' creatures were not to be regarded as safe in this respect and they could have been infested as well. Today no raw meat can be regarded as safe, and even the latest poultry regulations will not prevent the sale of poultry meat infected with *Salmonellae*. The Israelites were well accustomed to boil or roast their meat, and had the major purpose of the dietary laws been the prevention of disease, the most valuable instructions would have been about adequate cooking. It must be agreed, however, that there was some gain in choosing for diet those animals and birds that were least likely to be infested with harmful organisms. A further distinct gain came from the prohibition that applied to the touching or eating of a 'clean' animal if it had died of itself or been killed by some other animal. In this connection a non-Israelite living in the camp was permitted to eat such an animal, so it is obvious that the health of the community as a whole would not be protected by the prohibition.

If we accept that clean meat begins with a clean live animal, the Mosaic Code certainly points us in the right direction, and in the years that have followed the orthodox Jew has developed this 'seed thought' to a point where his present method of meat inspection is more rigorous than any other. For example, a carcase fit enough to conform with the latest EEC regulations may still be rejected by a Jewish inspector if he suspects that at any time during its life the animal may have been ill, even though at the time of slaughter it was in good health.

A study of the cleansing ritual laid down for those who had either eaten 'unclean' flesh or touched the carcase of an 'unclean' creature reinforces the view that the defilement is ceremonial rather than microbial. The person concerned had to stay apart from his fellows only for the remainder of the day and, after washing his clothes, he was 'clean' again by the evening. Such a cleansing ritual would have done nothing to prevent the development of disease if the meat or carcase had been infested. Furthermore, if an 'unclean' animal died and its body came into contact with any object inside a tent, that object became 'unclean' until the evening. If it was made of wool or fabric, it had to be steeped in water for the remainder of the day and by the evening it was 'clean', but if it was a clay cooking pot or oven, it could not be cleaned by steeping in water and had to be destroyed. The destruction of the clay oven or cooking pot seems hard to understand when, from a health point of view, all that would have been needed would have been to light a fire in the oven and to boil some water in the cooking pot. Further evidence supporting the view that the dietary defilement is primarily ceremonial is found in the fact that even a 'clean' animal became 'unclean' when it was used as a sin offering (Lev. 6:28; 16:26; Num.19:7,8,10).

It would seem reasonable, therefore, to regard the dietary laws as having a primary religious or ceremonial significance. God is concerned about purity. Healthwise the dietary law did provide some immediate benefit to the Israelites in that their meat was less likely to carry infection.

Delivery in childbirth: Leviticus 12

Childbirth was another cause of defilement, the state of total 'uncleanness' lasting for seven days for a boy and fourteen for a girl, followed by a longer time of partial 'uncleanness' lasting thirty-three days for a boy and sixty-six days for a girl. Throughout this period the mother might not enter the Temple for worship.

To suggest that childbirth must always produce some infectious state capable of transmission to others is just not true. Even if it did, why would the infection last twice as long for a girl as for a boy? We are left with no good medical reason for the exclusion of the mother from Temple worship or normal social contact. Childbirth has not rendered her a hazard to anyone. The religious significance of this particular state of 'uncleanness' is substantiated by the fact that in the terminal cleansing ritual the mother had to offer a sin offering before she could be pronounced 'clean'. Further support for this comes from the fact that the isolation period was double where the birth of a girl was concerned. The religious significance of the seven or fourteen days of impurity is linked to the rule for menstruation, the discharge of blood being taboo. The reason for the longer time of 'uncleanness' in the case of a female child may possibly be related to the fact that the girl will herself menstruate in the future, but it is more likely to be associated with the inferiority of females in that culture. The period of impurity was not because childbirth was a danger to others, or because it was a sinful happening—indeed childbirth was greeted with great joy and thanksgiving. It was a reminder that God is pure and any defilement symbolically separated the individual from God.

DISCHARGES: LEVITICUS 15

Bodily discharges from the male and female genital tracts, whether normal or abnormal, physiological or pathological, caused varying degrees of defilement. The two natural discharges were seminal emission and menstruation. These would not normally convey any infection and yet, in the case of a seminal emission, the man had to wash his clothes and person and remain unclean until the evening. If the emission occurred during sexual intercourse, his wife also was defiled and had to join him in his period of isolation. When a woman menstruated she became unclean for seven days. Any thing or anyone touching the woman during the seven days also became unclean, and whoever touched her bed or whatever she may have been sitting on was also rendered unclean. This 'secondary uncleanness' lasted only for the day of the contact. If, however, her husband had sexual intercourse with her at the time of her menstruation (though this was strictly forbidden), he became unclean for seven days.

It is hard to see how the state of 'uncleanness' caused by these two physiological happenings was other than ceremonial 'uncleanness'. Seminal fluid may, rarely, carry infection, e.g. the virus of hepatitis B, but infection by this means is going to occur only during sexual intercourse. The same could be true of the menstrual flow, but transmission is again very unlikely unless through sexual intercourse. We must conclude, therefore, that no real health benefit was obtained by this part of the code, rather that it was a ceremonial provision, although Gordon Wenham[5] has given an alternative view.

The third bodily discharge that caused defilement was that from the male urethra due possibly to gonorrhoea or non-specific urethritis. These infections appear to be the only ones mentioned in the Mosaic Code of 'uncleanness' which can be unequivocally identified. Even so, their infectivity is virtually only through sexual contact. But in the Levitical account the state of defilement could be transmitted if the man touched another with an unwashed hand or by spitting. Anything he sat on and his bed also became unclean, and anyone touching these articles was also made unclean. The state of 'uncleanness' for the patient lasted until seven days after all symptoms had subsided, but the secondary uncleanness incurred by contact with the man or his furniture lasted only for the day of contact. In this case the man had to stay outside the camp until his period of exclusion came to an end and when he finally returned he had to bring a sin offering.

Here we seem to be dealing with a straightforward case of sexually transmitted disease (venereal disease). Its isolation until a cure was possible was a valuable health gain. At this stage we may ask why a urethral discharge from the female was not included in the list of unclean discharges. A possible answer may be that the urethra in the female plays no part in the act of generation whereas the male urethra does. That there was also a ceremonial aspect is emphasized by the methods of secondary defilement through remote non-infectious contact and by the presence of a sin offering at the end of the isolation period. There is a balance of evidence, therefore, for both views.

The fourth bodily discharge was that of menorrhagia, a condition in which the duration of the menstrual flow extends well beyond the normal four to seven days. In fact, in some cases, it may continue right through the cycle. All the regulations that applied to the menstrual 'uncleanness' applied here, with the added factors that the state of defilement remained for seven days after the symptoms had ceased and that a sin offering was then obligatory. A chronic infection may have been present but the most likely causes are fibroids, hormone imbalance and similar non-infectious conditions. Once again we have to accept that there is no good case medically either for isolation of the victim or for the cleansing of those who have made contact with her.

One interesting concept in this section of the code is that of remote transmission of defilement to others. This defilement was not necessarily caused by sexual contact but by touching the unclean person or the furniture made unclean by contact with the patient. This concept of indirect transmission of 'uncleanness', though of little or no value healthwise in these particular instances (since infection is not spread in this way in venereal disease), is of real value when dealing with certain cases of infectious disease. It should be noted, however, that if some microbial infection was transmissible by this indirect contact, there is no requirement laid down for the cleansing of the potentially infected bedding, clothing or furniture, except for the washing of clothing or leather stained by semen.

On the whole there seems little doubt that the main import of this section of the code dealing with discharges, though it has a positive health gain where a male venereal infection is concerned, is ceremonial or typical. The defilement attributed to the natural physiological discharges and to a non-infective menorrhagia, coupled with the fact that an infective discharge from the female urethra was *not* included, is hard to understand if the primary purpose of the code is the prevention of infective disease. The sin offering that was obligatory following urethritis or menorrhagia emphasizes the spiritual and moral aspects of the 'unclean' state.

What then is the lesson in this section? Is it that any activity of the genital tract in male or female is accompanied by a break in communion with God? Rabbinical teaching is that the uncleanness ascribed to normal male sexual activity did not apply to laymen, and merely involved absence from the 'camp', by which was meant the Sanctuary proper and the levitical encampment around the Sanctuary. It also involved abstention from sacrificed food. Thus this passage does not imply that sexual activity is sinful, but simply that God is holy and consequently when dealing with him his servants should be symbolically pure.

In the New Testament the apostle Paul advises husbands and wives not to deprive each other of their marital rights. However, sexual intercourse outside of marriage is strongly condemned.

CONTACT WITH DEATH: NUMBERS 19

Contact with human death produced a state of uncleanness that demanded an isolation period of seven days and also an application by sprinkling of the 'water of purification' on the third and seventh days of the isolation period. If a person died inside a tent, all who lived in the tent, or who entered the tent, became unclean, even if they did not actually touch the body. The state of uncleanness extended also to any container in the tent that was not covered, but if its lid was fastened it remained clean. This defilement due to human death could be acquired also merely by touching a bone or a grave.

There is a natural abhorrence of anything that is dead, based probably on the rapidity with which decay sets in. Having said that, however, there is little justification for regarding one who has just died as infectious or contagious. A living patient suffering from any infectious disease is a hazard, but once he is dead the risk of transmission is minimal. Special handling precautions are really essential today only in the case of viral hepatitis, AIDS and possibly lassa fever. Such patients, however, would be infinitely more dangerous in life than in death. Contact with a dry bone or a grave would normally be no more likely to infect than would contact with the bare earth.

That defilement through human death was regarded as ceremonial rather than microbial is supported by the ruling concerning the container in the tent of the deceased. With its lid fastened it remained clean, though its outer surface would have been just as liable to contamination (if some lethal microorganism had been floating around inside the tent) as would its interior if the lid were off. The outer surface would in fact have been more likely to have been contaminated and more likely to have been handled.

The cleansing ritual introduces a new concept—the use of the water of purification which had to be sprinkled on the unclean person on the third and seventh days of his isolation period. This water of purification was a watery suspension of ashes which themselves were the end product of the burning of 'a red heifer, without defect or blemish and that has never been under a yoke'. Slaughtered outside the camp in the presence of the high priest elect, it was then burned, and while it was being burned some cedarwood, scarlet wool and hyssop were added to it. The resulting ashes were then taken to a ceremonially clean place outside the camp. They were to be kept by the Israelite community 'for use in the water of cleansing; it is for purification from sin'. From the point of view of hygiene no antiseptic effect, or even a mechanical cleansing effect, would have been produced by the ritual sprinkling on day three and day seven. At the end of the isolation period, however, there was a final washing of the clothes and bathing of the person, which might have had some minor benefit. The most useful part of the procedure would have been the exclusion period of seven days, which could have served as a precautionary quarantine period for a few diseases, but would have been much too short for many others.

Death did not honour God, and primarily for this reason he ordained that contact with human death rendered a person unclean. To help dispose of the remains of a dead person would often involve godly virtues of kindness and selflessness, but the law remained to remind the Jews that their God was holy and could not be associated with imperfection.

DERMATITIS ('LEPROSY'): LEVITICUS 13 AND 14

This subject is fully dealt with in chapter 4. Here I would draw attention only to the fact that once again an illness that was at worst of only minor infectivity, and could well have been non-infective, was treated to some extent as a dangerous and highly contagious disease. The isolation enforced on the unfortunate sufferer was desperately harsh and there is little doubt that the ceremonial significance attached to this group of skin complaints far outweighed their clinical importance, as is shown by the elaborate, costly and prolonged cleansing ritual applied to the recovered case. The final washing and complete shaving of the patient, repeated after an interval of seven days, emphasizes the gravity of the situation. This 'dreaded skin disease' was the punishment of Miriam, Gehazi and Uzziah. In each case the sin was the pride and covetousness of heart that wanted something special for one-self. This pride of 'place' and 'grace' was clearly regarded as an ever-present evil, requiring the deepest form of ceremonial repentance.

Other matters

In Deuteronomy 23:12–14 the burial of human excreta is made obligatory though, even in this case, the reason given is the presence among the people of a holy God. In the absence of more sophisticated methods of sewage disposal, the burial of human excreta is an absolute 'must'. Carried out thoroughly, it must have done much to prevent the spread of intestinal diseases. Even here, however, one notices the omission of what many would regard as a vital addition: 'Now wash your hands.'

In Numbers 31:19–24 soldiers returning from war, and their captives, are told to undergo a period of exclusion and purification. The material spoils of war also have to be purified either by fire or by water before they can be brought into the camp. All concerned, animate and inanimate, have also to be sprinkled with the water of purification. In Deuteronomy 21:10–13 women taken captive are required to undergo a process of cleansing and quarantine before they can be taken into the family.

Conclusions

The Mosaic Code of uncleanness as given in the Pentateuch deals with a variety of events that were said to cause defilement. Only in the case of gonorrhoea are we certain that we are dealing with a transmissible disease, and even here there are many aspects of ceremonial defilement as well as of actual infection.

The principle of isolation is introduced, but the periods of isolation allotted to each defilement would often not affect the transmission of disease if disease had been present. Nothing is said about the control of the spread of many of the major causes of infection that affect the world today. Tuberculosis, diphtheria, whooping cough, malaria, mumps, chicken pox, measles, german measles, poliomyelitis, influenza, plague and many other infections would, if introduced into the community, have been unaffected by the strictest observance of the code. Some of the hand-borne diseases might have been less prevalent in those families where hand-washing had become a way of life, but this would have been only an accidental, though happy, consequence of the ritual. Only gonorrhoea and non-specific urethritis would seem to have been diminished by observance of the code. It seems reasonable, therefore, to conclude that the Mosaic Code on uncleanness, as given in the Pentateuch, was primarily ceremonial and only at times of practical use in the prevention of disease, though there are certain basic points of hygiene associated with the ritual.

The Jew of today, however, is guided not so much by the Pentateuch as by the Talmud, and in this there has been considerable development of certain aspects of the Mosaic Law. For example, the simple prohibition of cooking a kid in its mother's milk has now grown to an extensive and complex code of rules whereby dairy produce is never consumed with any form of meat. Indeed, separation of these two articles of diet is carried out to such an extent that in many institutions there are two separate kitchens. The same occurred in respect of the many washings that were involved in the cleansing rituals. Hence we find that in the Gospels the disciples are rebuked for not having washed their hands before eating grain which they had plucked as they passed through a wheatfield. In the same manner the meat eaten by the orthodox Jew of today is subject to a much more rigorous code of health inspection than was laid down in the Pentateuch.

It does seem, therefore, that though the primary purpose of the code was to help in the separation of a holy nation unto a holy God, it also had its incidental value in the development of some forms of hygiene that are of benefit today. These may be summarized as follows:

1. ISOLATION The segregation, if not complete isolation, of patients with some kinds of illness or defilement may have helped to introduce the concept of the isolation unit in the treatment of infectious disease. However, the idea itself did not seem to dawn on the Israelites of those early days because we find that when God did permit the occurrence of an epidemic as a form of judgment, the disease swept through the community with great rapidity. In such cases there seems to have been no attempt to isolate either patients or contacts.
2. TRANSMISSION That disease can be spread by means of infected garments and bedding may have been suggested by the description of how defilement arising from bodily discharges was spread through contact with clothing, furniture and utensils.
3. DISINFECTION Every case of defilement had to pass through a

terminal process of cleansing which often involved the washing of the person and of the clothes. These washings with water may, or may not, have been of much value if microbial infection was still present, because we do not know how thoroughly the washing was done, nor if any attempt was made to use very hot water as a method of sterilization. Even though much of the terminal disinfection process was inadequate, or even useless, in the presence of a virulent infection, the 'seed thought' was there and the process today is one of value.

4. QUARANTINE AND OBSERVATION This principle was used during the diagnosis of doubtful cases of skin disease and the concept is still in use in true infections today.

It may be argued that the development of these ideas would have taken place in any case as a result of observation and trial and error, but certainly the Jewish mind was given a healthy stimulus in the right direction. An Israeli community physician recently said that she found it much easier to impart the basic rules of hygiene to an orthodox Jew brought up in the old traditions than to the non-orthodox Jew.

By developing certain ideas along a relatively easy path, the Jew has made some gain on the physical level, a gain that is not to be despised. However, in choosing the easier path he may have lost on the spiritual side by failing to discern the true spiritual meaning of the Mosaic teaching on defilement. It has always been easier to make clean the outside of the cup than to cleanse the inner defilement of the heart.

The Mosaic Law was given primarily to ensure that a holy people could dwell in harmony with their God. Holiness is not an optional extra, but is to be a way of life. Without it we cannot see the glory of our Lord. Holiness is like a good marriage—it has to be worked at. In the terminology of the New Testament it is the work of the Holy Spirit, but he does require our cooperation. Paul points the moral in the last verses of 2 Corinthians 6 and the first verse of chapter 7: 'We are the temple of the living God. As God has said, "I will live with them and walk among them, and I will be their God, and they will be my people." "Therefore come out from among them and be separate", says the Lord. "Touch no unclean thing and I will receive you. I will be a Father to you and you will be my sons and daughters", says the Lord Almighty. Since we have these promises, dear friends, let us purify ourselves from everything that contaminates body and spirit, perfecting holiness out of reverence for God.'

4

LEPROSY IN THE BIBLE

STANLEY G. BROWNE

For years Christians have been to the fore in caring for leprosy sufferers. They have generally based their attitude to the disease and its victims on the example of our Lord, who actually touched those suffering from leprosy (Mark 1:41), and have considered that his instructions to the twelve disciples ('cleanse the lepers' (Matt. 10:8)) were intended to be binding upon Christians down the ages. They have seen in the Authorized Version of the Old and New Testaments not only the justification for thinking of leprosy as a disease apart, but also a sufficient motive for showing especial concern for its victims.

On the other hand, there were those who have thought it improper (and even futile) to attempt to cure those afflicted with leprosy, regarding it as a divine punishment for sin and hence not amenable to treatment by medical means. Many Christian writers and preachers, from Origen onwards, have considered leprosy as 'a type of sin', a model or symbol of sin. Until recently, the facts that certain kinds of leprosy were relentlessly progressive and that no treatment seemed effective in healing the ulcers of hands and feet, certainly gave credibility to the widespread belief, enshrined in sayings and proverbs the world over, that leprosy was quite incurable.[1]

Recent research into leprosy—its aetiology, pathology, transmission and treatment—has brought the disease out of the mists of popular superstition and into the realm of specific communicable diseases that should be and are being investigated and appraised scientifically.[2] The role of the long-suspected cause, *Mycobacterium leprae*, is being deciphered, and Koch's postulates (sometimes attributed to Henle) are being fulfilled one by one. While many unsolved mysteries of immunology and transmission remain to challenge workers on the field and in the laboratory, leprosy is now assuming its proper place in the range of mycobacterial infections.

Much confusion exists concerning the meaning to be placed on the word 'leprosy' as it occurs in various English versions of the Bible. The difficulties that have for long been apparent are not lessened by the differences in the translations that have recently achieved varying acceptance and popularity. Some of these follow the traditional renderings of the Authorized Version, while others introduce novel translations. The crux of the matter lies in the original root-meanings and changing connotations of Hebrew and Greek words, and their verbal equivalents in modern English.[3] Another, and very practical aspect of translation concerns the implications of any identification of the word used in the Scriptures with a specific disease. If the well-defined disease known today as 'leprosy' is made to carry the connotation of ritual defilement, of uncleanness and of punishment for wrongdoing—then many human beings, who already suffer from the physical disease of leprosy, will have to bear in addition the results of the mistranslations and misinterpretations that over the years have caused deep distress and pain to millions.

Leprosy in the Bible and in Bible Times

What, then, in these days is the leprosy of the Bible? Is biblical leprosy the same as the disease we know today as leprosy? Further, why should a disease entity be singled out for special mention in Holy Writ? Has the specific disease called leprosy any ritual or theological significance?

The short answer is that true 'leprosy' is not explicitly or indubitably referred to in the Bible. If the Hebrew and Greek Scriptures were being translated *de novo* today into English or any other language, by scholars equally versed in historical linguistics and medical semantics (and having no subconscious presuppositions) a word other than 'leprosy' would be diligently sought as the equivalent in denotation and connotation of Hebrew *ṣāra'at* and Greek *lepra*. This is an impossible task. In fact, many serious scholars regard the words as untranslatable, since they embrace incompatible concepts.

The main reason for the bald statement that leprosy is not referred to in the original Scriptures is that it was not until 1847[4] that leprosy was clearly separated as a clinical entity from many other conditions that up to then had not infrequently been confused with it. Somewhat later, Hansen[5] published the initial results of his researches, and identified *M. leprae* as an organism consistently present (although in highly variable concentrations) in all kinds of lesions that were, by clinical definition, leprosy. The original Hebrew and Greek words and their Latin equivalents naturally lack the scientific precision and delimitation of the word 'leprosy' (and its cognates) as now used in English. These old words were generic, non-scientific, inclusive, imprecise, 'lay' terms. Words that were appropriately exact in a bygone age and in other cultures, are unlikely to be coterminous with terms used today by Western scientific man in the twentieth century.

Our main purpose here is to examine the word 'leprosy' as found in the Old and New Testaments, and to attempt to discover the meaning and delimitation of the basic concept denoted by the word in its various contexts. Only thus will it be possible to arrive at an understanding of leprosy in the Bible. In general, 'leprosy' in the Bible is a pathological condition, usually a disease set in a context of illness and affliction and of bodily infirmities (2 Sam. 3:29; Matt. 10:8; 11:5). It is a term denoting ritual defilement or uncleanness. It suggests a surface blemish and stigma and taboo. The ceremonially defiled object is not so delineated on grounds of modern ideas of infectiousness or hygiene or of morality. It is unclean.

We must at the outset humbly confess the fallibility of retrospective diagnosis, especially when insufficient medical hints are given, and words of disputed meaning are used (as in Leviticus 13 and 14). Moreover, patterns of disease do tend to change with the passage of time and among different races, as witness tuberculosis and syphilis, measles and scarlet fever. It is not possible, on strictly linguistic grounds, to assert categorically that leprosy was, or was not, included among the conditions that had to be identified by the priest as defiling, and which called for temporary or permanent exclusion from the community.

THE WORD 'LEPROSY' IN THE OLD TESTAMENT

The word 'leprosy', together with its cognates 'leper(s)' and 'leprous' in the Authorized and most subsequent versions in English, is a translation of Hebrew *ṣāra'at* in all texts where it occurs. Twenty-nine of the occurrences are in chapters 13 and 14 of the book of Leviticus. No other 'disease' is accorded equal prominence in the Bible. The derivation and root meaning of *ṣāra'at* have long been matters of debate. The suggestion of such authorities as Driver[6] and Snaith,[7] supported more recently by Wilkinson[8] was that the primary root carried the meaning of 'collapse' or 'strike', and came to mean 'stricken of God'. According to Driver, *ṣāra'at* could be rendered as 'a stroke inflicted by God' for a transgression of the Law; its meaning embraced both the prostrating experience itself and the visible consequences of such a visitation.[9] This derivation from the Arabic is now disputed by many scholars on several weighty grounds, and an alternative suggestion is made that a more likely root is *sir'ā*, which may be translated as 'hornet' or 'wasp'.[3,10] The appearance of a victim of *ṣāra'at* may recall that of a person stung by a wasp, or a swarm of wasps or hornets, just as the sufferer from urticaria (nettle rash) may feel and look as if he had been stung by nettles.

Whatever the derivation of the term, *ṣāra'at* is seen in Leviticus 13 and 14 as a disfiguring and dreaded condition of a surface—the human skin, or cloth or leather, or the walls of houses—that rendered the person or object ceremonially unclean.

To the Israelites, *ṣāra'at* was a condition amenable only to divine intervention. God alone was the source of healing for disease ('I am the Lord that healeth thee' (Exod. 15:26) and 'who healeth all thy diseases' (Ps. 103:3); and leprosy was a visible mark of God's power or displeasure. Thus, Job's misfortunes and sicknesses were not to be interpreted as punishment for wrong-doing (Job 42:8,10), and the *ṣāra'at* that struck Moses was a manifestation of God's power and presence (Exod. 4:6,7). The notion that all sickness was necessarily a punishment for sin, however, was rejected by our Lord (John 9:3), though the possibility was entertained (John 5:14).

Difficulties arise in determining the exact equivalents of many of the Hebrew words used in Leviticus 13 and 14 to describe the clinical appearance of people afflicted with *ṣāra'at* or with conditions that had to be differentiated from *ṣāra'at*. These words are variously translated by: rising (v.2), scab (v.2), bright spot (v.2), dry scall (v.30). Wilkinson[11] analyses the root meanings of these four basic concepts in the table opposite.

Other ill-defined terms also occur in this passage, for instance: somewhat dark (v.6); quick raw flesh (v.10); boil (v.18); freckled spot (v.39). The diagnostic assistance that these terms may seem to afford at first sight and to the layman, is illusory. No physician, relying solely on them, could today make an accurate diagnosis of the various skin conditions referred to.

The identification of *ṣāra'at* and its diagnostic separation from

HEBREW	AV	RSV	NEB	NIV	Occurrences in Lev. 13 and 14.
se'eth	rising	swelling	discoloration *or* mark	swelling	6
sappahath	scab	eruption	pustule	rash	2
bahereth	bright spot	spot	inflammation	bright spot	10
methek	dry scall	itch	scurf	sore	11

other conditions that were not ritually defiling, provide the *raison d'être* for the detailed information in these two chapters. In the case of *ṣāra'at* of the human skin, the victim himself, or his family and friends, would have their suspicions aroused by the presence of one or several of the following departures from the normal: swellings or nodules in the skin; a crusted or scabbed skin rash; inflamed spots or larger areas of skin; scurf of the scalp or beard area.

The individual suspected of being attacked by *ṣāra'at* would be brought to the priest, who would look for the specific indications of the ritually unclean and defiling condition. These were: some change in the pigmentation of the skin and hair—both hair and skin would be white; some thickening or infiltration of the skin; extension of the abnormal skin, and possibly ulceration.[8,11]

The striking feature of this rather confusing list of instructions drawn up to help the priests is that no recognizable disease, or diseases, emerge that can be unhesitatingly categorized into either the *ṣāra'at* or non-*ṣāra'at* classes. Because of the repeated references to whiteness of skin and hair, leprosy as we know it today definitely would not be regarded as *ṣāra'at*, if it had existed in Mosaic times or later.

Since the Mishnah achieved its present form as late as the third century AD, the laws of leprosy had already fallen into disuse with the destruction of the Temple. Chief Rabbi Adler states, 'The uncleanness of the leper seems, according to the Talmud, to have been ordained for the purpose of securing Levitical purity, and not with the view of preventing contagion.'

The possibility of cure as well as cleansing was held out in Leviticus—not only clinical arrest, but complete restoration. Cure is a matter of ritual cleansing and coincided with the disappearance of the signs that had led to the priestly diagnosis of *ṣāra'at* in the first place. The ritual was recognized and respected by our Lord. In the Talmud[12,13] instructions are laid down regarding ceremonial or ritual uncleanness of *ṣāra'at* that are on a par with those concerned with handling a corpse, or with menstrual uncleanness (Num. 5:2). It is interesting that our Lord superseded the three Mosaic prohibitions recorded in Numbers (Num. 19:22) and Leviticus (Lev. 22:4). He touched a sufferer from *lepra* (Mark 1:41); a woman with an issue of blood touched the hem of his garment (Matt. 9:20); and Jesus Himself touched the bier of the widow's son at Nain (Luke 7:14), and took by the hand the daughter of Jairus (Matt. 9:25), who was thought to be dead.

The apparent interchangeability of 'healing' and 'cleansing' in certain, admittedly rare, contexts may suggest that the distinction between these two ideas may not be as definite as at first appears. Thus, in Leviticus 14:3, the word 'healed' is used of the affliction *ṣāra'at* and in Leviticus 14:48 the same word is used of the *ṣāra'at* of a house. (The only New Testament reference to 'healing' of *lepra* is in Luke 17:15.)

Furthermore, the clinical features put forward as of differentiating value in enabling the priest to make a positive diagnosis of *ṣāra'at* are not applicable to true leprosy; for example, whiteness of the hair (leucotrichia) does not occur in leprosy. Hairs may break or fall out, and hair follicles may be replaced by scar tissue, but—in contradistinction to the usual state of affairs within a leucodermic area—the pigmentation of the hairs is unaffected. Another supposedly differentiating feature is some kind of swelling deep in the skin or spreading deeply (Lev. 13:3–28). This sign is of no real help in the diagnosis of any known conditions, and especially in the recognition of early diseases from which *ṣāra'at* had to be differentiated. One may hazard a guess at some of the possibilities. Conditions that were not *ṣāra'at* may, for example, have been erysipelas adjacent to a boil as in Leviticus 13:18, infection following a burn (v.24), a ringworm or sycosis of the scalp or beard (v.29), a pustular dermatitis (v.36), a favus or desert sore (v.42).[14]

Ṣāra'at was not a condition of human skin only. It could also appear as a mildew on wool or linen, or on any object made from skin or leather, or as a pigmented fungus or lichen on the walls of dwellings (Lev. 14:33–53). It is interesting that the French still refer to leprosy of walls (*la lèpre des murs*). It could thus be a dry-rot, or sheets of felt-like texture with a greenish-yellow or red surface.[9] While the lay or priestly mind of Moses' day might have been able to embrace these scientifically diverse concepts in a generalization of ritual 'uncleanness' or 'defilement', to our way of thinking their juxtaposition only reinforces the contention that a specific human disease, i.e. leprosy, could not have been the object of these laws. There is, of course, nothing in common between *M. leprae* and the various parasitic fungi that cause mildew on cloth and leather objects in damp situations. The underlying and visible basis for the 'uncleanness' in Leviticus seems to be depigmented patches on the human skin, or coloured patches on the surface of an inanimate object.

When *ṣāra'at* was suspected in human beings, the priest was enjoined, if in doubt, to temporize and re-examine after a period of seven days' exclusion from the camp—a procedure that could be repeated if necessary. In the case of inanimate objects, the same instructions were to be observed—re-examination, followed (if the suspicions were confirmed) by removal and destruction. However, the lesions of true leprosy are of such indolent development that seven days is far too short a period in which to note any change in appearance.

The word *ṣāra'at* was sometimes associated with *negha'* (= disease), and the combination is seen to refer to the place affected (Lev. 13:3), the man afflicted (Lev. 13:14), or the affliction itself (Lev. 14:35–37).

The other Old Testament references are equally imprecise, and afford no certain clue to clinical diagnosis.

God could by direct and miraculous intervention cause *ṣāra'at* to appear. Thus, in the case of Moses (Ex.4:6), it was a sign both to him and to the people; for Miriam (Num. 12:10–12), it was a salutary warning or punishment. The appearance and disappearance of 'leprosy' at the direct behest of God in these two instances, probably explains much of the subconscious attitude towards 'leprosy' of both Jews and Christians.

It thus cannot be denied that *ṣāra'at* was felt to be a sign of God's power to test or to punish, and its sudden appearance was a horrifying demonstration of the immediacy of the divine power. The Israelites are reminded of what 'the Lord thy God did unto Miriam' (Deut.24:9); Aaron pleaded with Moses, and Moses 'cried unto the Lord' for Miriam's healing (Num. 12:10–13); Gehazi was punished with the *ṣāra'at* of Naaman, and his descendants 'for ever' were likewise afflicted (2 Kgs. 5:27); and *ṣāra'at* was an evident sign of God's displeasure, as shown in the words of the curse of David on Joab's house (2 Sam. 3:28,29).

We note, in passing, that Moses prayed that Miriam might be 'healed' (Num. 12:13) (not cleansed), the word employed being that ordinarily used for wounds and illness. We also note incidentally that the word 'white' should not appear in Numbers 12:10, or in 2 Kings 5:27: it does not occur in Exodus 4:6. The reason for the use of an epithet in the Authorized Version is to signify a visible abnormality: in the case of Moses, Miriam and Gehazi, the skin change was striking and recognizable.

Leprosy lesions are never achromic, but whiteness of the skin and the affected hair is stressed several times in Leviticus 13. Some have seen in *ṣāra'at* a kind of vitiligo (the 'white leprosy' of medieval Europe and modern India), but this banal, if unsightly, condition would scarcely give rise to a degree of fear warranting the exclusion from the camp of every 'leper' (Num. 5:2), or suggest a resemblance to a macerated fetus. 'One dead, whose flesh is half consumed' (Num. 12:12) is not suffering from vitiligo or a benign and transient skin rash, or psoriasis (the 'white leprosy' of medieval England and of Arab countries). It may be remarked, in passing, that today the identification of an achromic area of skin as leprosy evokes the whole range of fear and revulsion associated with real leprosy.

The exact nature of Naaman's *ṣāra'at* cannot be deduced from the record (2 Kgs. 5:1). The rash may possibly have been scabies, for which the sulphur-containing waters of Rabbi Mayer (near Tiberias) are reputedly curative to this day, sufferers being exhorted locally to 'dip seven times'.[15] The transmissible disease that subsequently afflicted Gehazi (and his descendants) could also have been scabies, caught by contact with the garments he coveted (2 Kgs. 5:27). It seems that Gehazi continued his service after being smitten with *ṣāra'at* (2 Kgs. 8:4,5). We simply have insufficient clinical details to enable us to hazard a diagnosis of Naaman's *ṣāra'at*, and the reference in Luke 4:27 is similarly imprecise, Greek *lepra* being substituted for Hebrew *ṣāra'at*.

It is noteworthy that Naaman had a skin condition that was recognized and identified, but there is no suggestion that because of it he was excluded from high office, or from the palace and temple in Syria, or from access to king and prophet in Israel; nor was he denied the help of a Jewish serving-maid in enforced exile. He was suffering from *ṣāra'at*, but not apparently from the *ṣāra'at* of ritual defilement or Mosaic uncleanness. According to the Talmud, 'all can contract uncleanness from leprosy-signs excepting gentiles and resident aliens'.[12] On the other hand, the word 'clean' is used of his condition (2 Kgs. 5:10,12,14) as well as the neutral 'take away from him his *ṣāra'at* (vv.3,6,7): his flesh was 'to be restored' or 'to return' (vv.10,14). Elisha, moreover, accepted without question the diagnosis of *ṣāra'at* made by an unknown Syrian physician, or by Naaman himself. In Luke 4:27, the word 'cleansed' is used by our

Lord of Naaman. It is not the historicity or authenticity of the record that is in question—only the precise meaning and implication of the Hebrew text in a non-Jewish setting.

The 'four leprous men' (2 Kgs. 7:3) lived outside the city because they were unclean by reason of *ṣāra'at*. They were evidently mobile, and there is no hint of any neuropathic ulceration of the feet.

Azariah (2 Kgs.15:5) or Uzziah (2 Chr. 26:19–21), had a *ṣāra'at* lesion on the forehead, which became red and swollen when he was angry. The precise nature of the lesion is uncertain, since no clinical details of diagnostic value are given. The text implies that Uzziah was free from *ṣāra'at* until the Lord 'smote him', and the priests observed the forehead lesion rising up before their eyes. The diagnosis of *ṣāra'at* was readily and rapidly made by the priests and the victim himself, and the unfortunate king was isolated in a 'several house' ('lazar house', in AV margin) 'until the day of his death'.

Further evidence of the importance accorded to *ṣāra'at* is found in the injunction of Deuteronomy 24:8–9. The Israelites were advised to follow carefully all the instructions of the levitical priests. *Ṣāra'at* could also be invoked in a curse, a dire prediction, as in 2 Samuel 3:28–29. David cursed the house and descendants of Joab, and *ṣāra'at* and other unclean states were wished on the descendants in every generation.

Persons suffering from *ṣāra'at* are excluded from the camp of the Israelites (Lev. 13:46). No descendant of Aaron suffering from the condition recognized by the priest as *ṣāra'at* may eat of the holy things unless and until he has been pronounced clean in the accepted way (Lev. 22:4).

Although the word *ṣāra'at* does not occur in the book of Job, in medieval art and literature Job is frequently represented as suffering from leprosy.

None of the references to *ṣāra'at* includes any of these specific signs and symptoms of leprosy: anaesthetic areas of skin, progressive ulceration of the extremities, depressed nose, and facial nodules. These obvious departures from the normal would be noticed by observant laymen, and were, in fact, noted in other lands when true leprosy occurred.

This concatenation of converging lines of internal evidence—both positive and negative—should do more than just raise a suspicion that the *ṣāra'at* of the Old Testament was not leprosy. The references suggest that *ṣāra'at* is primarily and predominantly a state of ritual uncleanness or ceremonial defilement characterized by visible surface blemishes.

LEPROSY IN OLD TESTAMENT TIMES

Until recently, leprosy was considered to be a familiar disease in Mesopotamia and the Orient in antiquity, and some authorities[16] are convinced that authentic descriptions of the disease go back as far as the third millenium BC. The four lepers outside Samaria (2 Kgs. 7:3–10) and King Uzziah (2 Chr. 26:19–21) according to Harrison, suffered from true leprosy. However, recent research—in particular, the identification of specific bony changes due only to leprosy—has radically altered the picture, and it may now be stated with more or less certainty that the specific disease known today as leprosy did not exist in the lands of the Bible at the time of Moses and the patriarchs, or even in the exilic or post-exilic period. The oft-quoted references in the Ebers' papyrus (c.1550 BC) to 'uchedu' (ukhedu) and to Chons' swellings, are now held to be too vague to be indicative of leprosy. There is evidence that in both Akkadian and Sumerian the words used for serious skin disease could also be applied to guilt.[17]

It has been suggested[18] that imprecise and uncertain references in an Old Babylonian omen text to an incurable skin condition characterized by widespread whitish scales and necessitating excommunication and banishment, may have been true leprosy, since hypopigmented skin areas, scattered 'dots' (possibly papules) and a malodorous smell are all mentioned.

The human features portrayed on a Canaanite clay jar found in the temple of Amenophis III (c.1411–1314 BC) have been thought by some—on insufficient grounds, in the writer's opinion—to be so reminiscent of the leonine facies of lepromatous leprosy that they provide evidence that the disease existed in Palestine at that time.[19] It would seem most inappropriate for such a representation to figure on a jar intended for the storage of grain.

There is a suggestion that Nubian slaves, taken to Egypt about 480 BC by Persian hosts, may possibly have brought leprosy with them from the Sudan, but no precise clinical description is extant.

The earliest indubitable references to leprosy come from India,[20] and are dated as late as c.600 BC, although they must embody earlier oral tradition. The *Susruth samhita* summarizes traditional knowledge about leprosy and mentions chaulmoogra oil as a treatment. Both skin and nerve signs are recognized, and the disease (even in its common milder forms) is differentiated from leucoderma. Records from China and Japan are dated somewhat later than those from India.

The earliest descriptions of leprosy from India and China are surprisingly accurate and full, proving close observation and intelligent recording. Had leprosy existed at the time of Moses the law-giver, its cardinal signs could not have escaped the notice of observant priests and laymen in Egypt and Palestine, and would have received mention in a document intended to provide helpful information to those having the responsibility of pronouncing people or objects 'clean' or 'unclean'.

In the Western World, Hippocrates (c.400 BC) seems not to have been acquainted with leprosy; he does indeed refer to *lepra* in a context that suggests psoriasis, or (in another sense) an irritating blotchy summer prurigo or scurf.[21] The long history of the word *lepra* and its constant association with scurfy and scaly conditions of the human skin have left their mark on subsequent diagnostic criteria and language. The true nature of the more serious malady which Hippocrates calls 'the Phoenician disease' is unknown; some have imagined that it might be leprosy.

The suggestion has been advanced by Andersen[22] and others that the sudden appearance of the well-recognized signs and symptoms of true leprosy in the West coincided with the return of the armies of Alexander the Great from the Indian campaign in the years 327–326 BC. By that time leprosy had been prevalent in India for several centuries, but it was quite unkown in countries of the Mediterranean littoral. This suggestion has been invalidated by the fact that Alexander's troops stayed only a short time in India, and in an area (the Punjab) where the present prevalence rate of leprosy is low. Despite the contacts of Greek merchants with India and the East in pre-Alexandrian times, leprosy was apparently not introduced along the ancient caravan routes linking the Middle East with India and Mesopotamia.

The earliest records of leprosy in Europe are known only from later quotations of original works that have been lost. Straton, a disciple of the Alexandrian physician Erasistratos (c.300–250 BC) is quoted by Rufus of Ephesus (AD 98–117) as giving an accurate description of low-resistant leprosy. This is the first indubitable record of leprosy in Europe. It is called 'elephantiasis', a completely new disease. Some years later, elephantiasis was picturesquely designated 'leontiasis', by reason of the thickened corrugations of the facial skin, and 'satyriasis', when the cheeks and eyebrow region became swollen and prominent. While original texts from the third century BC referring to leprosy have been lost, enough is known to suggest that, once introduced, the disease followed the soldiers and traders from Athens and Rome into the countries of Europe and North Africa. Pliny the Elder asserts, with some circumstantial justification, that leprosy was brought into Europe by Pompey's army returning from the Egyptian campaign in 62–61 BC, the disease being already known and recognized in Italy.

Such, then, is the evidence. Leprosy was unkown in patriarchal times. It seems to have burst in on the Western World with apparent suddenness about three centuries before Christ. From sacred and profane literary sources we may now turn to skeletal remains.

It has been established, thanks to the researches of Moeller-Christensen,[23,24] that advanced lepromatous leprosy specifically and uniquely erodes the anterior nasal spine and the alveolar process of the maxilla, thus providing indestructible proof of its presence during the lifetime of the propositus. (Progressive reduction of the bony phalanges is secondary to peripheral nerve damage, and hence is non-specific). Systematic examination of some thousands of human skulls, variously dated, has enabled Moeller-Christensen to identify the specific changes due to leprosy. No evidence from Old Testament countries and times has yet come to light. Until recent excavations in Lower Egypt disclosed bony remains showing indubitable signs of leprosy[25] in skeletons from the second century BC, the earliest skeletal evidence of leprosy was in two Coptic mummies in the Nubian collection dated about the fifth century of our era.[26,27,28] The earlier evidence is in four skulls. According to intrinsic bony data these were of white representatives of the ruling class from the Ptolemaic period, and were discovered in the Dakhleh oasis.

While this argument from silence may carry some weight, it may be objected that persons suffering from leprosy might well have passed their days and ended their lives far from communal burying grounds. In certain countries (e.g. Eastern Nigeria and Bali) persons dying of leprosy were left unburied. In New Testament times the mentally afflicted might dwell 'among the tombs' (Matt. 8:28), and also those who were 'unclean' because of *ṣāra'at*.

Moeller-Christensen[29] 'failed to find the slightest trace of lepromatous bone changes among 1844 skeletons, mummies and skulls from Egypt dating from between 6000 BC and AD 600, and among 695 skeletons from Lachish, in Southern Palestine (760-600 BC).' We must await the results of further osteo-archaeological researches before a final pronouncement is possible; if leprosy indeed existed at all in ancient Egypt or in Palestine at the time of the prophets, it could not have been common.

To sum up, there are no positive proofs that leprosy is referred to in the Old Testament, nor is there any evidence from profane literary sources or skeletal remains.

If, then, *ṣāra'at* is not leprosy as we know it today, and did not even include leprosy, what could have been the diverse dermatoses comprised by the term *ṣāra'at*? It may indeed be idle to seek an exact equivalent, and misleading to suggest that, e.g. psoriasis or vitiligo should replace 'leprosy' as a translation of *ṣāra'at* in a clinical context. Moreover, the *ṣāra'at* of dwellings and cloth and leather still bedevil the lexicographer and etymologist.

To the deeper question, 'Why were these conditions regarded in this light, and hence subject to ritual or ceremonial discrimination?', it is impossible to provide a simple, convincing answer. It cannot be that *ṣāra'at* in its various manifestations was uniformly serious, nor could human *ṣāra'at* be considered as highly contagious or as threatening an epidemic of grave dimensions. Among unsophisticated peoples, any skin eruption—especially when present on the exposed face—may evoke an inordinate fear. It may be associated with taboo violation, and hence with the fear of punishment or retribution.[30] Again, a rational fear of a serious contagious disease (like smallpox) may have religious overtones. But leprosy is not explosively epidemic, or obviously contagious to a high degree.

When leprosy appears in a community, the disease brings to a focus existing fears and phobias[31] since it embodies many mysterious features—an oft-times unrecognized source of infection, haphazard attack, long silent period, protean clinical signs, inexorable march of peripheral ulceration once it appears, and a lingering life that is worse than death.

The taboo violation is sometimes particularized. In China, for instance, leprosy is thought to be the punishment for sexual misdemeanour, and is to be got rid of only by deflowering a virgin or by 'selling' it to as many people as possible.[31] It is the ultimate in moral degradation. In several cultures, leprosy is thought to be associated with venery; the satyriasis of the Greeks had a sexual component. In medieval English, the word 'leprosy' was sometimes equated with illicit sexual relations.

The fear of contagion is so strong among some peoples that the victims in parts of China and India were burned alive if rich, or buried alive if poor. In some districts in Eastern Nigeria, sufferers from leprosy actually asked to be buried while still alive, ostensibly to prevent their passing on the disease to others.

Leprosy is widely held in some countries to be transmissible to offspring, or to be evidence of wrong-doing in a previous incarnation. In some cultures, sufferers from leprosy are forbidden to marry, for fear of transmitting the disease to the next generation. On the other hand, according to the Talmud,[12] a non-Jew with *ṣāra'at* was not considered unclean and could live with a Jewish family. Furthermore, so far from being considered very contagious, suspected *ṣāra'at* in a bridegroom was not allowed to interfere with the seven days of honeymoon. After a week's cohabitation, the bridegroom was examined by the priest. The victim of *ṣāra'at* was regarded as 'unclean', i.e. defiled, or ceremonially contaminated. By extension and interpretation, a man with *ṣāra'at* was not to be touched, or even saluted; he had to keep at least two metres from a healthy person, or seventy metres if the wind was blowing from his direction.

Modern usage by the non-medical laity in Israel is in keeping with the unconscionable fear and loathing evoked by the word *ṣāra'at* in ancient times. Dermatologists and leprologists working in Israel today do not use the word *ṣāra'at* in referring to leprosy. It is not the contagiousness, but the mystery and the awfulness of *ṣāra'at* that strike terror to the hearts; *ṣāra'at* is 'leprosy', and 'leprosy is to be feared and dreaded as no other disease.

Leprosy in the New Testament

The words translated 'leper(s)' and 'leprosy' occur thirteen times in the synoptic Gospels, and not elsewhere in the New Testament. Like *ṣāra'at*, *lepra* (*lepros*) has an ill-defined non-specific connotation. In Attic Greek it means scaly, or scabbed, and it is one of a large family of words derived from a root meaning 'to husk, to scale or to remove the bark'. Some of the derivatives contain the idea of rough or scaly, whereas others carry the meaning of thin, scale-like.[32]

The references to leprosy in the Gospels may be arranged under six heads:

1. Matthew 8:2–4, Mark 1:40–45 and Luke 5:12–15. The man with leprosy, or 'full of leprosy' (Luke 5:12) came to our Lord in worship and entreaty. He was immediately and miraculously 'cleansed', and was instructed to fulfil his ceremonial obligations 'according as Moses commanded' (Luke 5:14). In passing, it is noteworthy that in the New Testament it is only 'lepers' who were cleansed; all other sick folk were healed.

2. Matthew 10:1–15. In sending out the twelve disciples our Lord enjoined them to 'cleanse the lepers' (Matt. 10:8); several ancient manuscripts of Matthew omit this phrase, as do the parallel passages in Mark (6:7–13) and Luke (9:1–6). Perhaps the inclusion of the injunction in Matthew's account is related to the purpose of the mission ('Go rather to the lost sheep of Israel'—verse 9) and the expected Jewish readership of the Gospel. In both passages in Luke (9:2 and 10:9, the missions of the twelve and of the seventy) the sick are to be healed, but those suffering from *lepra* were not regarded as suffering from an ordinary disease that required healing, but from a defiling condition for which cleansing was needed. In the similar series of instructions given by our Lord to

the seventy (or seventy-two, peculiar to Luke 10:1–16), there is no mention of leprosy. The various general references to our Lord's healing of the sick might in a modern context be held to include those whose sickness was due to leprosy; but Jewish belief and practice regarded leprosy as different from ordinary physical disease and excluded the 'leper' from the community, sending him to the border country between Galilee and Samaria (Luke 17:11).

3. Matthew 11:5 and Luke 7:22. The two emissaries of John the Baptist both see and hear our Lord's attestations of his Messianic mission, including the fact that *leproi* are cleansed. There was a widespread belief in Judaism that leprosy would be totally eradicated at the coming of the Messiah. This account implies a repeated or habitual practice of 'cleansing the lepers' on the part of our Lord. Whatever the reason, special emphasis is placed here on the cleansing of those suffering from leprosy.

4. Luke 17:11–19. Note that all ten *'leproi'* were 'cleansed' (v.14), as they went: one returned 'healed' (v.15). The wording suggests that the terms 'cleanse' and 'heal' might have been used loosely and synonymously. It is not actually stated that the Samaritan went to the priest after all: note that it was a non-Jew who saw that he was 'healed' (v.15). This differential use of 'cleanse' and 'heal' for Jews and non-Jews respectively has been thought to be significant.[33] But the Samaritans accepted, as much as the Jews, the Pentateuch and the Mosaic Laws.

5. The house of 'Simon the leper' (Matt. 26:6; Mark 14:3) was in Bethany. Numerous conjectures have been made at various times concerning his identity. It is unlikely that he was the same person as 'Simon the Pharisee' who also lived at Bethany (Luke 7:36–38). Had he died and bequeathed his house, with his name (John 12: 2–8) to Lazarus and his sisters Mary and Martha, or had he had to abandon his house because he had *lepra*? Scripture provides no answer.

6. Luke 4:27. Many sufferers from leprosy (*'leproi'*), in Israel at the time of Elisha remained 'uncleansed', except for Naaman. (2 Kgs. 5:1,2)

In none of these instances are any clinical details given to indicate what is meant by the diagnosis of *'lepra'*. Apart from the one example of 'healing' (Luke 17:15) and two of the use of the neutral phrase 'the leprosy departed from him' (Luke 5:13), the verb used ('cleansed') signified ritual purification, and those concerned were enjoined to fulfil the demands of the Law. Our Lord respected the Mosaic Law in regard to the ceremonial requirements that had to be fulfilled before 'cleansing' could be officially pronounced. He ignored the derivative injunction against approaching, and touching, and talking with those afflicted with *lepra*. He showed spontaneous concern and a deep compassion for their lot, and treated them as human beings in need.

It is a moot point whether 'Dr.' Luke could properly have used the medical term '*elephantiasis*' instead of the lay word '*lepra*' in his Gospel. *Elephantiasis* was in use at the time to denote leprosy, and *lepra* was also in use to denote several skin conditions characterized by scaliness (scurf, summer prurigo, pityriasis, psoriasis, seborrheic dermatitis, etc.). Although non-medical contemporary writers use some of the medical terms formerly thought to be peculiar to Luke, it may be significant that Luke does not use the medical term in current use for true leprosy; perhaps his sources did not differentiate between *elephantiasis* and *lepra*, and in any case Luke was writing for a Gentile audience. His Gospel was, of course, intended primarily for the layman, providing him with an accurate historical record 'of all that Jesus began both to do and to teach' (Acts 1:1).

What is the disease called '*lepra*' in the New Testament? Was it, or did it include, leprosy? There are no means of ascertaining with certainty, but some help in answering these questions may be derived from philological, historical and archaeological considerations.

Leprosy in New Testament times

As we have already seen, true leprosy had been present in Europe for about three hundred years before the time of our Lord. It was not called '*lepra*' but '*elephantiasis*'.

'*Elephantiasis*' can with reasonable certainty be identified with true leprosy. It is a chronic disease characterized by widespread defined skin swellings, ulcerated destruction of the extremities, and facial disfigurement. It is regarded as incurable in its later stages, and contagious.

On the other hand, all references to '*lepra*' seem to derive from the earlier Hippocratic concepts of a scaly, desquamating skin condition, with no indication that any such disease included the signs of true leprosy. It is only later that these two distinct medical concepts—of true leprosy (called 'elephantiasis'), and a group of scaly skin conditions (called '*lepra*')—became confused. The confusion seems to originate with the writings of Galen (AD 130–201).

With this explanatory background, we may turn to the version of the Old Testament, the Septuagint, translated into Greek from the Hebrew by a group of Jewish Alexandrian scholars about 300—150 BC. Seeking a verbal equivalent for the lay term *ṣāra'at*, they chose '*lepra*' and used this term in all texts where *ṣāra'at* appears in the original. '*Lepra*' was at hand to represent a generic concept of scaliness. It was an emotionally neutral descriptive word, containing no suggestions of ritual uncleanness or defilement. The word '*elephantiasis*' was not chosen by the translators as a rendering for *ṣāra'at*.

All synoptic references appearing in English versions as 'leprosy' are translations of the lay term *lepra*. It is therefore impossible to identify the disease or diseases that kept men apart from their fellows in first-century Palestine.

Ordinary people and ordinary healers (apart from Alexandria-trained physicians) could not be expected to possess knowledge enabling them to differentiate between the conditions comprised under the term '*lepra*', but they may have recognized the gross manifestations of advanced leprosy—the leonine face, the ulcerating nodules, and the paralysed extremities. And in any case, in Palestine the current Aramaic language, both spoken and written, must have carried some at least of the overtones of ritual defilement of the Hebrew *ṣāra'at*. The references to 'cleansing' in all the New Testament passages (except in the case of 'Simon the leper' Matt. 26:6; Mark 14:3) where 'leprosy' is mentioned, would support this suggestion. *Lepra* was considered to be different from all other illnesses, wounds or physical abnormalities: for these latter, 'heal' (or its derivatives) is used seventy-two times in the New Testament, and 'whole' thirty-two times.

The nomenclature is further confused by the existence of *elephantiasis Arabum* (now known as Bancroftian filariasis), and by the later addition of *Graecorum* to the word *elephantiasis* when used to designate the original *elephantiasis* (which, of course, was true leprosy). The exact date when the term *elephantiasis Graecorum* came into general medical use is not known. Celsus (53 BC to AD 7), writing in Latin, refers to true leprosy by this term, and Aretaeus of Cappadocia some seventy years later and Galen (AD 133–201) were acquainted with it.

To the question, 'Did the "*lepra*" of the New Testament include true leprosy?' there can be no definite answer. It probably did, since true leprosy certainly existed in Greece, Italy and North Africa at the time of our Lord.

Although no indubitable proof exists, it is more than likely that true leprosy was brought to Palestine by the followers of the Ptolemies or the Seleucids, as suggested by Hulse,[34] and that leprosy was among the groups of diseases embraced by the common term '*lepra*'. No positive help comes from archaeological findings in Palestine. No evidence from inscriptions or pottery is forthcoming, and no skeletal remains are extant showing the specific bone damage due to leprosy.

The subsequent history of the Greek word *'lepra'* is instructive.[32,35] In his translation of the Bible into the vulgar Latin tongue (The Vulgate), Jerome (AD 383) took over the Greek *lepra* and used the transliterated form as the Latin eqivalent of *ṣāra'at* of the Old Testament and *lepra* of the New. Under the influence of the Vulgate translation, the word 'leprosy' and its cognates subsequently entered versions in the languages of Western Europe.

Leprosy in the New Testament was an obvious and visible physical blemish in the skin of human beings; its disappearance was to be noted by patient, priest and ordinary people. It does not affect cloth or leather or the walls of houses.

Although the disciples were bidden (Matt. 10:18) to 'cleanse the leper', we read of no such instance in the Acts or the Epistles; there is no reference to *'lepra'* outside the Gospels, although the 'scales' that fell from Saul's eyes (Acts 9:18) are the same as the flaking skin of *lepra*.

The silence of the Acts of the Apostles and the Epistles concerning leprosy should be viewed in the light of the primary purpose of these books, written as they were for a largely Gentile audience and documenting the spread of the gospel in the Roman world. The Gentiles, unversed for the most part in the niceties of the Levitical Code and the ritual connotation of *lepra*, had, as far as is known, no formulated attitude to leprosy and its victims. Nor in early patristic literature can miraculous cures or cleansings of *'lepra'* be found. If such an activity had been regarded as necessary authentication of apostolic authority, the silence of the records is remarkable. The earliest record of a hospital built especially for sufferers from leprosy is one founded in Rome early in the fourth century during the reign of Constantine; and later in the same century, around AD 372, St. Basil is said to have built such a hospital in Caesarea.

Leprosy in Medieval Times

In English, as we have seen, leprosy remained a generic term until it was precisely delimited clinically by Danielssen and Boeck in 1847, and bacteriologically by Hansen in 1872–1874. In medieval English, 'leprosy' could be used with the definite or the indefinite article, and was singular or plural. It could refer to diseases of man and of animals and plants, the fungus of growing crops, the mildew of damp stored grain, and the mange of domestic pets. By extension, it was applied to beggary and indigence, and even venery, and could be used in the sense of a plague—i.e. a pestilence, epidemic or visitation. Leprosy was certainly known in

Britain in the Middle Ages, and was already indigenous when some of the Crusaders (1096–1200) returned, having caught leprosy in the near East. The dimensions of the endemic have probably been much exaggerated by some historians[36], who base their estimates on the number of hospices built for 'lepers'.[37]

The squint windows of medieval churches have an interesting history. In some instances, such as the one in the Stavekirk, Bergen (Norway), there is historical justification for associating them with sufferers from leprosy. The term 'lepers' squint' did not come into general use till last century. However, the phrase *leprosi animi* was applied to persons considered to be sick and unclean in soul by reason of sin against God, and who were therefore excluded from the Mass. Those suffering from leprosy of the body were excluded from the village as well as from the church.

Notwithstanding the imprecision of the term 'leprosy' as used by non-medical people writing in English in the Middle Ages, the researches of Andersen[22] and Moeller-Christensen[23] in special burial-grounds in Denmark and elsewhere reveal that most of the skeletons unearthed show the specific signs of lepromatous leprosy in the skull.

Monastic exegesis, ill-based and extravagant, invested both the patriarch Job and the beggar Lazarus (Luke 16:20–21) with leprosy (Lazarus is an abbreviation of Eleazar, and carried the meaning 'God has helped'). On no discoverable grounds, Lazarus of Bethany (John 11:1) was pronounced a 'leper', and made the patron saint of those thus afflicted; hence the derivatives, the disease of St. Lazarus, lazar house, lazaret, lazarine, leprosy, etc. It may be of importance that Luke, a careful writer, uses a medical term translated 'full of sores' (Luke 16:20) that does not appear elsewhere in the New Testament; he may have wished to distinguish the condition from *lepra,* and thus perhaps explain why Lazarus was allowed to beg and not excluded from contact with his fellows. It is of interest that Simon the leper (Matt. 26:6; Mark 14:3) lived in Bethany, and his condition may have played a part in the attribution of leprosy to his fellow-townsman, Lazarus, in medieval art and literature.

In some European countries, and to a much less extent in England, the infamous 'lepers' mass' was celebrated. The unfortunate person diagnosed as having leprosy was indeed reckoned 'as one dead'. Hooded and shrouded, he had to listen to a priest reading over him the awful words forbidding him henceforth 'to enter church, market-places, the mill, the bakehouse, the assembly of people . . . I forbid thee to go abroad without thy leper uniform'.

In some circles, victims of so-called leprosy were called 'Christ's poor' and 'Christ's dear children', and singled out for special merit-earning acts of compassion, high-born ladies being assiduous in kissing their feet. The extravagant and sentimental attitude may be traced in part to a widespread belief that our Lord himself had leprosy. Jerome in the Vulgate translates the Hebrew *naga* of Isaiah 53:4 and 8 by 'leprosy' ('Et nos putavimus eum quasi leprosum') in the sense of 'stricken of God'.[36] John Wycliff rendered this into English as 'and wee heeldun hym has leprous'.

The role of the Bible in the perpetuation of the stigma of leprosy is not easy to define. It may be at once admitted that relics of medieval superstitions and attitudes have been at times justified by reference to the Mosaic code, and by applying the *ṣāra'at* regulations to leprosy. And it cannot be denied that serious prejudice against leprosy sufferers has in historical times been reinforced by the wholesale transfer of the corpus of *ṣāra'at* beliefs to the perfectly innocent victims of a mycobacterial disease. In some countries, a sophisticated *raison d'être* is thought to be found in the Scriptures for long-held and pre-Christian attitudes to those suffering from leprosy. The harshest measures of persecution, compulsory segregation, deprivation of social and legal rights and forcible separation of families, may be traced in many of the prejudices extant in Christendom today. Leprosy is burdened with the incubus of an unscientific past, and with unscriptural accretions in addition to medical and ritualistic accidentia that were considered by the Jews and subsequently by generations of Christians to be proper to *ṣāra'at* and *lepra*, but which are totally inapplicable to leprosy.

But it would be quite wrong, and historically unjustifiable, to attribute wholly to the influence of biblical and Christian teaching the widespread stigma attaching to leprosy. Stigma and concealment may be subtly introduced by Western culture, as in Papua New Guinea,[38] replacing the fear of the evil spirit thought to be responsible for striking a person with leprosy. Apart altogether from any ritual significance, and notwithstanding the eclectic or vague meaning of *ṣāra'at*, the victim of advanced untreated leprosy often does present a repulsive, even nauseating appearance, a travesty of the human form. In many non-Christian lands and non-Christian civilizations, there exist an innate dread and fear of true leprosy, compounded of the physical appearances of the advanced disease and also the accumulated body of folk-lore surrounding its origin and cause. It is this fear of the evil spirit responsible that leads to cruelty perpetuated on the victim of leprosy. A whole amorphous mass of beliefs and superstitions, of taboos and prohibitions, may surround the disease today.

Because of the real offence inherent in the word 'leper', with its implications of uncleanness and moral turpitude (as seen in the pejorative and journalistic uses of the word), the World Health Organization, the International Leprosy Association and other representative and influential bodies have banned the word from their publications. For the same reason, repeated attempts have been made—but without general success—to popularize an alternative to the word 'leprosy' itself and its cognates. Thus, the term Hansen's disease (or Hansenitis) is in use in certain countries; but the coining of such eponymous naming of disease is not much in favour these days, and in any case, Hansen was not the first to describe leprosy, nor did he suffer from it himself. Derivative words and phrases (as 'hansenomatous Hansenitis' for 'lepromatous leprosy') would be both awkward and cumbersome. Other suggestions like dermatoneural mycobacteriosis or bacterial neurodermatitis, have little to commend them and are too long for general adoption. And, in any case, the newly-coined expressions must themselves be explained to the layman or the patient.

The suggested changes in nomenclature would be meaningless to the majority of people afflicted by leprosy. The indigenous social concepts of a feared disease—recognized, if not precisely delimited or pathologically defined—are independent of the actual words used to designate it. When it is appreciated that true leprosy, together with the diseases sometimes mistaken for true leprosy, evokes a characteristic pattern of ideas and reactions in diverse contexts and in different cultures, the whole question is seen to be more one of fundamentals than of nice verbal distinctions.

What was the 'something' that gave rise to the fears that resulted in the Levitical legislation? Could it—despite the clinical imprecisions and the archaeological silences—have been leprosy? Or, perhaps more convincingly, could human leprosy have gradually become burdened with the incubus and opprobrium that was formerly spread over all blemishing conditions of the skin and of cloth, pelts and house-walls regarded as connoting ritual defilement? Unfortunately it is at present impossible to provide reasonable answers to these questions.

Leprosy in Modern Translations

Many recent English versions of the Bible use the word 'leprosy' or 'leper' as a translation of *ṣāra'at* or *lepra* even when the reference (in the Old Testament) is to cloth or leather or the walls of houses, despite the present medical precision of the disease. The difficulties of rendering any such term in a true and comprehensive way into a modern language are immense and almost insuperable.

Most modern versions follow the Authorized Version (AV) and the Revised Standard Version (RSV) in translating the Greek, *lepra*. The word 'leper' is used in the New English Bible (NEB) and the Modern Readers Bible (MRB). The Good News Bible (GNB) has (in Matt. 10:8, 11:5; Luke 7:22; 17: 11–19) 'those who suffer from dreaded skin-diseases' and the New International Version (NIV) translates, 'cleanse those who have leprosy', adding in a foot-note on 17:12, (as in other places e.g. Matt. 8:3; Mark 1:40) 'The Greek word probably designated other related diseases also.' The medical philologist might quibble about the word 'related' in this footnote, since the conditions historically confused with leprosy and included under the term *lepra* were not 'related' in any aetiological sense, e.g. psoriasis, pityriasis simplex, vitiligo, etc. The modern translations as a rule follow the distinctions observed in AV, and RSV, between 'cleansing' and 'healing', but NIV (in Matt. 11:5 and Luke 7:22) introduces the word 'cured', and GNB uses the ceremonial 'make clean' with the unceremonial phrase 'dreaded skin disease'.

The difficulties of identification of *lepra* are unresolved in these modern versions, but the instantaneous and recognizable change in appearance is as unequivocal as the instruction to follow the Levitical requirements of priestly confirmation of the cleansing of a ritually defiling condition.

Three possibilities are open to the translator.[39] He may use the equivalent for 'leprosy', if one exists in the language concerned, and thus fly in the face of the medical arguments here adduced. He may transliterate *ṣāra'at* or 'lepra' or both, using them as lacklustre loan words, with all the shortcomings and limitations that this would entail; in this case, a lengthy explanation of such a word would be necessary, couched in readily understandable language. Or he might try to find some descriptive word or phrase that would cover (a) a scaly disease of the human skin, (b) a fungal condition of walls, cloth and leather, and (c) ceremonial defilement. This task verges on the impossible, for words combining such disparate conceptions are of rare occurrence in any language.

The RSV and most modern translations follow closely the text of the AV in rendering *ṣāra'at* and *lepra* as 'leprosy'. The English translation of the Hebrew Bible suggests an alternative rendering of *ṣāra'at* that presupposes a root meaning of 'strike' or 'stricken'; for example, 'the hand of Moses was stricken with snow-white scales'. (The epithet might well have been 'snow-like'; the scaliness may be reminiscent of *lepra* rather than of *ṣāra'at*.) The New Catholic Bible translated by the Catholic Biblical Association (of the

United States of America) comes out boldly in a footnote to the effect that the Hebrew term used 'does not refer to Hansen's disease, currently called "leprosy"'.

The NEB presents an ambiguous and in some respects, a confused picture. In the New Testament the text follows closely the Greek original in all thirteen places where *lepra* occurs,[40] but the following footnote was added in response to representations made to the translators: 'The words leper, leprosy, as used in this translation, refer to some disfiguring skin disease which entailed ceremonial defilement. It is different from what is now called leprosy.' While most people—Greek scholars and leprologists particularly—would heartily agree with the first sentence, many would prefer the second to read thus: 'The term may—and probably did—include the disease now known as leprosy.'

The Old Testament portion of the NEB illustrates the difficulty of discovering and rendering the meaning of a word that is essentially imprecise.

The 'leprosy' of the AV when used of clothing and leather (Lev. 13:47–59) becomes 'mould', with or without the addition of 'stain' or 'rotting'; and the 'leprosy' of houses (Lev. 14: 33–48) becomes 'a fungus infection' or simply 'the infection'. In the context, a mould or mildew is the likeliest possibility, though it might be mentioned that in ordinary parlance 'infection' is usually limited to living subjects.

Regarding the translation of *ṣāra'at* affecting the human skin, regrettable inconsistencies appear. Thus the word 'leper' is retained in 2 Kings 5:1 (an alternative rendering being given: 'his skin was diseased'), and the word 'leprosy' is retained in 2 Kings 12:5 and 2 Chronicles 16:20. *Ṣāra'at* is also translated by other words and phrases; thus, the skin was diseased (Exod. 4:6), her skin diseased (Num. 12:10), foul disease (2 Sam 3:29), the disease (2 Kgs. 5:11), his disease (2 Kgs. 5:2–7), his skin diseased (Exod. 4:6).

In the difficult chapters of Leviticus (13 and 14), the translators offer the renderings 'malignant skin diseases' (fourteen times) 'chronic skin-disease' (once), 'skin-disease' (three times), the neutral 'the condition' (twice), and 'his disease' (once). The phrase 'malignant skin-disease' occurs also in Deuteronomy 24:8. There are serious medical reasons for rejecting the translation 'malignant skin-disease;[41] which today refers to cancerous growth, a cutaneous neoplasm. This phrase, moreover, conveys no suggestion that *ṣāra'at* was terrible and awful because it was ritually defiling. It is to be noted that the intrusive 'white' of Exodus 4:6, has been retained in this translation, though it does not occur in the original.

The GNB uses the phrase 'dreaded skin disease(s)' in Leviticus 13 and 14, and refers to 'Laws concerning skin-diseases; mildew; and mildew in houses'. It has the word 'cured' in Leviticus 14:1, and makes the general statement that 'these laws determine when something is unclean and when it is clean.'

In the cases of Moses and Miriam (Num 12:10–12) most versions (GNB, NEB) retain the epithet 'white', while the GNB amplifies the translation thus: 'skin suddenly covered with a dreaded disease and turned as white as snow.' Similarly, with Gehazi (2 Kgs. 5:27) the obtrusive 'white' appears in both the NEB and GNB.

The four leprous men (2 Kgs. 7:3–11) had 'a dreaded skin disease' (GNB), but the NEB gives an alternative in a footnote to the phrase 'four lepers', and states 'men suffering from skin-disease'.

In Deuteronomy 24:8 and 9, *ṣāra'at* becomes 'malignant skin-disease' in the NEB and 'a dreaded skin-disease' in the GNB whereas the RSV refers to 'attack of leprosy'. In 2 Samuel 3:28–29, *ṣāra'at* is translated 'a dreaded skin-disease' (GNB) or 'foul disease' (NEB).

Uzziah (2 Chr. 26:19–21) or Azariah (2 Kgs. 15:5) had 'a dreaded skin disease' according to the GNB; and the NEB has 'the Lord had struck him with the disease' and 'a dreaded skin-disease broke out on his forehead', the priests staring 'at the king's forehead in horror'. The diagnosis was apparently obvious to the priests and was made without hesitation by priests unaccustomed to such an awful sight. All versions agree on the permanence of the affliction and the need for lifelong separation from the community in a special house. In Today's English Version (TEV) New Testament, the words 'leper' and 'leprosy' are retained (despite the opprobrium inseparable from the former), whereas 'mildew' or 'infectious skin disease' is used for most references in Leviticus.

The heart of the difficulty is that both *ṣāra'at* and *lepra* present such a wide range of meaning that they are virtually untranslatable. There is no convenient simple word in English, nor a simple phrase that is 'scientifically correct and euphonious'.[6]

Biblical Leprosy and Missions

If, then, the biblical basis for equating *ṣāra'at* or *lepra* with the disease we know as true leprosy (and consistently associated with infection with *Mycobacterium leprae*) is so uncertain and tenuous, is there any justification for maintaining that Christ's command to his disciples to 'cleanse the leper' (Matt. 10:18) is valid for medical missionary activity among leprosy sufferers today? This is a question that must be faced.

If the words are to be taken at their face value, then the

missionary should 'cleanse' and not treat with drugs, those suffering from infection with *M.leprae*. Also, in the context of the other commands, he should raise the dead and cast out demons. He should follow the lifestyle of the twelve and the seventy sent out to preach and heal by our Lord.

More and more, leprosy is being investigated and treated like any other disease, by Christians and non-Christians alike. Knowledge of leprosy is being disseminated and the present generation of missionary-hearted Christians whose support for leprosy may have been based on inadequate or erroneous exegesis, is passing away. Other missionary work, and other medical missionary work (which in the past may have been somewhat overshadowed by the ostensibly more scriptural 'leprosy' work) will be able henceforth to make their appeal to the Christian public on the same general grounds as must in future be those of the appeal of missionary work among leprosy sufferers. This will be couched in different terms, depending on theological outlook; but it will essentially be the canalization of Christian compassion and Christian service for the disinterested and medically competent succour of the needy, the neglected, and the untended sick.

The words, 'cleanse the leper', will be given the same content in the future as they had in our Lord's day and as spoken by him. In an amplified paraphrase, they might read thus: 'Seek the outcast, the underprivileged, all those who suffer because of society's attitudes. Help them in all ways. Help to put them on their feet, and bring them back into the society that despised and ostracized them.'

Those afflicted with leprosy are in a special category of need by reason not only of their physical and mental suffering, but also of the neglect of their fellows and the positive discrimination of society against them. Christians will thus continue to 'touch' those afflicted by leprosy, bringing them sympathy and healing, and drawing them nearer health and nearer God.

5

The Value of Human Life

DAVID R. MILLAR

The Christian believes that man is more than just a superior animal at the top of an evolutionary pyramid. He is a unique being created by God 'in his own image' (Gen. 1:27). The Glory of God can never be revealed fully in a man, but we have a responsibility to our Creator to be like him in character.

'Your attitude should be the same as Christ Jesus' (Phil. 2:5). In considering the value of human life, therefore, we cannot ignore our spiritual nature.

Most people, whatever their beliefs, set a higher value on human than on animal life, but in the imperfect world in which we live our judgment of human worth is sometimes conditioned by other factors. These may be social, economic or cultural, or may arise from scientific developments, which compel us to examine, or even reverse, previously held principles. Everything created by God is good (Gen. 1), and the discoveries of science, in one sense, merely reveal to us more of his perfect plan. However, ever since the Fall (Gen. 3), man has had the capacity to change God's world for either good or evil, and, as a result, we now have an unjust and unequal society.

Human Values and Medical Dilemmas

In treating illness doctors have to make a balanced judgment between the simple relief of symptoms, while awaiting natural recovery or death, and the use of those drugs, surgical operations and machines which are available to support life or modify disease. In a state-controlled health service with tight budgets on the one hand, and the enormous and open-ended expense of some treatments on the other, the value of human life sometimes truly has to be measured in pounds sterling. The use of cytotoxic drugs in malignant disease, the management of renal failure, cardiac transplantation, and the intensive care of the tiny neonate, all present ethical dilemmas which include the assessment of cost balanced against human worth. In private medical care the cost of treatment has to be judged by the patient, his relatives or his insurance company, but in the National Health Service it is the doctor, as the representative of society, who has to decide whether treatment is justified and how he can allocate resources to the most deserving patients.

While we in the West talk of 'scarce resources' the money which the governments of the poorer countries of Africa and Asia have to spend on health, per head of population, is tiny by comparison. They may have to choose whether to spend these inadequate funds on an acute hospital catering for the sick who live in, or who can travel to, the larger centres of population, or on perhaps more cost-effective but less prestigious measures to relieve and prevent drought, famine and pestilence in country areas.

The most stark example of selection for life-saving treatment is presented to the surgeon in wartime, or after other major disasters. Military surgeons use the term 'triage' for the process of first treating the seriously injured who can be saved while leaving those with relatively minor injuries to fend for themselves, and those suffering from horrendous wounds to die. Similar judgments have to be made by relief organizations in areas of famine.

Some people are given greater value in human terms, because of their social standing. Illness affecting a head of state, a sports hero, or a pop-star attracts the fullest coverage from the news media, whereas thousands of Third World refugees may die before the Western world even notices their plight.

We have seen already that, in the highly sophisticated world of modern medicine, a shortage of, say, organ transplants, of kidney machines, of specialist surgeons or of staff trained in intensive care may result in the need for choice between a number of patients in need of treatment. Doctors working in these areas have to judge the ultimate *quality* of the patient's life and, inevitably, consideration is also given to his value to society in general, and his family in particular.

Especially at the extremes of life, in the neonatal intensive care unit and with the elderly, but also with all critically ill and injured patients, one may have to consider whether any treatment at all is appropriate. Such judgment of life and death must give regard to the quality of the survivor's future existence, his capacity to tolerate unpleasant resuscitative measures, the cost and availability of such treatment and the burdens placed on the relatives.

Thus, it is sometimes the case that life is best respected by allowing it to end. However, there may be some difficulty in determining when it has ended.

Life support machines can now maintain circulation and respiration almost indefinitely, so brain death, carefully defined, has come to be accepted as the most reasonable criterion for the end of human existence. Life for an adult with a dead brain is considered not to be worthwhile, and pregnancy is not worth prolonging when a brainless (anencephalic) fetus is discovered.

Civilizations may well be judged by how they handle these dilemmas of life at its very beginning and its end, and the Christian doctor must look to the Bible for guidance. Biblical truth is unchanging, but we are fallible in our interpretation of scripture. One relevant question which has taxed theologians and scholars over the years is when human life, as a person in the image of God, starts.

The Value of The Fetus

(a) THE BEGINNING OF LIFE

From 400 BC, when Aristotle first suggested that life started when the mother felt fetal movements, until 1803 when an abortion law was introduced in England which dealt with the fetus before the time of 'quickening', there was no legal protection for the early human fetus. Even the Roman Catholic church, until just over a hundred years ago, regarded human life as starting with 'ensoulment', which papal edicts of the thirteenth and sixteenth centuries had pronounced to occur at forty days of pregnancy for a male fetus and eighty days in the case of the female. (These intervals are the same as the periods of ritual cleansing after the birth of male and female children as laid down in Leviticus 12:1–5). These ideas were abandoned only in 1869 when abortion was declared to be sinful from the time of conception. Theological and legal concepts of the beginning of life had to be changed as a result of advances in medicine and biology. More recently, fetal imaging—especially with ultrasound—has shown us the baby's heartbeat as early as three to four weeks after implantation and limb movements can be detected shortly afterwards. This information has strengthened the case for protecting the fetus in the early weeks of its existence.

Other recent advances in reproductive biology, however, have created new difficulties for those who wish the embryo to have maximum protection from the time of conception. It has been known for many years that in the vast majority of pregnancies which end by spontaneous abortion in the first three months of gestation, an embryo with human form has never developed. To use the language of Psalm 139:13, they were never 'knit together' properly in the womb. We call them 'blighted ova'. A large number (perhaps a half) of all human embryos are also lost in the menstrual flow prior to their implantation, and before the diagnosis of conception is possible by ordinary means. So (as Gardner discusses in his monograph on abortion),[1] if full value as a human being is to be attributed to the egg at the moment of fertilization, then the majority of beings in the after-life will never have experienced life outside the womb.

In an apocryphal book, Ezra similarly expresses to God his feelings of futility at fetal loss (2 Esdras 8:8, 14, NEB):

> The body moulded in the womb receives from you both life and limbs: that which you create is kept safe . . . for nine months.
> . . . But if you should lightly destroy one who was fashioned by your command with so much labour, what was the purpose of creating him?

Another difficulty in claiming personhood from conception is that it is known that the cleavage of the single pre-embryonic cluster of cells to form identical twins may be delayed until after implantation—that is, some two weeks after fertilization. Thus we should have to accept the difficult notion of a single person dividing into two (or more) people who are identical biologically but who, after birth, develop their separate selves.

Yet another difficulty has been caused by the introduction of synthetic sex steroid tablets capable of so altering the endometrial 'soil' that the human 'seed' does not implant. These 'morning-after' pills have also made it impossible to apply the legal and statistical requirements of the Abortion Act (1967), because neither the prescribing doctor nor the patient know whether fertilization has occurred. So it has been decreed that this form of fertility control is exempt from the law on abortion. However much the Christian doctor may object to this untidy method of birth control, it is going to be used increasingly by our colleagues and patients.

At a slightly later stage of a suspected pregnancy an intrauterine device, or a suction tube is sometimes inserted into the womb to induce abortion, again before the diagnosis of pregnancy is established. The latter technique is called, rather euphemistically, 'menstrual extraction' and has been performed without satisfying the terms of the Abortion Act. This omission could result in a charge under section 58 of the Offences Against the Person Act (1861) which clearly states that the *intent* to procure abortion is illegal, whether the woman is pregnant or not. So, we can offend against a person who does not exist! The law, as well as science, can produce anomalies when considering the status of the very early human embryo.

The latest medico-legal and ethical dilemma in this area has been created by the development of 'in-vitro' fertilization (IVF). What is the value of a human embryo produced in a glass dish by the union of a sperm (perhaps from a deep-freeze) and a cultured oocyte, sucked several hours previously from a functioning ovary? This creation of man could not be called even a potential person, unless it is transferred to a receptive uterus, because it inevitably dies within a few days if left in the culture fluid.

Despite recent advances in the laboratory and in the intensive neonatal care unit, there is still a gap of five calendar months between the age of the oldest embryo grown in a dish, and the youngest fetus, of about twenty-four weeks gestational age, which has so far survived after premature birth. Like other biological gaps this will certainly be narrowed, but the *Brave New World* concept of 'test-tube babies' is still a very remote fantasy.[2]

Advances in reproductive biology are often greeted with suspicion by the general public on the grounds that Nature is being tampered with. In one sense, however, the technique of IVF and embryo transfer is closer to the natural event than is, say, an artificial kidney or even intravenous feeding.

The Warnock committee, which reported in July 1984,[3] recommended that IVF should be controlled by a licensing body, and that embryos not transferred to a woman within fourteen days (so-called 'spare embryos') should be kept alive no longer than this time, unless frozen for future use. They proposed certain restrictions on research on embryos up to the fourteen-day stage. Among many other legal and ethical recommendations about artificial insemination, egg donation and surrogate motherhood, they suggested that a frozen embryo not 'in utero' by the date of its father's death should be disregarded for the purposes of inheritance from the latter. In other words, they suggest that the embryo should not be a legal person, at least until it is implanted in the womb.

Those who attribute full personhood to the embryo from the

moment of conception reject such views and regard the discarding of a 'spare' embryo from a culture dish to be on a par with infanticide. We have already seen that this rigid view presents its own ethical dilemmas.

The leap from Aristotle's view of the origin of life in mid-pregnancy back to the time of fertilization may have been too great. If we accept brain death to be the best criterion for the end of life, could we then, quite logically use the *onset* of brain activity, in the second month of intrauterine existence, as a measure of the start of human life?[4]

This is the critical argument in the abortion debate and, therefore, will be considered below at greater length, under three headings, biblical, legal and medical.

(b) THE BIBLICAL PERSPECTIVE

(i) New Testament

The fact that Jesus chose to be born from a virgin's womb, and to be fully human throughout his earthly life, strengthens our belief in the value he placed on our humanity, but does not contribute greatly to the arguments about the sanctity of other human embryos. Jesus took human form, but his parthenogenetic conception was unique.

The Gospels are concerned mainly with the birth, life and teaching of our Lord and there is nothing about induced abortion there. Nor do the Pauline epistles mention this problem although attempts to terminate pregnancy (certainly with drugs, if not instruments) were prevalent in Rome in Paul's day.

Luke's Gospel does, however, give us one rather lovely example of fetal awareness. Mary visited Elizabeth just after the annunciation and it is recorded that John the Baptist, at six months of intrauterine life, leapt with joy when his mother heard that the incarnation of our Lord would soon take place:

> When Elizabeth heard Mary's greeting, the baby leaped in her womb, and Elizabeth was filled with the Holy Spirit (Luke 1:44).

Luke implies that this fetal emotion was provoked by Elizabeth's spiritual excitement, but it is not impossible at that stage of pregnancy for John to have heard the prophecy himself.

Birth is the event which transforms fetal existence into neonatal life. Life, in this new sense, involves not only physical separation from the mother and independence, but also respiration. The fetus makes breathing movements in the womb, but the 'breath of life' is the oxygen of the air—the life force which God breathed into Adam's nostrils (Gen. 2:7).

Some talk of the fetus as just a 'potential' human, but a potential for life could apply also to the newborn, and our true personality is only gradually revealed throughout childhood. The ultimate in human worth has been defined as the ability to worship and form a relationship with our creator God. By that criterion perhaps we never reach our full potential!

Life, like death, is an emotive word, and one of the difficulties with this biblical interpretation of the subject is that, in the Scriptures, three or four different words are used, both in Old Testament Hebrew and New Testament Greek, to express different meanings of the one English word.[5]

For example, *bios* (Gr.) is used for bodily or vegetative existence, a property of all living things; *psyche* (Gr.) may be translated as 'soul-life' as well as heart, mind, or the breath of life, whereas *zoe* (Gr.) introduces a spiritual concept and may be translated as 'resurrection-life'. The distinction between the two last forms can be illustrated by quoting Jesus himself:

> I have come that they may have life (*zoe*) and have it to the full. I am the good shepherd. The good shepherd lays down his life (*psyche*) for the sheep (John 10:10, 11).

Psyche is the living being whereas *zoe* is the life of that being. To attribute each of these words respectively to life of the body, the mind and the spirit, though superficially helpful and attractive, is too simplistic. There is a considerable overlap in their meanings and usage, and if the distinctions are pushed too far it can be just as confusing as trying to consider the human soul as separate from a body/mind entity.

Bios is present in the sperm and the egg *prior* to fertilization, and life, in this sense, is a continuum. *Psyche* and *zoe* appear sometime later, but conception, implantation, quickening, birth etc., are all equally arbitrary possible times for their appearance. The main justification for choosing conception is that genetically a new individual is formed at this time. This is the origin of 'self' in the immunological sense, but not necessarily 'personhood' in the theological and philosophical sense.

Perhaps we are not meant to understand these mysteries of life.

> As you do not know the path of the wind or how the body is formed in the mother's womb, so you cannot understand the work of God, the Maker of all things (Eccles. 11:5).

(ii) Old Testament

The first chapter of Genesis establishes the principle that God cares about his creation, and particularly about 'man in his own image'. We should join the psalmist in blessing our Creator.

> For you created my inmost being. You knit me together in my mother's womb . . .
> I praise you because I am fearfully and wonderfully made . . . when I was woven together in the depths of the earth your eyes saw my unformed body (Ps. 139:13–16).

Clearly, therefore, we must have a deep respect for human life from its origin. (Declaration of Oslo W.M.A. 1970).

Schaeffer,[6] Wenham[7] and other writers on the abortion issue use the term 'sanctity of human life' and they affirm an unbreakable link between the acceptance of the existence of God and the unique value of human life, insisting that the fetus must be regarded as a person, in the fullest sense, from conception. They invoke the sixth commandment and Genesis 9:6 ('Whoever sheds the blood of man by man shall his blood be shed') and claim that these verses refer equally to induced abortion and to murder, as the killing of 'innocent' life. However, in both Exodus 21 and Deuteronomy 7 (chapters which follow shortly after those containing the ten commandments) and in many other parts of the Old Testament there are biblical instructions to take human life, either as a punishment for a whole variety of crimes, or to destroy the enemies of Israel.

Thus, although scripture places a very high value on human life, on some occasions it sanctions killing as being justified. The principle is that homicide may be deserved both as a punishment for the sin of murder and to protect a nation, or an individual, from an evil aggressor.

Dunstan[8] proposes the term 'justifiable feticide' as an ethical explanation for some forms of legal abortion, when the fetus may be regarded as an aggressor against the mother. Although it is difficult to hold the fetus personally responsible, the pregnancy (or fetoplacental unit) can be seen as sometimes threatening the mother's life or health. When termination of pregnancy is the chosen way to protect the mother's vital interests, fetal death is an inevitable result, but not the primary aim, of the procedure. For example, in the rare case where pregnancy is ended because of severe maternal illness *after* the time of fetal viability, strenuous efforts are made to keep the baby alive.

This justification for abortion is clearly untenable when the reason is that the baby is severely malformed. When a Christian gynaecologist performs a legal abortion, in good faith, he would be more likely to argue that the fetus is less fully human, or less fully a person, in comparison with the mother. This medical argument is expanded in a later section.

Much is made, by those taking a fundamental position against abortion, of the fact that Isaiah and Jeremiah were both chosen in the womb:

> Before I was born the Lord called me—from my birth he has made mention of my name (Isa. 49:1).
> Before I formed you in the womb I knew you (Jer. 1:5).

The latter quotation does not mean that Jeremiah was known to God before his conception. Until embryology was more fully understood a distinction was often made, in Scripture and in other literature, between a formed and unformed fetus. The change was sometimes equated with quickening, or another supposed time of ensoulment. It is much more likely that these verses indicate a pre-existent divine purpose for the prophets rather than any particular identification with them at a fetal stage. The same phrase, 'set apart from birth', is used by Paul in Galatians 1:15 for his own predestination, although he was not aware of that calling until the events on the Damascus road many years later (Acts 9).

These verses re-establish the principle that God is in charge of his world without helping us to define the status of the fetus.

The only verses in the entire Bible (Exod. 21:22, 23) which deal with the process of induced miscarriage are the subject of argument and are therefore worthy of some discussion.

> If men who are fighting hit a pregnant woman and she gives birth prematurely (or has a miscarriage), but there is no serious injury, the offender must be fined whatever the husband demands and the court allows. But if there is serious injury you are to take life for life, eye for eye, tooth for tooth etc.

Firstly, the situation referred to is an accidental rather than a deliberate abortion. Before the appearance of the New International Version (quoted above) all biblical translators were clear that the mother had lost her child, and all commentators assumed that 'no serious injury' referred to the mother. Now Schaeffer[6a] and others claim these words refer to the child, and they assume he survives the premature delivery. This distinction seems unlikely, but is important because the biblical penalty for the miscarriage is simply a fine imposed by the husband and some arbitrators, whereas recompense for any other injury is meted out by the Law of Retribution—a life for a life—including, Schaeffer concludes, the life of the child. In fact, Wiseman[9] states that the 'Lex Talionis' was never taken at its face value, because of the great respect the Jews had for life.

I see these verses as being evidence that the Bible does diminish the significance of abortion compared with homicide. Mosaic law can be compared with other legal codes of around 2000 BC. The Hittites had a graded series of fines for abortion of approximately one shekel per month of pregnancy, while the Sumerians had a stiffer penalty for causing miscarriage in the wife of a nobleman, compared with the wife of a commoner or slave.

(c) THE LEGAL PERSPECTIVE[10]

The law upholds the view that the fetus, though deserving protection, is not as important as the mother. Any child born dead before the twenty-eighth week of pregnancy is not registered as a stillbirth and can be disposed of, but a child of any size which shows even fleeting signs of life must be recorded as a live birth, and must be buried.

So the civil law regards death a minute before birth as being less important than a minute afterwards. Similarly, the penalties for the murder of a child, infanticide by the mother, child destruction 'in utero' and criminal abortion become progressively less severe. However, abortion outside the terms of the Abortion Act is still a felony.

There is some confusion between the provisions of the Abortion Act (1967) and the Infant Life (Preservation) Act (1929). The latter describes as 'child destruction' the intent to kill the child ('in utero' or at his birth) at a stage of pregnancy when he was capable of being born alive. So the ludicrous situation may arise with late induced abortions, that, although it is anticipated or even intended that an unwanted or abnormal child will die, if when born the baby unexpectedly shows signs of life, there is a statutory duty to try to keep him alive by all reasonable means. Then the mother and child have, by law, to be attended by a midwife for ten days and an offence is committed if the baby's birth, and subsequent death, are not registered, or if his body is incinerated elsewhere than in a crematorium.

Another legal anomaly resulted from the passage of the Congenital Disabilities Act (1976). This gives a living child the right to claim damages for any injury sustained at any stage of his intrauterine existence. A stillborn child has no such posthumous rights, so a child which could be aborted within the law at, say, twenty-four weeks of pregnancy may, if he survives the operation, and until he reaches the age of twenty-one, sue the abortionist for any birth injury. Persons who wished that their lives had been terminated before birth have also taken doctors to court, particularly in the USA, because of their 'wrongful life'. The practical effect of the law is that very few abortions are undertaken after twenty weeks of pregnancy.

We have already mentioned that the law on abortion is to do with intent, and a subsequent defence that the woman was not pregnant is untenable. Thus, the same legal system protects the undetectable embryo and gives him retrospective rights should he survive, but, at the same time permits doctors to kill him and deny his rights as long as the criteria for abortion and child destruction are met. The American Supreme Court has gone even further by declaring the fetus a non-person and giving every woman a right to abortion.[11]

(d) THE MEDICAL PERSPECTIVE

In obstetrics it is difficult to manage pregnancy and labour without accepting the concept that some babies are more precious than others—at least to their parents. For example, the same degree of fetal distress in labour would lead, on the one hand, to a caesarean section for a forty year old mother with twenty years of infertility, but might not result in any intervention in the case of a sixteen year old girl whose baby was destined to be adopted.

Another criterion of value to the mother, and to society, is *physical and mental normality*, so that serious malformation is accepted as a reasonable ground for legal abortion. The anencephalic fetus, incapable of independent existence for more than a few minutes, is regarded as a candidate for termination of pregnancy at whatever stage the diagnosis is made, to save the mother the distress of carrying her hopelessly deformed child to term. The respected authors of the standard textbooks of operative obstetrics have long accepted perforation of the hydrocephalic head (and deliberate brain damage to ensure stillbirth and vaginal delivery and to avoid the need for caesarean section) as a legitimate and ethical procedure. In such cases we are dealing with a child who, in the unlikely event of his surviving, would lead but a short life with severe mental handicap. Similarly, when the mother is miscarrying in mid-pregnancy, nothing other than a vaginal delivery would be contemplated for a baby who was considered too immature to survive—so there is also a concept of fetal worth in relation to *gestational age*.

We mourn a neonatal death more than a stillbirth, and a late miscarriage more than an early spontaneous abortion. But even with sophisticated diagnostic equipment we can define no precise physiological milestone during fetal development, from conception through to birth, which could be used to define a sudden change in fetal value as a human being. So, many Christian gynaecologists rationalize their opinions about induced abortion by employing what Stirrat[12] calls *a sliding scale of values,* which includes many factors, the most important of which is gestational age. This is our first consideration, mainly because of the wording of the Abortion Act (1967) which legalizes abortion when two doctors agree that the risk to life or health of the mother would be greater if pregnancy continued. Thus the main reason why so many abortions are now done legally is that the techniques employed to empty the womb, at least in the first trimester, have so improved that the procedure can be regarded as safer than childbirth.

But we look also at the mother's total health in making such decisions. Her age, maturity, fertility, marital and social status, intelligence and occupation are also factors on the sliding scale. In effect, we are judging the woman's capacity as a mother, and balancing it against progressively increasing fetal value.

Gynaecologists are often accused of 'playing God' when they judge on maternal and fetal values, but theirs is a very imperfect system of choice. Fortunately, in judging their actions, God will not use the imprecise sliding scale of values imposed by fallible doctors upon the fetus as they wrestle with the dilemma or abortion.

When they do abort legally, on social grounds, gynaecologists are not saying, with the situationists, that they are doing 'right'. They just find some appalling circumstances in this fallen world where they decide they ought to adopt the less harmful alternative, which some say is wrong and others call the lesser evil.

Legal abortion will never increase our respect for life. Despite selectively destroying many thousands of babies thought to be 'at risk' socially, the incidence of baby battering continues to rise. The need for induced abortion is a social evil, but what is wrong for the community may not always be so wrong for the individual.

The Value of the Newborn

Only when the child exists independently from the mother does the law regard it as a person and give it the full protection of human rights. Infanticide is equivalent to murder, with the exception that the penalties are reduced for the mother who kills her own child while in an unbalanced state of mind soon after the birth.

The view is often expressed that a more liberal attitude to

abortion will inevitably lead to a diminished regard for the life of the newborn. But those doctors who sometimes terminate pregnancy because of serious social problems never consider these same factors before striving to keep alive a premature baby. In fact, our colleagues in neonatal intensive care units create new ethical dilemmas by the very success of modern techniques of prolonging life and treating previously lethal neonatal disease. As a result, when their treatment has failed they sometimes have to withdraw ventilatory support from a child with severe brain damage, caused by birth injury or post-natal asphyxia.

Since the Abortion Act the perinatal mortality rate in England and Wales had continued its downward trend, and has even tended to fall more rapidly, partly because many 'at risk' babies have been removed by abortion. However, some 130,000 abortions a year (one fifth of all births) is a very extravagant loss of life in order to achieve a modest improvement in birth statistics.

But concurrently with the abortion holocaust there have been dramatic advances in treating infertility, preventing miscarriage and premature labour, and preserving the lives of tiny neonates. The efforts of our paediatric colleagues and the immense cost of their treatment in some measure serve to balance legal abortion in an assessment of how today's experts in perinatal medicine value the baby.

The principal ethical dilemma which paediatricians face is that of treating grossly deformed infants. This problem is diminishing as more and more babies with spina bifida and Down's Syndrome are identified by antenatal diagnosis and removed by selective legal abortion. But destroying babies before they are born can be regarded only as a first and unsatisfactory step in preventing congenital abnormality. There is hope that 'in vitro' techniques may lead to a better understanding of embryology and contribute to a true prevention of defects. On the other hand, the pursuit of perfection in fetal development can become an evil influence leading first to relatively trivial abnormalitites being regarded as unacceptable, and later to such frightening prospects as the selection of fetal sex and other eugenic manipulation.

When an abnormal baby is born the criteria for surgical intervention to correct defects, or preserve function, are becoming clearer. Such treatment is not so much a 'life and death' issue as is sometimes supposed. For example, many children with spina bifida survive when treated conservatively and the need for surgery must be constantly reviewed.

The claim that deformed babies are being systematically eliminated by narcotic drugs and starvation in special care units is exaggerated. Where sedatives are prescribed it is usually because a severely deformed or critically ill child is causing extreme distress to both parents and the nursing staff by clinging to his pathetic existence for a few more days than expected. As Vere[13] has said, we have a mandate in medicine to curtail disease to save life, but not to curtail life to restrict disease.

The Value of Childbearing

In the twentieth century many may regard the Lord's instructions to Adam (Gen. 1:28) and to Noah's sons (Gen. 9:7) to 'Be fruitful, multiply and fill the earth' to be a divine mission which is almost complete.

Nevertheless, God is concerned about the continuation of the human life he has created and scripture acknowledges that children are a gift from God.

> Sons are a heritage from the Lord,
> children a reward from him (Ps. 127:3).

We can learn a lot about the maternal instinct by studying the infertile wives of the three Jewish patriarchs Abraham, Isaac and Jacob.

Sarah was so frustrated by her childlessness that she provided Abraham with a surrogate mother, the slave girl Hagar, only to find herself despised by the pregnant girl (Gen. 16). Sarah finally conceived long after she had passed the menopause (Gen. 21).

Rebecca's brothers said, 'May you be the mother of thousands', but she was barren for twenty years of marriage to Isaac before his prayer was answered with twins (Gen. 25).

Rachel said, 'Give me sons or I will die' (Gen. 30) but God 'remembered her and opened her womb' to conceive and give birth to Joseph only after Jacob had produced ten sons with his other wives. She believed that this birth had taken away her disgrace, but she went on to die at the birth of her second son Benjamin.

Clearly infertility was regarded as a reason for despair and humiliation. In those days there were no fertility drugs, no artificial insemination and no 'test tube' babies, but these three women, as well as praying earnestly to conceive, were also prepared to go to considerable lengths, even to using subterfuge, in order to obtain a child.

We have now reached the stage when childbearing is almost regarded as a feminine right, and scientific medicine can help to satisfy demands for children, if necessary, by borrowing one, or both gametes, or even a womb from a donor.

In the course of all infertility investigations there comes a stage, when, if the measures taken are unsuccessful, the couple should be advised that enough has been done. Some prospective parents stop short of requesting artificial insemination by a donor and many still feel that 'in vitro' techniques are too 'unnatural'. Perhaps the extreme lengths to which other couples now go to create 'wanted' life serve as a balance to the wanton destruction of 'unwanted' life by abortion.

Contraception is at the other end of the fertility spectrum, and is not discussed in the Bible. The condemnation of Onan (Gen. 38:7–10) was not because he practised coitus interruptus but because he failed in his duty, under Mosaic law, to provide a child for his widowed sister-in-law.

In the early part of this century when contraceptive measures were being introduced they were opposed vigorously by the Church before informed discussion had taken place. Gradually a Christian consensus was achieved and family planning is now a norm, at least within marriage. Nevertheless, the provision of birth control to the unmarried, and particularly to teenagers, remains highly controversial. On the one hand, some claim that contraception indicates responsibility, reduces illegitimacy and abortion, and increases the value of children by making them 'planned'. Others feel sure that the rise in irresponsible sexual behaviour, divorce, venereal disease and cervical dysplasia can all be blamed on the introduction of oral contraceptives.

The truth, in this complex area, is difficult to obtain from statistics, but the changing attitudes of society are reflected in the fact that the sixteen-year-olds of today behave like the twenty-year-olds of ten years ago. This change cannot be attributed to an almost imperceptible trend towards earlier puberty. It does seem to be related to the reduced discipline imposed on teenagers, especially within broken homes, to the influence of the media, and to the rejection of, or a failure to understand, the virtue of chastity.

The Value of the Elderly

The European Convention on Human Rights in 1953 confirmed that 'Everyone's right to live shall be protected by law. No one shall be deprived of life intentionally, save in the execution of a sentence of a court following his conviction of a crime for which this penalty is provided by law.' Most doctors subscribe to this view. Minority support for voluntary euthanasia is largely based on two misconceptions; firstly that pain in terminal disease cannot be adequately relieved without shortening life, and secondly that doctors have a duty to preserve life at all costs. The true meaning of euthanasia is death without suffering, and that should always be the aim of terminal care by the correct use of therapy, directed not only towards the body, but also the mind and the spirit. The doctor must sustain life wherever possible, but this duty stops short of prolonging the distress of the dying patient, or maintaining the circulation of an individual with irreversible brain death.

The patient at the end of his life cannot be treated in isolation. Relatives and friends are usually closely involved in any decisions. In many parts of the world the elderly normally live with their families and the care of parents and grandparents is regarded as one of the most important filial duties. Although the 'nuclear family' of modern Western society frequently has no place for the elderly, it is part of the Christian tradition to honour and respect old age. The infant Jesus was presented to Simeon and Anna when he was first taken to the temple (Luke 2).

It is tragic to die isolated and neglected and the hospices of Britain, largely established and staffed by Christian doctors and nurses, have a tradition of love and concern which serves to give their patients a peaceful and a happy end. As Cicely Saunders has said, 'When a man asks for death someone has failed him'.

Conclusion

This chapter has concentrated on the beginning of life because that is where the major ethical dilemmas still exist, but the young, the sick, the disadvantaged and the elderly may all become partly, or totally dependent on those around them for Christian love and caring in their times of need.

There is an argument quite prevalent today that we are on a 'slippery slope' which starts with lack of respect for the fetus and leads through mercy killing to genocide.

We need to be alert for any evidence that this trend exists but in some respects modern Western society is more caring and less prejudiced than it was a hundred years ago. These virtues are, however, balanced by an unhealthy pursuit of pleasure and money and a humanistic doctrine of self-interest.

In contrast Jesus summarized Christian doctrine to be firstly the love of God, and secondly the love of one's neighbour as oneself (Mark 12:30, 31). In the context of this chapter the fetus, the handicapped child, the sufferer from kidney-failure and the senile are all our neighbours.

Sexual immorality and a lack of respect for human life are symptoms of a sickness of a society which has moved away from Christian principles. Those who seek a return to a more responsible society would be better employed in explaining these principles and encouraging their re-acceptance, rather than exaggerating the symptoms of the disease.

6

Homosexuality

RICHARD WINTER

Homosexuality may be defined as 'preferential erotic attraction to a member of the same sex which usually, but not inevitably, involves some physical expression of this attraction'.[1] We often consider people to be clearly heterosexual or clearly homosexual—either the one or the other—but it is now recognized that there is a whole spectrum of sexual orientation, ranging from those who are exclusively heterosexual, and have never had a homosexual inclination or thought in their lives, to those who have never felt any erotic attraction to a member of the opposite sex. It is much more helpful, therefore, to think in terms of 'homosexual tendencies' rather than 'homosexuals'. It is too simplistic to categorize a person by only one aspect of his identity. Our sexuality pervades much of what we do and who we are, but we are much more than sexual beings. As Steinbeck has written: 'The homosexual as such does not exist, but persons who at times fantasize, feel or act homosexually do.'[2]

Historical aspects

Homosexuality is not a new phenomenon. The writings of Plato and Socrates show that, in pre-Christian Greece, love between males was thought to be superior to love between men and women. Women were regarded as inferior and confined to domestic life, whereas the love of a man for a boy was the road to intellectual maturity and ultimate truth. But, as Coleman points out,

> There were also more sensual, exploitive and commercial aspects in which the national tolerance for an educational process between older and younger men enabled pederasts to pursue homosexual lust for younger boys, despite the largely ineffective prohibitions of the law.[3]

In ancient Rome, although the tradition of family life was strong and homosexual behaviour was prohibited by law from the third century BC (a law probably rarely invoked), sexual licence was common among the ruling classes and many Roman emperors were practising homosexuals. In contrast, Jewish culture firmly held to the importance of family life and there were heavy penalties for anything that threatened to disrupt it. Adultery, bestiality and homosexuality were all punishable by death.

Since the time of Christ nearly all Christian theologians have agreed in condemning homosexual behaviour, seeing it as part of the disorder and brokenness of a fallen world and a deviation from the divine intention in creation. Tertullian, Augustine and Aquinas all saw it as 'against nature', and English Canon Law, codified in the twelfth century, maintained the prohibition of homosexual practice.

In pre-Reformation times sexual sins were regarded as the worst of all evils, and much early Christian and medieval thought was affected by a neo-Platonic dualism in which the body was considered inferior to the spirit. Celibacy was the ideal and sexual promiscuity of any sort was an expression of gross carnality. Tertullian, after joining an ascetic Christian community, determined to prevent adultery, fornication and homosexuality, wrote:

> 'All the other frenzies of passions, impious both towards the bodies and towards the sexes—beyond the laws of nature, we banish not only from the threshold, but from all shelter of the church, because they are not sins but monstrosities.'[4]

Thomas Aquinas saw homosexual practices as more serious than other forms of sexual lust because they corrupt the natural order of heterosexual union most directly. He was influenced by Aristotle who had argued that homosexual behaviour was closer to animal than to human behaviour and therefore a type of bestiality. This, coupled with the superstition that the seminal fluid contained the embryo, reinforced the attitude that homosexuality was 'the most horrific sin'.

Reformed theologians such as Calvin and Luther spoke very strongly against homosexuality but stressed 'that homosexual practice is no more or less serious than fornication, adultery or other expressions of sin.'[5] More recently Helmut Thielieke concluded that 'homosexuality is in every case not in accord with the order of creation . . . Yet, the predisposition itself, the homosexual potential as such, dare not be any more strongly deprecated than the status of existence which we all share as men in the disordered creation that exists since the Fall. . .'[6]

Legal, Ethical and Medical Considerations

The laws of England have in the past been largely grounded in Christian values. Thus Henry VIII introduced the death penalty for sodomy and after several repeals by other monarchs the Act 'finally became a permanent part of English law when it was re-enacted by Elizabeth I in 1563, the preamble stating that since the repeal "divers ill-disposed persons have been the more bold to commit the said most horrible and detestable vice of buggery aforesaid, to the high displeasure of Almighty God"'.[7]

The death penalty remained in force until 1861 when life imprisonment for sodomy and lesser terms for indecent assault were introduced. However, homosexuals who continued their activities in private were still virtually ignored until, in 1885, a new Bill was presented to Parliament for 'further provision of the protection of women and girls and the suppression of brothels and other purposes'. At a late stage a new clause was added to the Bill with the supposed intention of protecting men and boys from assault as well, for behind the scenes of upright Victorian society there was apparently considerable 'commercial exploitation of the young for both homosexual and heterosexual gratification'.[8] The clause read as follows:

> Any male person who in public, or private, commits or is party to the commission of, or procures or attempts to procure the commission by any male person of any act of gross indecency with another male person, shall be guilty of a misdemeanour . . .[9]

The main purpose of protecting the young was achieved by the Act but it was not immediately recognized that the wording of this new clause cast the net far wider than had originally been intended. In 1885 Oscar Wilde was brought to trial and, although not molesting the young, was accused of 'the worst of crimes'. A move in 1921 to include lesbianism under the same law failed. It was thought to be relatively uncommon and also presumably less likely to involve children. Until recent years female homosexuality has somehow avoided the attention paid to male relationships.

This century has seen a gradual change in the public attitude towards homosexuality. This has come about partly through the increasing dominance of humanist thinking and, more recently, because of the loss of any absolute values of right and wrong. 'If it feels right, do it', is the overriding consideration in much of modern behaviour. This changing pattern of public morality, together with an enormous rise in the number of prosecutions for homosexual offences in the years after World War II, forced a re-evaluation of the law and under the Sexual Offences Act of 1967 'homosexual behaviour between consenting adults in private' was accepted as being no longer a criminal offence. As a result, homosexuality and bisexuality are now virtually accepted in our Western cultures as normal varieties of human behaviour, and in 1973 the American Psychiatric Association amended its list of diagnostic categories in mental illness and removed homosexuality from the list of abnormalities. Many young people today are taught that we are basically bisexual and that sexual orientation is a matter of choice. For many it *is* a clear choice, but for others the choice is not so obvious. For them, in their early years, there has been a marked preference for relationships with members of the same sex and an avoidance of close relationships with the opposite sex.

The Extent of the Problem

It is difficult to know just how common homosexual activity is. Many people, at some time in their lives, experience some degree of passing homosexual attraction for another person. It is particularly common in adolescence and in abnormal stress situations, such as war and prison, where members of the same sex are confined for long periods in each others' company. With its acceptance as an alternative lifestyle in our culture it is increasingly common. In most cities in England and North America 'gay bars' and 'baths' are an accepted part of the social scene. The homosexual movement is a growing political and social force with the ultimate aim of making homosexuality completely acceptable.

Kinsey, in his 1948 study, estimated that 4% of American males (i.e. 1 in 25) were exclusively homosexual, 10% had been practising homosexuals for more than three years during their lives, and 27% had had some homosexual experience.[10] It has been estimated that 1 in 45 adult women is exclusively homosexual. The homosexual movement insistently states that 10% of the population is homosexual, but this is an ideological statement intended to advance the belief that 'gay is good', and has little scientific validity. In general, and there are exceptions to this, men tend to be more promiscuous and have shorter relationships with intense physical contact, whereas women tend to be less promiscuous and there is more stress on companionship and friendship than on the physical relationship. For this reason homosexual relationships between women tend to last longer. Kinsey's figures are often used to provide a statistical norm for human behaviour. With the loss of any external framework of values we are left only with science and statistics or the whim of an arbitrary authority to provide the points of reference for our conduct in this world, but it is only in very recent years, and in particular since the passing of the 1967 Act, that homosexuality has been accepted by society, by the law of the land and by many churches as a legitimate option. In this increasingly tolerant atmosphere 'gay' societies, 'gay' churches and the 'gay' Christian movement have all flourished. Apart from the more conservative few, many doctors, psychiatrists, and lawyers now see nothing abnormal about homosexuality. This is in striking contrast to most medical and psychiatric literature of ten to fifteen years ago which still described homosexuality as abnormal and deviant. Homosexuals themselves felt that the medical profession was behind the times and in 1973 Gay Information published *Psychiatry and the Homosexual: A Brief Analysis of Oppression*.[11] But the climate was changing as Ruitenbeek wrote, also in 1973, in *Homosexuality: A Changing Picture:*

> A great deal has happened to our thinking about homosexuality. Regardless of Bieber, Socarides, Hatterer *et al* who still advocate the pathology concept *vis à vis* homosexuality there are now increasing numbers of psychoanalysts and psychiatrists who strongly feel that homosexuality should be considered as just another form of sexual behaviour, another variety of sexuality, if you will, and who indeed no longer view heterosexuality as *the* preferred lifestyle.[12]

Homosexuality was no longer a 'questionable and treatable condition' but a 'natural alternative'. Psychiatrists began to help their patients to be better adjusted homosexuals rather than attempting to change them to heterosexuals.

It is important to recognize that for some homosexuals, the campaign for freedom has much wider political and social implications. Some choose a homosexual lifestyle as an act of protest against the nuclear family, traditional sex roles or even capitalism. Many in the homophile movements are not concerned only with affirming the homosexual person but also with rejecting the family structure as the basis of society. At an early Festival of Light meeting on homosexuality the speaker was heckled by members of a homosexual movement whose first shout was, 'death to the family'.[13]

Christian Viewpoints

In the last twenty-five years there has been a growing division of opinion among Christians. The major Protestant denominations have debated the issue for many weary hours and there appears to be disturbingly little agreement. A Methodist report, *A Christian Understanding of Human Sexuality*,[14] which was not accepted by the Methodist Conference, affirmed that homosexual activities are not 'intrinsically wrong'. 'For homosexual men and women, permanent relationships characterized by love can be an appropriate and Christian way of expressing their sexuality.' The Church of England's Report from the working party of the Board of Social Responsibility[15] also approved of loving homosexual relationships, but this view was severely criticized by other members of the Board of Social Responsibility in Part II of the Report. Obviously a variety of views exists but three main streams of thought are now clearly recognizable.

(1) The homosexual condition is a result of being part of a broken, 'fallen' world and it is the practice of homosexuality which is sinful. This view is based primarily on the creation ordinance that 'a man shall leave his father and mother and cleave unto his wife and the two shall become one flesh' and supported by other scriptures which condemn homosexual practice. The Nottingham Statement of the National Evangelical Anglican Congress in 1977 acknowledged:

> . . . the growing problem of homosexuality and our need for a better informed understanding of this condition. There should be a full welcoming place in the Christian fellowship for the Christian homosexual. Nevertheless we believe homosexual intercourse to be contrary to God's law and not a true expression of human sexuality as he has given it. More thought needs to be given to the pastoral care appropriate to those with this particular need.[16]

The second and third views are closely related in not condemning homosexual relationships, but one sees them as the lesser of two evils and the other as God-given and good.

(2) Homosexual relationships are accepted as non-ideal, as the lesser of two evils. Loving relationships are better than continuous sublimation or temptation to sin. It is better they would say, to have a loving homosexual relationship than to burn with unfulfilled

homosexual desire or to have promiscuous homosexual relationships.

H. Kimball Jones writes in *Towards a Christian Understanding of the Homosexual:*

> The church must be willing to make the difficult, but necessary step of recognizing the validity of mature homosexual relationships, encouraging the absolute invert to maintain a fidelity to one partner when his only other choice would lead to a promiscuous life filled with guilt and fear. This would by no means be an endorsement of homosexuality by the church.[17]

(3) According to the third view the Bible is not relevant to our contemporary social situation. Homosexual relationships are God-given and to be accepted with joy, usually within loving relationships. In a relationship of commitment and love, writes Norman Pittenger,

> I cannot see . . . why two persons should be condemned for committing sin, when they desire, as almost invariably they will desire, to *act on* their love—and that means, of course, to engage in physical acts which for them will both express their love and deepen it.[18]

The statement of conviction of the Gay Christian Movement is that

> Human sexuality in all its richness is a gift of God gladly to be accepted, enjoyed and honoured as a way of both expressing and growing in love, in accordance with the life and teaching of Jesus Christ. Therefore it is our conviction that it is entirely compatible with the Christian faith not only to love a person of the same sex but also to express that love fully in a personal sexual relationship.[19]

The second and third views tend to stress God's love and acceptance almost to the exclusion of teaching on righteousness and judgment of sin. Many writers on this subject see the watershed as being the publication in 1955 of D. Sherwin Bailey's book, *Homosexuality and the Western Christian Tradition*.[20] His views are used extensively by the Gay Christian Movement and the Christian Homophile Movement. Although accepting that the traditional Christian view has been to condemn homosexual practice, he severely criticizes the traditional interpretation of the Scriptures which refer to homosexuality.

It is to an examination of the scriptural references to homosexuality that we now turn because the key issue in this whole debate is the interpretation and authority of the Bible. Even among evangelicals there is some diversity of opinion on this matter and it is on such a moral issue as homosexuality that the debate might well come to a head.

Biblical passages

A. Old Testament

1. Sodom and Gibeah

Two very uncomfortable stories in the old Testament have usually been understood to express strong condemnation of homosexual acts. In Genesis 19, Lot offers hospitality to two visitors who are, in fact, angels. The men of Sodom come banging at the door demanding, 'Where are the men who came to you tonight? Bring them out to us so that we may know them' (v.5). Lot pleads with them not to 'do this wicked thing' (v.7), and offers his 'daughters who have not known man' instead of the visitors. Fortunately they are protected by the angels and Lot and his family are told to flee the judgment that is coming on the city.

In Judges 19, the wicked men of Gibeah come to the door of a house where a stranger had been given hospitality for the night. They demanded, 'Bring out the man who came into your house that we may know him' (v.22). The host reproves them for 'acting so wickedly' and doing 'so vile a thing' (v.23). The host's daughter and the visitor's concubine are offered instead. The concubine is raped and murdered by the men.

In no way do these incidents justify Lot or the other men for offering their daughters or the concubine to the men, but they do emphasize the evil of homosexuality.

The New International Version clearly translates 'that we may know them' as 'that we can have sex with them.' This has been the traditional understanding of this expression and of the references to 'acting wickedly' and 'so vile a thing'. Sherwin Bailey, however, questions any reference to homosexuality here, claiming that the Hebrew *yadha*, to know, though occasionally used in relation to sexual intercourse, is more frequently used for 'to get acquainted with', implying that Lot was guilty of a serious breach of hospitality. Lot had received two strangers who had not been introduced to the other men of the city.

When dealing with the different uses of a word, one principle of biblical interpretation is that the context can help to decide the meaning. For instance, Bailey agrees that the word refers to sexual intercourse in Genesis 19:8 and Judges 19:25 when it refers to women (the daughters and the concubine) but insists on a different meaning when it refers to the men.

Now it is true that Sodom's sin was much more than just sexual. Ezekiel 16:49 speaks of the sin of Sodom as arrogance, gluttony and failure to help the poor and needy. But in Jude 7 the sexual aspect is explicitly stated, 'In a similar way, Sodom and Gomorrah and the surrounding towns gave themselves up to sexual immorality and perversion.'

Sherwin Bailey admits that in the rabbinical literature, Philo and Josephus present the homosexual interpretation of the sin of Sodom but he claims that this is uncommon in the rest of the rabbinical literature. R. T. Beckwith maintains that Bailey is certainly wrong in this and quotes numerous other rabbinical sources which refer to the sin of Sodom as being of a sexual nature.

2. The Levitical laws

> Do not lie with a man as one lies with a woman; that is detestable (an abomination) (AV)) (Lev. 18:22).
>
> If a man lies with a man as one lies with a woman, both of them have done what is detestable (that which is an abomination (AV)). They must be put to death (Lev. 20:13).

The word 'abomination' (*toebah*) implies more than a breaking of Jewish law and custom. It emphasizes something that is 'incompatible with the nature of the Creator' or a reversal of what was intended. It is a very strong word used with reference to the offering of children to idols.

But Bailey and others believe that the Old Testament laws are not relevant today. Scanzoni and Mollenkot in *Is the Homosexual My Neighbor?* write:

> 'Consistency and fairness would seem to dictate that if the Israelite Holiness Code is to be invoked against 20th Century homosexuals, it should likewise be invoked against such common practices as eating rare steak, wearing mixed fabrics, and having marital intercourse during the menstrual period.[21]

In understanding the Old Testament law we can look at three things: (i) How did it apply in its own context and culture? (ii) What underlying ethical principles emerge from the law? (iii) Are the Old Testament laws reinforced or abrogated in the New Testament? Jesus said that he had not come to destroy the law but to fulfil it.

Obviously the ceremonial and sacrificial laws are no longer relevant for today, having been completely fulfilled in the ultimate sacrifice of Christ. But the law is given for our good, so that we might live within the limits of the way we are made. What then can we say are the underlying principles in relation to sexuality which emerge from the Old Testament? We find strong prohibitions, not only against homosexuality, but against incest and adultery. These prohibitions are all a restatement, in a negative sense, of the original command in Genesis, 'A man shall leave his father and mother and cleave unto his wife and the two shall become one flesh' (Gen. 2:24). This is the fundamental divine principle in creation to which we return again and again. It is not so much the prohibitions of homosexuality which run through the whole Bible, but the affirmation of the Creator's intention for men and women that should be the focus of our attention. This intention is affirmed and safeguarded by the prohibitions in the teachings of Jesus and Paul and is as relevant in the twentieth century as it was at the creation.

New Testament: Paul's condemnation of homosexuality

1. Romans 1:18–32

In the context of strong statements of the judgment of God on a culture that suppresses the truth of God Paul writes:

> They neither glorified him as God nor gave thanks to him, but their thinking became futile and their foolish hearts were darkened. Although they claimed to be wise they became fools and exchanged the glory of the immortal God for images made to look like mortal man and birds and animals and reptiles.
>
> Therefore God gave them over in the sinful desires of their hearts to sexual impurity for the degrading of their bodies with one another. They exchanged the truth of God for a lie, and worshipped and served created things rather than the Creator—who is forever praised. Amen.
>
> Because of this, God gave them over to shameful lusts. Even their women exchanged natural relations for unnatural ones. In the same way the men also abandoned natural relations with women and were inflamed with lust for one another. Men committed indecent acts with other men, and received in themselves the due penalty for their perversion.

In verse 20, there is emphasis on the fact that 'ever since the creation of the world' God's character has been known, his divine intention expressed. All distortions of that original creation intention are unnatural and sinful. Some would say in response to this that Paul is referring only to idolatrous, unloving homosexual relationships, not to the caring, responsible behaviour of Christian homosexuals who are motivated by 'love'.

But Paul's argument is that the whole 'natural' order is broken, twisted and distorted by man's disobedience at the Fall. We all have biases towards particular sins as a result of our genetic inheritance and our early environment. The sins of our fathers will affect the way we cope with life to a considerable extent. A homosexual inclination is no worse in God's view than a tendency to uncontrolled anger, or unbridled pride or covetousness.

Richard Lovelace writes:

> All human sexuality, in its heterosexual as well as its homosexual forms is disordered by the inherited drive towards disobedience which we call original sin, and by the broken social fabric of idolatrous societies. Human sin and God's punishment upon it have deeply affected the processes by which sexual identity is formed, with the result that none of us, heterosexual or homosexual, naturally desires to fulfil perfectly God's plan for our sexuality. We did not consciously choose to have the deviant sexual orientation which drives us towards fornication, adultery or homosexual practice. But we *are* confronted with the choice whether or not to act out our orientation and fulfil our natural desires, or whether instead to seek the control and transforming power of the Spirit of Christ to restrain and reorient our desires and our behaviour.[22]

Paul is referring to homosexual behaviour not homosexual disposition or temptation. It is those who do not resist the tendencies of their fallen, sinful nature that receive God's condemnation. Homosexuality is part of a list of other 'shameless passions' such as 'envy, murder, strife, deceit, malice, . . . arrogant, boastful . . . God-haters' (Rom. 1:26–32).

2. 1 Corinthians 6:9–11

> Do you not know that the unrighteous will not inherit the kingdom of God? Do not be deceived; neither the immoral, nor idolaters, nor adulterers, nor homosexuals, nor thieves, nor the greedy . . . will inherit the kingdom of God.

The Greek for 'homosexuals' in this passage is in fact the two words *arsenokoitai* and *malakoi,* words which imply, respectively, the active and passive partners in a male homosexual relationship.

Others challenge this interpretation and say that it refers to either homosexual, heterosexual or male prostitutes, not to those in a committed love relationship. We shall take up this challenge after looking at a passage from the first letter to Timothy.

We should notice that Paul's list includes many other sins besides homosexuality—the greedy are mentioned alongside adulterers and thieves! Paul is referring to those who do not struggle against their sinful tendencies, those who do not even think that these things are wrong. This way of life, says Paul, is evidence of the unrighteousness which God cannot accept in his kingdom.

3. 1 Timothy 1:8–11

> We know that the law is good if a man uses it properly. We also know that law is made not for good men but for lawbreakers and rebels, the ungodly and sinful, the unholy and irreligious; for those who kill their fathers and mothers, for murderers, for adulterers and homosexuals, for kidnappers and liars and perjurers . . .

Paul here is talking about breaking the commandments of God. To those who kill their father and mother, murderers—you shall not murder (Exod. 20:13). To adulterers and homosexuals (*arsenokoitai*)—you shall not commit adultery (Exod. 20:14). To kidnappers —you shall not steal (Exod. 20:15). To liars and perjurers—you shall not give false testimony against your neighbour (Exod. 20:16).

Notice that adultery and homosexuality are placed together here because they both undermine the creation intention of sexual intercourse being designed for the marriage relationship.

Sherwin Bailey draws a distinction between 'inverts' and 'perverts' saying that Paul is speaking to perverts only. An invert is someone with a fixed homosexual disposition. A pervert is someone with a basically heterosexual disposition who engages in homosexual acts. The Christian Homophile Movement has taken Bailey's argument and says that Paul is not talking about two people of the same sex who are 'in love'.

The problems with Sherwin Bailey's view are threefold:

(1) It rests on the assumption (specifically claimed by Bailey in relation to Leviticus and Paul) that the homosexual condition (invert) was not known in Paul's time. This is clearly not true.

> . . . Philo refers to those who 'habituate themselves' to the practice of homosexual acts, so also Josephus indicates that homosexual behaviour has become a fixed habit for some. Clement of Alexandria (3rd Century) refers to the interpretation of Basilides on Jesus' words in Matthew 19:12 concerning those 'eunuchs who have been so from birth' that 'some men, from birth, have a natural aversion to a woman; and indeed those who are naturally so constituted do well not to marry.'
>
> It is likely therefore that Paul and his readers were not unaware of the fact that there were some people for whom homosexual intercourse was not simply a freely chosen alternative but a fixed preference or settled lifestyle.[23]

(2) As we noted at the beginning of the chapter, we all lie on a spectrum (or Kinsey Scale 0–6) of homosexual orientation so that it is virtually impossible to draw a clear line morally between the invert and the pervert.

(3) This view ignores the difference between temptation and sin. Sin is allowing the temptation to develop in our thought life so that it

leads to action. Homosexual behaviour, not homosexual disposition, is condemned with other sins in both Old and New Testaments.

We can thus conclude that:

(1) We are all to some degree sexual deviants with aberrations in fantasy and behaviour.

(2) The norm for sexuality is heterosexual, based on scriptural teaching on creation. Homosexual tendencies, like tendencies to extreme expressions of anger or pride, are the results of the brokenness of the fallen world. 'Homosexual practice represents a move away from the "one flesh" ideal God intends for the most intimate of human relationships; heterosexuality represents movement towards it.'[24]

(3) Sexual sin is not worse than other sins, although some sins leave deeper and more lasting scars than others.

Causes of Homosexuality— Heredity v. Environment

As with many areas at the interface between medicine and psychology, controversy rages over whether a homosexual orientation is constitutional or a product of environmental influences. A recent review in the *British Journal of Hospital Medicine* concluded that at the moment the cause of homosexuality remains a mystery.[25] Numerous genetic and hormonal studies have been carried out to prove a biological factor but there are few positive results. The few hormonal disturbances that have been found may be the result, not the cause, of a particular sexual orientation. Twin studies can be quoted to support heredity *or* environment. There is no demonstrable abnormality of the chromosomes. A. W. Steinbeck, Associate Professor of Medicine at the University of New South Wales, after reviewing the literature writes:

> There is no genetic or chromosomal aberration underlying the disposition of homosexuality . . . these facts stress that the primary or basic origins of homosexuality, bisexuality, and heterosexuality lie in the developmental periods of the postnatal era, especially infancy and childhood. The pubertal hormones bring the dispositions to full or modified expression.[26]

There is considerable evidence pointing to a variety of influences in early life which seem to be related to the acquisition of a predominantly homosexual orientation. There is certainly not 100% correlation but significantly higher percentages are found when compared with control groups of heterosexuals.

The studies of male homosexuals produce a caricature family.

Father is not particularly interested, loving or approving. He is sometimes overtly critical and hostile. He tends to be weak when compared with mother and to have a low status in the family. Mother is the dominant disciplinarian. She tends to be over-protective and jealously guards her son's sexual development by restricting his heterosexual contacts. The parents' relationship is poor. The child is often isolated from his male peers and is perhaps teased for his lack of masculine interests. His first experience of erotic arousal in adolescence is with another boy or man.

One can see from this how a young man with an over-powering mother may develop inhibitions and lack of confidence and fear of failure in heterosexual contacts. With a critical, weak father, he may also lack confidence in himself and his masculinity and hence fear rejection. His desire for security and approval combined with the sexual drive of adolescence will rapidly push him into close relationships with other boys and men.

For a girl the picture is not so clear and few studies have been done. There is a fair relationship with father and poor relationship with mother. Loss of parents or parental fighting and drinking are common factors. As a child she is often described as a 'tomboy'.

Elizabeth Moberley, a Cambridge psychologist, believes that one major precondition of the development of a homosexual orientation is a deficit in the relationship with the parent of the same sex. If the needs for identification and approval are not met in the pre-adolescent phase, there will be incomplete emotional development. Approval and affection are found by the individual among his or her peers at a time when the body is developing sexually so that relationships rapidly become erotically intimate, thus hindering the development of other aspects of the friendship. Unless a close non-erotic relationship is possible, Elizabeth Moberley argues, that person will never develop emotionally beyond the pre-adolescent period.[27] Irving Bieber's psychoanalytical writings on this subject suggest that the presence of a warm, supportive father virtually precludes the possibility of a homosexual son.[28]

There are, of course, many people from the sort of backgrounds described above who do not develop overt homosexual tendencies and there are obviously many factors involved. For example, a particular event or relationship in one boy's life may be far more formative at the age of nine than at the age of eleven or vice versa.

A study from the Kinsey Institute of Sexual Research in California compared large groups of homosexuals and hetero-sexuals on a number of different factors. They claim that their findings point to a biological basis for sexual preference. They have no proof but they strongly suspect that the root cause of homosexuality is biological or, more precisely, hormonal. They claim that environmental influences do play some role in the emergence of homosexuality in bisexuals but not among those who are exclusively homosexual. The sexual preference of the exclusive homosexual simply seems to follow from a deep seated predisposition that has emerged during childhood or adolescence. The biological predisposition also produces gender non-conformity—in other words, boys who prefer hopscotch to football or girls who prefer cars to dolls. John Money, a leading American sex researcher, believes that there may be some strong predisposition built into the brain by prenatal hormones that makes it extremely easy for some people to be either bisexual or homosexual or heterosexual in their partner relationship. But he admits that this is only a theory and needs more research.[29]

There may indeed be a biological influence on temperament and the expression of masculinity and femininity, but their findings are only suggestive not conclusive. The authors of the Kinsey Institute study have a vested interest in undermining the traditional environmental explanations.

> Should it ever be discovered with more certainty that homosexuality is derived primarily from physiological origins, what might be the implications for society? First, those who argue that homosexuality is 'unnatural' will be forced to reconsider their belief, because something that is biologically innate must certainly be natural for a particular person, regardless of how unusual it may be . . . We might reach the point when all homosexual men and women will be as comfortable with their orientation as their heterosexual counterparts are with theirs.[30]

This is a morality based on 'whatever is, is right'—a statistical ethic, which ignores the biblical view of a fallen, abnormal creation.

But even if we do prove some biological predisposition, no one can argue that it gives rise to uncontrollable or compelling behaviour. Influences in childhood, adolescence and adulthood will work to reduce or enhance the effect of the predisposition. The biblical perspective stresses our responsibility for our behaviour. We are free to make choices. Yes, we *are* affected by our genes, hormones and our early family life, but not to the point of complete determinism.

Is Change Possible?

Until recently, it has been believed that for a strongly homosexual individual, change is impossible. Scanzoni and Mollenkott argue that for some people homosexuality is as natural as left-handedness. Surely, they say, God would not condemn people for an orientation which cannot be changed. Jim Peron writes, 'When we present to a constitutional homosexual a false hope that he can be changed we are lying.' The Gay Liberation Movement believes that any fundamental change is impossible.

In the face of these views, psychiatrist E. Mansell Pattison and his wife, Myrna Loy Pattison, write:

> When homosexuality is defined as an immutable fixed condition that must be accepted, the potential for change seems slim. In our study, however, when homosexuality was defined as a changeable condition, it appears that change was possible.[31]

The Pattisons' study, published in the American Journal of Psychiatry in December 1980, documented the claimed change in sexual orientation of eleven white males from exclusive homosexuality to exclusive heterosexuality through participation in a Pentecostal Church fellowship. Out of thirty subjects who claimed change, eleven were interviewed in detail and their information correlated well with information from the staff of the church crisis centre through which they had made the original contact with the church.

The eleven white men were aged between 21 and 35 years (mean 27). All had developed homosexual tendencies before the age of 15 and most changed to heterosexual orientation by the time they were 22 years old. Nine of the subjects had a Kinsey Rating of 6 (the highest, indicating exclusively homosexual physical and psychical responses) before change. Six out of the eleven were happily married at the time of the study. The length of time they had been married varied between two and seven years (mean four years). The change was gradual for all the subjects, with homosexual fantasies, dreams and impulses fading slowly over months and years and as their marital relationships developed.

The Pattisons describe the process of change very succinctly:

> 'When our subjects came in contact with the church's crisis service for homosexuals, they found a welcome reception as homosexuals. No attempt was made to make them change their homosexuality. Rather, they were presented with the invitation to commit their life to Christ and the church. All subjects had an explicit Christian conversion or rededication. They were then invited into small church fellowship groups where they studied the Bible and learned expected Biblical patterns of mature lifestyles.'
>
> 'All of our subjects soon became aware that they were psychologically immature and had poor interpersonal relationships . . . They were surprised to experience acceptance, non-judgmental evaluation, and non-erotic love from both men and women. These were new

> experiences for them and in turn they began to learn and practise these new styles of interpersonal relationships. As a result they began to identify with those they considered "mature Christian men" and to experience and practise non-erotic relationships with Christian women in the church . . . (There was no) immediate change in their homosexual dreams, fantasies, impulses or orientation; rather a gradual maturation into a secure and satisfying identity as a male with high self-acceptance . . . They began to experience non-threatening and satisfying interpersonal relationships with women (resulting in) a steady diminution in their homosexual feelings and a steady increase in their heterosexual feelings.'
>
> 'The process of change was not magical, spontaneous or dramatic. Change was embedded in an accepting, evaluative, and loving, non-erotic social milieu that provided expectations, ideology, and actual interpersonal experiences and thus promoted what they saw as personal growth into heterosexuality.'[32]

In 1979, Masters and Johnson, in *Homosexuality in Perspective*, reported a study of ten years' work in behaviour therapy and five years of follow-up of sixty-seven homosexual men and women all predominantly to exclusively homosexual on the Kinsey scale. 65% achieved successful changes in their homosexual orientation.[33]

Kinsey *et al* concluded that, in young men, change in sexual orientation was common, and that there was more ability to change than commonly accepted.[34] In a review of *Deviant Sexual Behaviour*, Bancroft wrote:

> If in fact we had evidence that either a homo or a heterosexual identity was an immutable and fundamental aspect of an individual nature, then any attempt to modify such an identity would be inappropriate and unjustifiable. But there is no such evidence, and we know that many individuals pass through a phase of homosexuality or bisexuality into a stable heterosexual role.[35]

Four factors stand out as crucial to change. Firstly, motivation: in all the studies mentioned there was high motivation to change. Secondly, belief that change is possible: expectations and assumptions are vital in the process of reorientation. The situation is similar to a self-fulfilling prophecy. If there is no belief that change is possible, or if adjustment to one's homosexual state is regarded as the only option, then it is unlikely that change will occur.

Thirdly, age appears to be an important factor. For any habitual way of relating to people or doing things, the longer we have maintained that habit, the harder it is to change. So, for people with homosexual orientation, change is most frequently seen in the early twenties. This does not mean that change is impossible after the age of twenty-five, but that for most it will be a harder struggle because behaviour patterns have become more fixed.

Fourthly, the environment of love and acceptance is necessary. In the church described by the Pattisons the subjects were accepted as no worse sinners than all the other members. Provided there was repentance and a desire to change, they were welcomed into the fellowship. They were also taught clearly that homosexual relationships were not part of the Creator's intention and that change to some degree was possible. Homosexual orientation itself was not condemned. In the fellowship they found friendships with all ages but particularly important was the possibility of non-erotic love from both men and women.

This possibility of love, approval and acceptance without the complication of a physical sexual relationship may be the major healing factor in the situation. It may allow the person to grow beyond a period of 'arrested development' and enter more mature relationships with both men and women. The distorted perceptions that were formed by his relationships with parents may be gradually re-evaluated, corrected, and a much greater range of possibilities in relationships opened up. Skilled counselling in the area of relationships and sexuality may also be very valuable in assisting the process of change.

It is important, too, to see this process of change in the context of the fact that we are all 'being changed into the image of Christ' (2 Cor. 3:18). All of us have been bent and broken by the 'sins of our fathers' stemming back to Adam, and by our own choices. The process of sanctification is a restoration of the broken image, a slow and sometimes painful process which will not be complete until we are with the Lord.

For many the change will not be very great and they may have to struggle against 'thorns in the flesh' for most of their lives. A homosexual orientation is a particularly difficult 'thorn in the flesh' as it may mean coming to terms with being single. There are, of course, many people with a heterosexual orientation who have to accept singleness as well. The impression is often given in Christian teaching that the fulfilment of one's sexuality comes only through 'becoming one flesh' (Gen. 2:24) with another person. But this is not so. It is not everyone's 'right' to have a sexually intimate relationship. Jesus never married and yet he was fully human as well as fully divine. Paul advocates the single life as a high calling. Our fulfilment as men and women is rooted in the creation 'in God's image, male and female' (Gen. 1:27). Our culture bombards us with the view that friendships have always to be exclusive and physically intimate to be normal. The church must take up the challenge to show a different view of friendship and love.

Ideally, within the fellowship of the church family, some of the damage to our broken sinful nature can be repaired. Renewed confidence in friendships with both men and women can replace totally self-gratifying or fearful relationships. The New Testament emphasis is that as we learn to serve and love others, rather than seeking for our own needs to be met and our own rights satisfied, we shall begin to experience relationships as the Creator intended.

For those who can change only a little, there is the biblical call to celibacy. Some who are able to change considerably may be able to marry. For some who do not want to change, and persist in homosexual relationships after a number of warnings, the New Testament pattern of church discipline and (at least) temporary exclusion from fellowship is demanded by Scripture. But we must be careful that we do not fall back into an attitude of condemnation which has driven away from the Church and away from the living God so many people with homosexual leanings who were seeking help.

In conclusion I should like to quote Richard Lovelace's excellent summary of the causes of the growing acceptance within the church of homosexual practice. He sees this as due to: 1) a 'false religion' opposed to biblical revelation and the authority of Scripture; 2) an 'antinomian ethic' that undercuts the balance between the law and the gospel; 3) a 'cheap grace' that ignores repentance; and 4) a 'powerless grace' that denies the possibility of change.[36]

7

Demon Possession: Medical Perspective in a Western Culture

ANDREW SIMS

> We wrestle not against flesh and blood, but against the rulers, against the authorities, against the powers of this dark world and against the spiritual forces of evil in the heavenly realms (Eph. 6:10).

> Your enemy the devil prowls around like a roaring lion looking for someone to devour. Resist him, standing firm in the faith (1 Pet. 5:8).

Psychiatrists (and their predecessors in medicine and philosophy) and theologians have traditionally found each other incomprehensible. Nowhere has this lack of understanding been more acrimonious and damaging than with the whole topic of demons, demon possession and exorcism. While the protagonists quarrel and regard each other as respectively atheistic or anachronistic, the victims or patients suffer both from their unpleasant, abnormal experience and also from the opprobrium of their fellows. There is nothing new in this conflict; scientific and theological man has certainly been arguing on this subject since the early seventeenth century, and the two predominant theories for the causation of abnormal psychic phenomena, the *theurgical* and the *organic*, had different eras of popularity well before that.[1] King James I ascribed many mental symptoms to witchcraft and wrote, 'One called Scot an Englishman, is not ashamed in publike print to deny, that ther can be such a thing as Witch-craft'.[2] Perhaps so much moral indignation has been ignited into flames of flagrant antagonism because each side sees the other, not only as mistaken, but as challenging their whole scale of values. The devout might express their anxiety thus, 'If rationalists declare their scepticism concerning demon possession, perhaps their disbelief will spread to other people and to all other areas of religion'. 'If these fanatics see demons everywhere, what will they not do to their unfortunate victims to purge them of their non-conformity?', is the fear of the humanist physician.

Falret, a distinguished French psychiatrist, gives voice to the latter sentiments in the mid-nineteenth century:

> 'Before the erection of special establishments, the lot of the insane was subjected to numerous vicissitudes.—Considered alternatively, according to the manner of the time, as privileged beings, as inspired by Heaven, as possessed by demons, as sorcerers or heretics, and even as criminals, they were the objects of the most absurd superstitions, and the most cruel punishments. We find them at first shut up in the sanctuary of the temple, often mingling in the religious ceremonies; again subjected to exorcisms, to the rack, burned at the stake . . . '[3]

An important thread that must not be ignored running through all discussion of demons and witchcraft is the whole area of sexuality. This is very obvious in the manifestations of the *possessed*; for example Huxley, in his description of the affected nuns at Loudun in the early seventeenth century, quoted earlier documents which stated, 'Three of the nuns announce, without beating about the bush, that they have undergone copulation with demons and been disflowered.'[4] However, this often single-minded morbid preoccupation with sex is by no means confined to the victims. In the infamous textbook by Sprenger & Kraemer (1487) on the identification and treatment of witchcraft, *Malleus Maleficarum* (the hammer of witches), the authors frequently reveal both their belief that witchcraft was intimately involved with sexuality—copulation with the devil—and their own unhealthy prejudices in this area.[1] Veith has considered that much of the emphasis upon demonic causation of mental symptoms, especially those of sexual disturbance, originated from the writings of Augustine and his later commentators.[5] A sick person with emotional needs and physical distress became, for the theologians, someone more or less wilfully possessed and in league with the devil.

In a society where sexual taboos are restrictive, alternative routes have to be found for sexual drives to gain expression. Freud showed how unconscious but irrepressible sexual urges manifested themselves in straitlaced Viennese society at the end of the nineteenth century.[6] Similiarly, it was often in just such societies with the strictest prohibitions concerning sexual behaviour and the most effective methods of ensuring conformity (such as the late seventeenth century Puritan villages in New England or the circumscribed life of a convent in a small French town) that the sexual excesses of both victim and exorcist were most likely to explode into notoriety.

It is often thought that the pre-reformation Church was riddled with demon-spotting, witch hunts and a morbid need to identify sorcery; this is certainly a mistake. Belief in demons and other supernatural powers was prevalent in many parts of Europe, and probably originated through syncretism with various pre-Christian religions, often only partly absorbed into Christianity through conversion by the sword rather than the word. Such beliefs, however, did not become prominent within the organs of power in the Church until the end of the fourteenth century. Even then, such a sane opinion as Oresme could refute the belief that sorcerers were capable of invoking demons, although he certainly did not rule out their existence.[7] Cohn has pointed out that the great witch-hunt occurred during the sixteenth and seventeenth centuries equally in Catholic and Protestant countries; that it was founded upon a myth, inasmuch as there never was a global secret subversive organization of witchcraft; that it fulfilled the political ambitions of the establishment and also, perhaps, the psychological needs of the victim.[8] There was never a cohesive organized sect of witches or wizards; the intense dread inspired in the minds of people at these times was based entirely upon a collective myth. There are many lessons that can be learned relevant to the modern interest in demons and the identification of those believed to be demon-possessed.

In this chapter I shall not attempt to review the voluminous theological and pastoral literature on exorcism; (my own list of such references contains 113 items). It is deliberately directed at a medical readership and restricts itself to medical and, more specifically, psychiatric aspects of the subject. There is a vast amount of anecdotal information available from cultures other than that of the western European society, but I thought it best not to attempt to describe these phenomena as they occur outside my personal experience. Medical missionaries differ radically in their experience of possession in patients in the Developing World. This clearly merits a separate and detailed description which is outside the scope of this chapter.

Bavington has reviewed this area in his interesting historical account of missionary work involved in mental health. 'It is often difficult to know where to draw the line between "mental illness" and "spiritual problems" and indeed there is no clear line to be drawn since there is much overlap. Attitudes to psychiatry have ranged from a dogmatic condemnation of the subject as "of the Devil" to a rather cautious and reserved acknowledgment of its place and value. These attitudes have perhaps been particularly strong among missionaries influenced more by the prevailing local view of mental disturbance as "evil" or "Satanic". It is often stated that cases of demon possession are more common in the mission field because, it is held, of the more immediate and powerful presence of "evil" and "heathen darkness"—a blatantly ethnocentric view. While not wishing to deny the possibility of spirit possession, from my experience of many years in Pakistan I can hardly think of a single case of alleged possession which could not, at the same time, and from a psychiatric perspective, be recognized as either epileptic, hysteria, schizophrenia or, more rarely, some other diagnostic category. Making such a diagnosis does not, of course, exclude other possible levels of aetiology.

'In most Third World countries much mental illness, even if locally given the label "madness", is usually believed to be the result of evil spirits or the influence of magic, perhaps arranged by someone wishing evil on the victim. Also, indigenous forms of help for the sufferer are traditionally non-medical, such as various exorcism practices or ritual measures to counteract magical or spiritual forces. It is understandable then that Christian missionaries felt some reluctance to enter this arena from the medical angle . . .[9]

While making disclaimers, I would emphasize the tentative nature of what is written here. This is a difficult subject, and I freely acknowledge that I have at times been groping for explanation when current knowledge is decidedly misty. These are my current views; they could well be modified by future experience. Neither the interpretation of the meaning of symptoms to the patient, nor the understanding of the origins of human behaviour is straightforward. I have avoided second-hand accounts of abnormal phenomena because they are notoriously prone to alternative explanations.

Having examined the historical setting, we must now explore the biblical background further if we are to formulate a Christian mind on the subject.

Biblical Background

'Satan went out from the presence of the Lord and afflicted Job with painful sores from the soles of his feet to the top of his head' (Job 2:7). From such biblical excerpts we read that evil is not just the haphazard absence of good; nor is it a purely internal, unorganized tendency of the individual to serve his own interests rather than those of others—*the flesh*. Evil is present everywhere in this world; it is organized, co-ordinated and concerted; it is directly opposed to the will of God; it appears at times to be in total command in the world but is ultimately subject to the power of God. Not only is evil ubiquitous but it is also centralized in such a way that this power may be regarded as a person—*the Devil*. It is thoroughly biblical, evident from church history, and in conformity with our own experience to believe that the Devil sets about his work in many guises. Three common diabolical strategies are: (1) that the Devil does not exist at all; after all, we cannot see him and he is therefore perhaps just a projection of our own internal conflicts; (2) he is ludicrous, or anachronistic. By representing him with horns and a tail, any idea of his posing a serious threat is immediately discredited; (3) the opposite of the previous two; if the Devil, in the form of demons, is everywhere upturning natural phenomena so that no part of the created order may be seen as free from diabolical influence, effective and constructive action in the world becomes impossible. This last view results in a negotiated compromise in which the world and all activity in it is ceded to the Devil, while the religious person retains a right to retreat into *spiritual life* whatever that means. This effectively removes Christians from any effective intervention in public affairs—the end-result of *pietism*.

We get the clearest account of the status and limitation of power of the Devil in the gospel accounts of the experience of Jesus. Throughout his human life Jesus submitted himself to his Father's will. His first public step on this path was to be baptized, when he was filled with the Holy Spirit. Immediately following this, he spent some weeks in solitary communion with God, during which time he was intensely aware of the reality of the Devil in opposing the will of God (Luke 4:1–12). He resisted this force by standing firmly on the truth as outlined in the word of God in the Old Testament; 'It is written: "Man does not live by bread alone"'. 'It is written: "Worship the Lord your God and serve him only"'. 'It says: "Do not put the Lord your God to the test"'. To a greater or lesser degree this is the normal experience of all Christians. As they are filled with the spirit of God so they become increasingly aware both of the 'spiritual forces of evil in the heavenly realms' (Eph. 6:12), and of the God-given power to resist these forces.

The Greek word *diabolos*, the Devil, means, in fact, the *accuser*.

Demons (devils) *daimonion* were believed in and accepted as being influential in many parts of the Greek-speaking, ancient world surrounding the Mediterranean. There are several examples in the Gospels of the word meaning *possessed with the Devil, daimonizonai*; for example, in Mark 5:1–20 we have this as an explanation of the abnormal behaviour of the 'man with an evil spirit' who lived in a graveyard in the region of the Gerasenes. Such accounts are not, in fact, case histories and we are not given enough information either to make or repudiate a diagnosis. The description of the man in the tombs is quite compatible with schizophrenia, but far from pathognomonic. The account of the boy in Mark 9:14–29 sounds like epilepsy, but is not necessarily so. Anyway we know that epileptiform convulsions are a common end-state of many different disease processes. We also know that psychological factors are important in precipitating an attack or an episode in those already predisposed to epilepsy or schizophrenia.

Fortunately one cannot be dogmatic about the medical details in these gospel accounts. We do not know whether these descriptions refer to neurological or psychiatric illness unrecognized at the time and described in the terminology of that epoch as demon possession, or whether there was a 'flurry of demonic activity' during this time of outpouring of God's power. Of course, these two views need not necessarily be opposed. We believe that all evil, all disease, ultimately comes into the world through activity of the Devil, and the fact that Jesus casts out evil spirits in order to effect cures in the Gospels does not preclude those conditions having what we would nowadays regard as an organic aetiology. We are so often strung up on the horns of the dilemma of our Cartesian dichotomy; modern western man finds it important to decide whether a phenomenon is *physical* or *psychological*, and he often discounts the *spiritual* element altogether. Jesus' acts of healing were not quasi-medical in their execution but supernatural. He cured people neither just symptomatically nor via a specific operation upon the diseased organ. His approach was spiritual and he treated the whole person. For example, in the curative touch of the woman suffering from menorrhagia (Luke 8:42–48), healing occurred through no medical or surgical procedure but through her faith, as revealed by her touch and Jesus' power.

In Luke 11:14–28 there is an important discussion on how Jesus counteracts the power of Beelzebub: 'But if I drive out demons by the finger of God, then the kingdom of God has come to you'. Implication here is that the spiritual power of the devil can be overcome only by the Spirit of God, not by some magical act. This requirement for the replacement of the spirit of evil in a person by the Spirit of God is further made clear in this passage: 'When an evil spirit comes out of a man, it goes through arid places seeking rest and does not find it. Then it says, "I will return to the house I left". When it arrives, if it finds the house swept clean and put in order . . . it goes and takes seven other spirits more wicked than itself and they go and live there. And the final condition of that man is worse than the first.'

The teaching of Jesus makes it quite plain that there is a coordinated and personalized force of evil. It is only the superior power of the Spirit of God that ultimately can combat this force. Individuals are given a degree of freedom as to which of these opposing forces they serve, but 'no servant can serve two masters' (Luke 16:13).

In the Gospel, Jesus talks not only about Satan, the father of lies, but also about demons and their activity in the world. One accepts these statements on demonic intervention absolutely on the authority of Jesus. Clearly, that epoch was quite different from the Old Testament times that preceded it, in that there are not found in the Old Testament the large number of references to demonic influence that occur in the New Testament; nor has this frequency of demonic intervention been found subsequently to the same extent either in the early growth of the Church or in more recent times. The emphasis in both the teaching and the work of Jesus Christ upon the conflict with Satan and the frequent warfare waged against demonic influence conforms with the spiritual nature of the work, witness and kingdom of Christ. 'My kingdom is not of this world . . . but now my kingdom is from another place' (John 18:36).

One cannot be sure that what is being called demon possesion in the latter part of the twentieth century is identical in all respects with what Jesus was dealing with. The presence of evil then and now is undoubted; the query is whether the phenomena that some parts of the Church would now call demonic are the same as those of the first century. The following considerations would make us hesitate in equating the account of Jesus dealing with demons with modern experiences for which the same terminology has been used:

1. There is no clear evidence of historical continuity of such a phenomenon universally understood in the Church from the first century to the present; much more, it has been episodic in nature, for instance in Renaissance Catholic and Protestant Europe, Puritan New England in the past, and the Pentecostal Renewal in this century. Quite often the assertion of a recrudescence of demon

possession made by Church leaders of one generation has been completely discounted by orthodox and biblical Church leaders at a later time.

2. In some of the problem situations ascribed to demon possession, there is no evidence of direct spiritual conflict in the victim at that time, nor is there any obvious association with demonic influence.

3. In the gospel stories we are not given enough evidence to make diagnoses. However, there are some clues that the phenomena experienced by those whom Jesus claimed were demon possessed, were not similar to the phenomena which we would identify as those of mental illness, whereas our modern phenomena of possession are certainly close to the symptoms of some major mental illnesses. The boy with fits in the Gospels would seem to have suffered from epilepsy, not a psychiatric illness; the daughter of the Syrophoenecian woman was described as a *little* girl and therefore really outside the age range in which a psychotic illness is likely. These are only faint clues, not firm evidence.

4. When the transcultural evidence is examined carefully, the assertion that demon possession is 'extremely common in the undeveloped world' becomes less tenable. Sometimes the missionary has accepted uncritically the explanations given by local people for symptoms and behaviour that could have other medical explanation. For example, Bavington, quotes Dr Hughes who worked in Shillong, northeast India, who had spotted one effective medical response to an apparently spiritual problem: 'I recognised hyperventilation tetany as the basis for lay-diagnosis of spirit possession. Fancy lecturing ministers and elders in a general assembly on the recognition of tetany and giving them grounds to believe that they were not enchaining the spirit by refusing to accept the evidence presented by the possessed. A shot of calcium gluconate could exorcise the most persistent "spirits".'

5. Only to invoke demonic influence in those situations where certain physical signs or bizarre behaviour are obvious seems to do an injustice, and to belittle the enormous spiritual conflicts of the vast majority of people who do not show these manifestations. If the work of Satan is confined only to these very rare and exotic examples, we dangerously underrate his activity and we cast the blame for spiritual conflict in the majority of cases back onto the individual rather than seeing them as being involved in one battle of a global or cosmic warfare.

6. Theological authorities who take a conservative position on the interpretation of scripture are divided on this issue. Presumably those of us who are not theologians should therefore be cautious.

7. Even among those who purport to see evidence of demon

possession quite frequently, there is considerable disagreement as to what phenomena are and what are not regarded as evidence.

Perhaps the clearest demonstration of the use of the word *demon* is in the first letter to the Corinthians where Paul is contrasting feasts to idols and the Lord's supper (1 Cor. 10:14–22). In verses 19–21 he writes: 'Do I mean then that a sacrifice offered to an idol is anything, or that an idol is anything? No, but the sacrifices of pagans are offered to demons, not to God, and I do not want you to be participants with demons. You cannot drink the cup of the Lord and the cup of demons too; you cannot have a part in both the Lord's table and the table of demons.' So Paul makes the point that the idols themselves, the symbolic visual representation of pagan gods, are nothing; but the pagan gods themselves, the concept of a power other than the true God, the 'demons', are real, and a Christian cannot be in communion with God and with pagan gods. This teaching is quite explicit and leads us to the consideration of what these demons are in our secular but largely pagan society. I would suggest that the false gods, the demons of our day, include the major philosophical sects which tempt and sometimes undermine the faith of Christians and lead non-believers away from the true God. These include materialism, atheistic humanism, communism, nationalism, and so on—as well as superstitions which affect only a very small minority.

If this be so, it would be more appropriate for an individual, wishing to remove the influence of demons, actively and deliberately to reject the false influences he is involved with (rather than passively receiving a ritual of exorcism), and combine this with 'participation in the blood of Christ . . . participation in the body of Christ . . . partaking of the one loaf' (vv. 16, 17).

There are two particular dangers in the tendency to see demons everywhere. First, accounting for a behaviour by the presence of a demon removes personal responsibility from the victim of the demon's activity. If a person loses his temper, or even kills someone else because of the influence of a putative demon, it is not ultimately that person's fault; in such a case exorcism would become more appropriate than confession. Second, if the demon is seen as being present there, inside person A, it is therefore not, by definition, also present inside person B. This divides the faithful into those who have a devil—the *possessed*, and those who have not, and who may therefore regard themselves as above blame. The reality, of course, is that all have sinned, and that the devil exerts his influence in much more subtle ways on both parties—the person who feels himself to be possessed and the person who feels himself to be blameless.

The Nature of Referral to Doctors

It is our purpose to consider *possession states*, or the *perception* of the *presence* of *demons* and the *occult* by the victim, as these phenomena are presented to doctors. We are not, in this chapter, concerned with these topics in general terms but specifically in their medical manifestation. People may *believe themselves* to be possessed; it may be *believed by others* that they are possessed; the individual may quite deliberately in some way have *invited* a demon or power of evil to possess him. These three situations are altogether different and require separate consideration by the doctor. The first question for the doctor to ask the person who believes himself to be possessed is: Why? On what evidence do you come to this conclusion? In my experience this will reveal *cause* in the majority of cases seen by a doctor. In response to this question many patients will describe passivity experiences highly suggestive of a diagnosis of schizophrenia; or other bizarre delusional evidence may be described by the patient to account for his belief that he is possessed. On other occasions an association will be drawn between a series of unfortunate happenings and some, perhaps quite trivial, association with the occult in the past; in such cases the subject is less likely to be convinced that he is truly possessed than in the delusional case with passivity described above.

There are some people who did not originally believe themselves to be possessed—such an idea had never occurred to them—but someone else, often belonging to a sect or group of people who regard such happenings as frequent, had considered this to be so and told the victim of their opinion. This other person, the *demon identifier*, may have come to this conclusion when he or she discusses the series of misfortunes of the victim and discovers that the latter had in the past some slight exposure, perhaps accidental, to the occult. A man was burgled and broke his leg in the same week; a friend of his, who was always looking for such influences, discovered that he had played with a ouija board as a teenager fifteen years before and caused him great consternation by suggesting that these misfortunes were evidence of demonic oppression and required some form of exorcism. Rather impressionable, anxious parents were very much disturbed by their two-year old crying throughout the evening; they asked their vicar to visit them and the child at home, as they believed the child's distress to be demonic in origin. To his credit, the vicar suggested more mundane causes and, in soothing the parents, relieved the child's discomfort.

There are some who, like the fictional Dr. Faustus,[9] deliberately seek out possession or domination by evil. They may not give this any spiritual dimension, and they may not acknowledge it in public. Very often they do not believe in either demons or 'a devil', but they have, inside themselves, made a contract to do consciously and long-term, without compunction, what they know to be wrong in order to gain the benefits of such a course of action. This is quite a different situation from the person who does something he believes to be wrong, feels very guilty about it but is unable to refrain the next time temptation presents. Occasionally, working in either physical medicine or psychiatry, a doctor will incidentally come across a person who both believes in a force of evil or demons, and has by intention made some contract with this power. Such a situation should be conceptually differentiated from a medical or psychiatric condition; it is no more illness than any other religious belief. I am then describing two groups of people in this category *deliberately seeking out possession*; first, those who, believing in 'the devil', voluntarily enter into contract with him; second, those who do not believe in the personification of evil, but, knowing what is right and wrong, consistently and deliberately espouse evil.

If possession, or some related phenomenon, is suspected and yet the victim consults a doctor, the implication must be that either the patient himself or more often another person, believed that in this case illness rather than possession was the likely explanation. The situation may be brought to the attention of a general practitioner initially, but referral to a psychiatrist is likely, so that psychiatrists are the doctors most likely to see several such patients over the years. In my own experience referrals of this type have always been appropriately made; all of those seen where possession has been queried have proved to be mentally ill and in need of psychiatric attention.

There have in the past been some (fortunately very few) Christian doctors who have been prepared to carry out exorcism. Such doctors should examine very carefully their dual, and possibly conflicting, roles. Sometimes the role of doctor precludes his fulfilling a different role with the same person: for example, it is very unwise for the general practitioner to treat his wife medically. Similarly, the role of doctor and exorcist towards the same person should never be combined.

PEOPLE WHOM OTHERS BELIEVE TO BE POSSESSED

Two brief examples of this have already been given. In some churches with a particular interest or perhaps sensitivity in these areas, it has become quite common to suggest the likelihood of demonic influence. In a further case, a middle-aged woman who had been a very active member of a church which had an emphasis upon the physical manifestation of spiritual gifts was referred to a psychiatrist after years of anguish. She had become a Christian a few years before; her husband had objected to this, to her going to church, and to her teaching their teenage children about her faith. Her husband left her, and there was a series of catastrophes in her life including deaths in the family, marital problems of her friends and her own serious physical illness. When she subsequently became profoundly depressed she ascribed this to a 'Satanic element' and was discouraged by her confidants from seeing a doctor. When eventually she did come for treatment, she made a rapid and uncomplicated response to antidepressant drugs.

What contribution has a doctor to make in these situations? What should guide his response to the patient's complaint? There are often plenty of people to worry about a patient's condition, to create an air of consternation that may permeate the whole community or church. The great asset the doctor can bring to such a charged atmosphere is his professional mantle of detachment—calm, rational, enquiring, sympathetic but outside the drama and therefore able to retain a sense of proportion. Irrespective of his own beliefs the doctor must bring commonsense and the distillate of previous experience to help the patient. There are no guiding rules that he could have learned at medical school relevant to this situation except the method of educated curiosity and scientific enquiry. Cautious and painstaking observation, with the eliciting of a detailed history, should precede any theory or diagnosis of the patient's condition. In the long term a readiness to be sceptical is more likely to prove beneficial to the patient and those close to him than a naive acceptance of all his claims of possession at face value.

In addition to his qualities as an uninvolved participant, an objective scientist, and a physician using observation and the collation of evidence before launching into diagnosis, the Christian doctor should make practical application of basic theology; it is important that he knows the biblical principles. For example, he can know that if a Christian believer asks in faith for the Holy Spirit to come into and fill his life, and asks for forgiveness of sins and for the continuing presence of God, then the devil or a demon cannot be in possession of such a person (John 14:15–31). '. . . The Father will give you another Counsellor . . . the Spirit of truth . . . he lives with you and will be in you . . . Because I live, you also will live . . . the prince of this world is coming. He has no hold on me . . .'. Jesus Christ, the Truth, brings freedom from lies, and one of these lies is the superstitious part of the belief in demons. Jesus said 'the devil . . . was a murderer from the beginning, not holding to the truth, for there is no truth in him'. All superstitions are lies, and it is a part of the truth that comes in Christ to realize that they are false and that they have no power. Jesus *is* the truth (John 14:6).

Those involved in Christian counselling should be very wary. There may be individuals who, despite reassurance, continue to feel or be influenced by others into believing that they are possessed, and they may doubt the genuineness of their own conversion and subsequent spiritual experience. It is wrong to collude with such people in their fears; they require gentle but consistent reminding of the biblical facts.

In the words of Charles Wesley, 'He breaks the power of cancelled sin'; that is, the sin has been forgiven and the authority of the devil already broken when a sinner accepts redemption in Christ. In such a case, for a believer to feel that he is possessed and overpowered by a demon must be the acceptance of a lie rather than the truth. It is knowledge of the scripture that reveals such a belief to be false. A Christian believer who has never intended to have dealings with the devil nor given himself over to a deliberate way of life of evil cannot, by accident, become possessed, and one should therefore look for alternative explanation if such are his feelings.

In such a case, where a believer without mental illness believes himself to be possessed, deliverance is not by exorcism but by the apprehending of orthodox biblical doctrine on the nature of the relationship between God and man and the practical significance of the word of Christ: theology not ritual. In fact, if ritual or ceremony is used in such a case by a well-meaning clergyman in order to reassure the subject, it may have the opposite effect; by asserting the need for ritual it reinforces the person's belief that a demonic problem exists. In this area, doctors need to be very clear in what they themselves believe and there is no substitute for detailed study of biblical principles.

The Faust Contract

Goethe recounts the old legend of a learned doctor who, knowing quite clearly what he is doing, sells his soul to the devil for the price of enjoyment, power and success.[9]

There are certainly some people who, believing in the existence of God and the Devil, quite deliberately choose to serve and relate to the latter. Some devil worshippers and Satanists are sincere in their belief rather than using it in any fraudulent way. They will not usually admit their beliefs readily to a doctor, and in fact, many of them reject traditional medical care, perhaps because of its Christian origins; they may only come to be receiving medical treatment because of some emergency presenting with physical or mental symptoms. In our experience they are agitated and apprehensive while in hospital; they may react with hostility, suspicion and distrust towards the staff. It is quite certain that they will not obtain peace of mind while their allegiance is to Satan, and the doctor is surely entitled to say this without transgressing his medical relationship with the patient.

Mental illness in such people may be reactive to the conflict and guilt engendered or secondary to other problems within their human relationships. It is also true that a person with a psychiatric condition, recognizing that something is wrong but not knowing what to do about it, may mistakenly seek an amelioration of symptoms using various means such as illicit drugs or joining minority organizations. An involvement with witchcraft may be an example of the latter, and therefore it is worth looking for a primary mental illness which could then be treated appropriately. If this is found, psychiatric treatment should precede any measures intended to help the person deal with his involvement with the occult. It is not at all uncommon for a person involved in witchcraft as an assistant to the main adepts to become acutely anxious about his involvement and show psychological or physical symptoms of anxiety.

Many of the contemporary adepts of witchcraft claim that theirs is a religion alternative to and older than Christianity, and should be regarded in our society as parallel with Buddhism or Islam in representing a substantial minority group. This is a mistaken notion for two main reasons. First, there is no uniform doctrine within witchcraft; it is not an identifiable religion with a core of beliefs. Each coven dictates its own practices with no central control and only minimal influence from other groups. Covens vary from the apparently innocuous to the extremely vicious; although the lack of clear information from many groups necessarily makes their practices suspect. Second, there is no evidence to support any historical continuity from Druidic times, or from the Ephesian worship of Diana. The persecution of witches in the fifteenth, sixteenth, and seventeenth centuries was thought to indicate that there was a substantial and organized following of witchcraft at this time. In fact, according to Cohn, this was a collective myth and there was no organized subversive cult of Satanism in Europe.[8]

A patient's self-description of feelings of guilt is not necessarily a reliable indicator of moral, legal or theological guilt. In most instances, when a person feels guilty, this is an appropriate acknowledgement that he has done something which contravenes his own moral principles. However, an identical subjective experience of feeling guilty may occur as a symptom in severe depressive illness following behaviour that is essentially not discordant with that person's own moral standards; that is, if he were well, he would not feel guilty on this occasion. A middle-aged woman described profound feelings of guilt and unworthiness. When asked what she felt guilty about she said that her house did not belong to her, her married daughters were illegitimate and she had stolen all the money she possessed. When one of her daughters remonstrated with her that none of these claims was true, she said, 'That shows how wicked I am, telling lies like that'. Guilt feelings occur as a symptom of depressive illness, an epiphenomenon, and not as evidence of a moral lapse. The distinction between an appropriate sense of guilt and pathological guilt feelings as a sympton is difficult, sometimes arbitrary, but always important; it must depend upon the demonstration of other clear evidence of depressive illness.

The position of those who have deliberately placed themselves under Satanic power or demonic influences and now regret this, is that they can be forgiven and reconciled with God through the propitiatory work of Christ. Such a person, who regrets his previous allegiance to powers of evil, cannot have committed the *unforgiveable sin* (. . . whoever blasphemes against the Holy Spirit will never be forgiven; he is guilty of an eternal sin: Mark 3:29) for one vitally important reason: 'If we confess our sins, he is faithful and just and will forgive us our sins and purify us from all unrighteousness' (1 John 1:9). It is quite clear that repentance and confession, committing oneself to the mercy of God, always results in forgiveness; the unforgiveable sin is unforgiveable only because the offender has removed himself from the influence of the Spirit of God so utterly as to be unable to ask for forgiveness.

There is quite clear biblical authority that the repentant Satanist can be forgiven. If such a person suffers from an identifiable physical or mental illness, he can also be treated in a manner appropriate to that particular diagnosis. The doctor should not be beguiled by the particular *content* of the mental illness or the nature of the presentation of physical illness into thinking that an entirely different order of treatment is required, or even into believing that no treatment at all is possible. A Satanist who contracts pneumonia following the celebration of a wintry Sabbath requires antibiotics;

the symptoms of psychotic depression will demand appropriate treatment with antidepressant drugs or electroconvulsive therapy.

The phenomenology of believing oneself to be possessed

Belief that one is possessed by outside influences is a psychic phenomenon and is therefore accessible to investigation by the methods of *phenomenology*; that is, the nature of the self-experience can be examined irrespective of whether the belief is true or false, and irrespective of whether there is mental illness present. This method of exploration was introduced into psychiatry by Karl Jaspers, and it relies upon a skilled and expert use of the capacity for empathy.[10] At the present time when the aetiology of most mental disorders remains unknown this process of eliciting the patient's subjective phenomena is the only rational way of ordering psychiatric diagnosis. By detailed questioning, the doctor attempts to build up such a clear impression of how the patient is experiencing symptoms that, when the doctor gives an account of the patient's mental state, the latter recognizes this as his own.

In using phenomenology in examination of the mental state for diagnosis, there is an important distinction between *form* and *content*.

This distinction may be thought esoteric but, especially with possession states, has considerable practical application. The form indicates the likely diagnosis; thus a delusional percept is characteristic of schizophrenia: the content arises from the socio-cultural background and predominant interests of the patient. A person who was previously very devout, on becoming mentally ill, may show religious content whatever is the nature or form of the abnormal mental experience. The self-description of 'being possessed by demons' is one of content, the precise form will vary according to the nature of the illness, if illness be present. An added advantage for the doctor in using this phenomenological approach is that it demands that he follow the vitally important principle of accepting his patient's experience and values as described by the patient himself rather than imposing upon him the theories and explanations of the doctor.

A person may believe himself to be possessed because, in the manner of Dr. Faustus, he has taken active steps to invite demons into his life. Clearly, to do this he must believe in demons and that such an occurrence as possession is possible. There is nothing intrinsic to holding such views to suggest that mental illness, if present, demonstrates psychosis, although there may be other evidence of such disturbance. A person with a neurotic disability may experience a possession state, so also may somebody with depressive psychosis and, most commonly, it occurs in schizophrenia. The form is different in these three conditions, each of which will now be described in more detail.

Neurotic involvement in the occult

Neurosis is not *disease* in the sense of being an organic disturbance of physiological function, yet it is a potent cause of disability in social relationships and functioning, and of disturbance in personal wellbeing. It can be seen as an inappropriate psychological or emotional reaction to a perceived stress, in that the person's behaviour is not effective in removing or coping with that stress. In personality disorder, the person himself or other people suffer as a direct result of his abnormality of personality. Personality is a long-term characteristic of the individual, and so personality disorder is likely to be manifested throughout life, although it will be modified by social circumstances. There is considerable overlap between neurosis and personality disorder; personality disorder predisposes to neurotic reaction.

There are particular attractions for the neurotic both in the social aspects of *belonging* to a Satanist group, and also in the nature of the *beliefs*. Neurosis impairs both the individual self-image and the ability to establish human relationships. This creates a craving for a sense of belonging. The neurotic looks at other people and envies them their freedom to establish mutually rewarding relationships, knowing that his own attempts are so often unsuccessful. The *shared secret* aspect of a minority religious group is attractive, and the external opposition which is the inevitable consequence of this strengthens the cohesiveness of the group. In a sense, therefore, the more the group or coven flouts standards of conventional morality, the more outside opposition and suspicion it will arouse and the greater the sense of unity and conformity among the devotees will be, so that the feeling of alienation the neurotic usually experiences with others will be submerged within the all-pervasive, all-controlling ethos of the group.

The sensationalism of the witchcraft cell or coven will be attractive to many with neurotic personality disturbances also. This is particularly apposite for the attention-seeking, sensation-craving element in the *hysterical* or *histrionic* personality disorder. Those of neurotic disposition will frequently describe conflict within the family in which they were brought up, arguments between themselves and their parents, and an unhappy childhood. This may well predispose to problems in the way they cope with *authority*. The non-conformity of demonism, the way it affects public morals, even those aspects which may be covertly illegal, will all be attractive to those with such long-term problems with authority figures.

The neurotic person has often had repeated experience of failure in achievement and in personal relationships so that he has come to believe that failure is inevitable, and, in his attitude to others, he is aware of his own inferiority and is expecting further humiliation. In the ritual of witchcraft and in the organization of a cohesive group such a person may find both a possibility of succeeding and an opportunity to dominate others in a way that has never been possible in the larger society. These different elements may mean that a neurotic person heavily involved with witchcraft may find a sense of fulfilment that he has not previously known. Of course, as Christians, we realize that the same psycho-social set may exist when the neurotic person joins a church, especially if this is a group with extreme beliefs and practices which may thereby arouse considerable local opposition.

A group dynamic has occurred surprisingly often in many minor heretical religious sects, including many covens, in which three distinct roles can be recognized. There is the *seer* whose visionary statements are often unintelligible to other people. Not uncommonly this person, whose productions may amount to no more than gibberish, is psychotic, and far from being the leader is actually a dupe who is being used by the interpreter and by the rest of the group. *The interpreter* is often the real leader who dominates the rest of the group. He or she is manipulative, controlling, and may often be neurotic with perhaps personality disorder of either hysterical or psychopathic type. The *followers* in the group may well include many people with neurotic symptoms and dependency needs as described above. A very good description of this dynamic of seer and interpreter occurs in C. S. Lewis' book, *The Last Battle*, in which an ingenious ape dresses his donkey stooge in a lion skin to become a simulated Aslan, or God; meanwhile the ape as his mouthpiece, in fact, completely controls him.[11]

The very need for which the person with neurotic problems has inappropriately sought fulfilment in witchcraft can be seen as an aspiration which could have been met in salvation through Jesus Christ, in faith, and through the fellowship of the Church. Obviously this is not a medical form of treatment, but the Christian doctor does well to introduce people who express such a need to a church where they will find help. This does not just mean saying, 'There is a church on the corner where you can go if you feel like it', but implies arranging an introduction with the minister or relevant person in the church.

Neurosis can be treated in that those who wish to receive treatment can usually be helped to more effective modes of coping. There is a range of psychological methods of treatment including dynamic, behavioural and cognitive psychotherapies. Social aspects of treatment are important; drugs have a much lesser part to play in management.[12]

In many instances the general practitioner can be just as, if not more, effective than a psychiatrist, but he does need to have knowledge in this area and appropriate training. He needs to have sufficient psychiatric knowledge and experience to have the confidence to treat those who can be helped and to have the judgement to refrain from becoming involved in potentially disastrous situations.

AFFECTIVE PSYCHOSIS AND THE OCCULT

Affective psychosis is typified by disturbance of mood which exceeds the normal swings, and may last for several months, being experienced as either depression, which is common, or mania, or rarely a mixture of both occurring synchronously. This mood disturbance may be accompanied by delusions, perplexity, disturbed attitude to self, disorder of perception and behaviour, and a strong tendency to suicide.[13] Between 1 and 4% of the population can be expected to have at least one attack of this illness at some time in their lives; it is commoner in women than men, and in older rather than in younger people.

With the depression of mood, there is a generalized lowering of vitality, retardation of mental and physical activity, loss of the ability to experience emotion, especially enjoyment, and also feelings of unworthiness and guilt; hypochondriacal ideas are also frequent. When this condition is severe there may be *delusions* of guilt or unworthiness, and also hypochondriacal or nihilistic delusions. Characteristic of the latter was the patient who said, 'I do not exist, the devil has taken me to Hell.' Suicidal ideas, ruminations and impulses are common, and there is always a serious risk of suicide in depression.

It is not surprising that with such symptoms, beliefs about possession and demonic influence are a not infrequent *content* of the illness in those whose religious views tend towards the possibility of such involvement. This is exemplified by 'a judge who believed his wife was possessed by the devil, became obsessed with religion and beat her. At one stage, he even claimed that they must both die because the devil was in them.'[14] This judge was a man of strong religious conviction and he suffered from recurrent episodes of manic-depressive psychosis. In a severe depressive state it is the patient who is likely to complain of being possessed by the devil because of profound guilt feelings, which may amount to delusions. Delusions of control or influence are not normally present; the claim to be possessed arises from mood and is metaphorical: 'I believe myself to be so evil that the only possible explanation is that I have a devil in me.' The feelings are those of guilt for which this is a logical explanation, rather than an actual experience of external control. In such a case the victim will not usually have taken any steps to encourage such possession; in fact he will usually describe having fought a battle against the devil over a considerable time, which he now believes he has lost. Although a non-medical person may take such an account at face value, a doctor should look carefully for other symptoms of depression. Vigorous treatment of depression is essential, and can be life-saving; failure to treat because the doctor is misled by the religious nature of the symptoms into thinking the condition is spiritual rather than psychiatric may be followed by the patient's suicide. In depressive illness antidepressant drugs are of proved efficacy and, where depressive delusions are present, the patient may require electroconvulsive therapy. It could reasonably be regarded as negligent to omit such physical treatments in severely depressed patients; however, this treatment is not enough in itself. As the patient recovers from the acute depressive illness, he needs to be able to accept himself as a person who has been mentally ill and to work out once again what are his beliefs, particularly those pertaining to his relationship with God and also possession by demons. Taking up his normal position in society, both at work and also perhaps as a member of a church, will be difficult because of the loss of self-esteem engendered by 'having been ill' and 'having held unorthodox beliefs'. Ideally, this *reincorporative psychotherapy* should involve cooperation and understanding between the minister and doctor.

POSSESSION AND SCHIZOPHRENIA

Among psychiatric illnesses schizophrenia is both the commonest cause to account for possession, and the most florid and bizarre in its presentation. The most important symptoms of schizophrenia in this context are delusions, hallucinations and passivity experiences.

Passivity experiences (or delusions of control) are those in which the person believes himself to be influenced or controlled from outside himself. Many authors, for example Jaspers,[10] have regarded the self-experience of the schizophrenic to be intrinsically different from normal, and ultimately *un-understandable*. In normal health we know with absolute certainty where *I* ends and *not I* begins; however, the schizophrenic has a loss, or interference or blurring of such *ego boundaries,* so that he perceives as 'outside himself' voices or processes which are actually going on inside his head; he believes his impulses are imposed upon him from outside; or he experiences his own thoughts being drawn out of him and broadcast whereas, in fact, they remain unknown to all save himself.

Watson[15] has regarded some religious experiences as being similar in nature to the symptoms of schizophrenia, but whereas the latter remain long-term the former are transitory. There are, however, more fundamental differences: (1) Religious experiences are regarded by the believer as being metaphorical or spiritual; the boundaries of self are not invaded. In fact the paradox for the Christian is that he is freer and more independent of external influence when Christ 'lives in him' than previously. (2) Religious experiences provoke sustained, meaningful constructive activity—'good works', 'a changed life', 'regular devotions', whereas the behaviour that results from a schizophrenic experience is often irrational in that it does not follow logically from the experience, bizarre in that it flouts popular *mores,* concrete in making spiritual values physical, and degraded in that it trivializes the sublime. A patient experienced 'the fiery darts of the wicked' (Eph. 6:16 AV) as 'pin pricks all over my head through which demonic thoughts are injected'. (3) The schizophrenic delusions and hallucinations are associated with a loss of ego boundaries; they are often based upon delusional evidence. (4) Religious beliefs are held alongside the possiblity of religious doubts; in this they are like other *abstract concepts*. Schizophrenic delusions and hallucinations are accepted without doubt in a manner reminiscent of *concrete reality*; one does not have doubts about the existence of the chair one sits on.

Form, the nature of the psychic phenomena, and *content*, the ambience of that form, were discussed earlier. Transcultural studies of schizophrenia have shown a remarkable constancy of the form of the condition, but the content is quite different in different cultures. To ascribe delusions and passivity experiences to demons, the sufferer has to believe in demons and to live in a subculture which accepts the notion of demons. A man brought up as a child in Sunday School and church in a small village believed that Satan, the Archangel, was 'taking away my body and mind and soul to Market Drayton'. He used to write to the 'University,

Radio-isotope unit' (such productions usually reached the University Department of Psychiatry), asking for 'radio-active materials and nuclear waste' to prevent this supposed activity of Satan upon him. The form of this illness included both delusions and passivity of thinking; the content contained both material about demons from the background of his early life, and the vocabulary of physics from his current watching of television. Most practising psychiatrists could readily supply similar examples. The diagnosis is not based upon the belief of the patient in demons, but on the presence of the distinctive form of the illness. Diagnosis is often most readily made in possibly-schizophrenic patients who use religious language by examining their mental state when they talk about areas of their life that are not intrinsically religious and in which they would not reasonably use religious expressions.

Passivity experiences or delusions of control are subjectively experienced as states of possession by powers outside oneself. When the content is of demonic or satanic possession it obviously poses a problem of diagnosis for the doctor or minister. The most useful indicators of schizophrenia in such a situation are the presence of clearcut schizophrenic symptoms in other areas of a patient's life, the concrete corporeal way in which the description of possession is phrased, the prolonged nature of this experience of being completely controlled (religious ecstacy states in a non-psychotic person are usually transient and evanescent), the evidence upon which the beliefs are based are also in themselves delusional, and finally the pattern of behaviour resulting from the beliefs are problematic and bizarre rather than lofty or altruistic.

Exorcism

In the Gospels, Jesus not only describes the effects of demons upon individuals but he also commands them to leave those who are possessed (Mark 9:25). He also gives to his disciples the authority to cast them out (Matt. 10.1).

However, there are very considerable dangers associated with exorcism as witnessed by the notorious case from Ossett, near Wakefield, in which a man killed his wife after an intense, prolonged and highly emotionally-charged ceremony of exorcism, believing her to be a demon that had to be destroyed. The exorcism had taken place over two full nights, by the end of which the man was in a dissociated state of mind amounting to insanity. Because of this risk of the situation getting out of hand, it is not unusual for responsible church leaders to seek a medical opinion when exorcism has been suggested.

We have already discussed many situations which at first sight would suggest demon possession, but prove on more detailed examination to reveal mental illness. There are also many similarities between the rituals associated with exorcism and certain techniques of psychiatric treatment involving *suggestion* and *abreaction*.[16] Hypnosis or drugs are used to achieve heightened suggestibility during a state of altered awareness in order to remove symptoms and produce marked change of attitudes; some states of possession develop, or are generated, in a similar way.[17] The techniques for exorcism are remarkably similar in many different cultures and with different religions all over the world.[18]

Both Anglican and Roman Catholic theologians and experts on possession and exorcism have produced lists of diagnostic signs whereby those possessed and requiring exorcism may be identified. Unordained members of charismatic fellowships have also looked for recognizable features—almost stigmata. Although it is wholly appropriate for the minister of religion to approach this very difficult area in the manner that enables him to function most effectively and be of most help to those he serves, I do not consider this appropriate for the patient's doctor. While being prepared to accept the possibility of Satanic possession and influence, and to work in sympathy with the minister of religion, the Christian doctor is being most helpful when he functions as a doctor, using his diagnostic skill and therapeutic ability to exclude the possibility of psychiatric disorder. When such illness is present, he treats it medically; when he blurs the distinction of role between doctor and minister in this area, he may imperil his patient and remove from him an objective and uninvolved potential source of support.

Those empowered by the church to carry out exorcism should know of the possibility of confusing spiritual problems with psychiatric illness. They should also know of the potential dangers involved in creating the intense emotional atmosphere experienced by a group of people during the ritual of exorcism. A failure of exorcism to relieve the victim's fears and anxieties will, in fact, increase his feelings of guilt, isolation and despair. Carrying out the ceremonial of exorcism on a person suffering from a psychotic illness such as schizophrenia is likely to exacerbate the condition both by increasing the intensity of emotion and by playing upon the delusions. In Barker's study of a large number of people in whom premonitions, predictions, auto-suggestion and Voodoo preceded the victim's death,[19] magical ritual was an important factor.

Psychological Explanations

All thinking or behaviour can be given a psychological explanation, that is, it is mediated in accord with psychological mechanisms. This does not mean that, for example, faith has no basis, but is 'only psychological'. Faith can be examined in psychological terms in the same way that the print of this book or the paper it is written on could be examined chemically; the chemical analysis of the materials can make no comment at all on the truth or otherwise of what is written in the book. Scientific explanation may describe the process, it cannot comment upon the message. A psychological, psychiatric examination of the experience of possession may give useful information about the presence or absence of mental illness.

There is not one, universal, psychological explanation but many; these depend upon the type of experience and the perspective of the psychological observer. One type of psychological explanation is based upon *psychodynamic* theory and stresses the importance of unconscious mechanisms. Another viewpoint is that of deterministic *behaviourism*. In the foregoing description of psychiatric syndromes a *phenomenological* or *descriptive psychopathological* approach has been used; i.e. an attempt has been used to categorize the experiences which the patient describes without attaching elaborate theory to these phenomena.

The fact that a patient's religious or demonic experience has a psychological explanation does not prevent it from also having a non-psychological explanation. A person describes 'hearing God clearly telling me' to do this. The psychiatrist will want to examine the form of the experience and other associated psychic experiences—is this an auditory hallucination or not? A person looking at this from a Christian viewpoint will want to consider the person's other religious beliefs and also what is the result in action of this supposed message from God—'by their fruit you will recognize them' (Matt. 7:16). These two approaches, far from being incompatible, are complementary.

Conclusions

There is a great emphasis upon truth in the Bible, and especially in the Gospel and Epistles of John. Jesus Christ both brings the truth (John 1:17) and *is* the truth (John 14:6). Conversely, the devil is the epitome of falsehood: 'the work of Satan displayed in all kinds of counterfeit miracles, signs and wonders, and in every sort of evil that deceives' (2 Thess. 2:9f). Jesus' teaching concerns truth in its entirety. 'If you hold to my teaching, you are really my disciples. Then you will know the truth, and the truth will set you free' (John

8:31f). Again, not having the knowledge of the truth that is in God is bondage or slavery (Gal. 4:8). The devil is 'a spirit that makes you a slave again to fear' (Rom. 8:15).

Demon possession is an example of how Satan uses evil to confuse with lies and with fear. Demons are the personification of the powers of evil. The truth in Christ removes these powers altogether, thereby removing the very existence of these demons, showing them to be lies of the devil. People without Christ live 'in the futility of their thinking. They are darkened in their understanding and separated from the life of God because of the ignorance that is in them due to the hardening of their hearts' (Eph. 4:17f). But we are encouraged 'to put off falsehood' (Eph. 5:6), 'Have nothing to do with the fruitless deeds of darkness, but rather expose them' (Eph. 5:11), 'Do not be foolish but understand what the Lord's will is' (Eph. 5:17).

Syncretism is a perpetual danger within the Church. There are still those who believe that there are other gods, demons who can work a malign influence even on those who asked for the Spirit of God to occupy their lives. It is the work of the devil to persuade people that these demons exist, that they have a power which is beyond the reach of God, and that despairing submission is the only possible response. It is the clear teaching of scripture that these are falsehoods from the devil, and the spirit of God brings freedom from their power entirely, so that they become known for what they are, illusion, a distortion of perception. This is made clear by the 'light in the Lord' and we are therefore 'to live as children of light' (Eph. 5:8). 'Everything exposed by the Light becomes visible, for it is light that makes everything visible. This is why it is said:

> Wake up, O sleeper,
> rise from the dead,
> and Christ will shine on you!
> (Eph. 5:13f).

Just as the child's fearful illusion that the wind-blown curtain is a malevolent figure disappears when the electric light is switched on, so the Light removes all superstitions in the clear beam of truth. As the lies are dispelled, so freedom comes into the spirit through the truth that is Jesus Christ.

> Hobgoblin nor foul fiend
> Can daunt his spirit;
> He knows he at the end
> Shall life inherit.
>
> Then fancies flee away
> He'll not fear what men say;
> He'll labour night and day
> To be a pilgrim.

John Bunyan, *Pilgrim's Progress*

8

Healing

ROGER F. HURDING

This century has seen an explosion of concern about health and healing. The extraordinary achievements of Western physical medicine, the rise of psychologies that emphasize the 'whole man', the founding of the World Health Organization following the carnage of World War II and the emergence of charismatic and renewal movements within the Christian church are among the indicators that health is 'an idea whose time has come'.

This 'idea', which Isaak Walton urged us to value 'next to a good conscience', needs definition if we are to understand the concept of healing. The word 'health' is from the same Old English stock that gave us 'hale' (as in 'hale and hearty') in the northern dialect and 'whole' in the midlands and southern parts of England. Although the word is commonly used today as synonymous with 'soundness of body', its original meaning included the concept of well-being in every aspect of human life. This comprehensiveness accords well with the biblical view of wholeness, as is brought out by Morris Maddocks in his book *The Christian Healing Ministry* when he writes that 'health can never be equated with human wellness and an absence of disease. Health is to do with the totality of creation, with the Creator himself'.[1]

If health in this wholesomeness, God-centred sense is our ultimate objective, then, by definition, we are declaring our 'unhealth' or 'dis-ease'—and this brings us to the notion of healing. What does it mean for you or me to be healed of, say, a duodenal ulcer, a depressive illness, a broken marriage, a resolutely nursed grievance or hurtful childhood memories? Perhaps we feel that to embrace mental, emotional and social 'unhealth' as candidates for healing is widening our scope too much and yet, if we are true to biblical perspectives on health, they must be included.

Usually, in medical practice, we do not talk of healing so much as cure. This, of course, is quite appropriate within the primarily physical framework of much of our work. We may say, 'Mrs. Jones seems to be cured of her pneumonia' or, 'If only we could find a cure for more forms of cancer'. To announce, 'Mr. Smith is healed', implies, quite correctly, something more far-reaching than, say, the cure of his varicose ulcer. Michael Wilson makes a helpful distinction here when he writes that to cure means a 'restoration to function in society' whereas healing involves a 'restoration to purposeful living in society'.[2] Mr. Smith, cured of his varicose ulcer, is able to function normally once more in that he can now cycle to his job, spend his day working on the factory floor and dig his garden at weekends. We might say that Mr. Smith is healed if he is not only mobile again but has discovered a new zest for living as a responsible husband, father, neighbour, participant in the community and member of the local church.

Let us now look at the Scriptures to gauge something of their teaching on the question of healing. In turn, we shall examine in outline the ways Christian attitudes to healing have waxed and waned through the centuries, before focusing once more on the twentieth century and its burden that health is 'an idea whose time has come'. In so doing we shall describe the polarization of views about healing within the Church and seek some biblically-based resolution of these contrary opinions.

Biblical Considerations

(1) God the healer

In the Old Testament, God reveals himself as Yahweh the healer, both in his words and in his actions. This divine character is seen when, following the triumphant celebration of the Red Sea crossing, Moses led the Israelites into a drought-stricken area and on to the undrinkable waters of Marah. There, in answer to anguished prayer, the water is sweetened and the Lord then declares to the people, 'I am the Lord, your healer' (Exod. 15:26).

However, it is important to come to terms with the thought that the Lord God is not only the source of healing but is also the One who 'sends' affliction and disease. In Exodus 15, Yahweh both declares his healing power and his ability to inflict the 'diseases of the Egyptians' on his people if they should be disobedient. We see something of this mysterious emphasis again in Habakkuk 3:5 where the prophet says of God: 'Before him went pestilence, and plague followed close behind.'

Perhaps it is in the book of Job that we have the key to this 'dark mystery'. The prologue in Chapter 2 indicates that Satan, who goes 'to and fro on the earth', is the bringer of disease. 'So Satan went forth from the presence of the Lord, and afflicted Job with loathsome sores . . .' (v.7). And yet we also read that the Lord God has said to the Adversary, ' "Behold, he (Job) is in your power; only spare his life." ' (v.6). It is as if Satan is like a wild and ferocious beast which, although roaming the earth, is kept on a chain. Unfortunately for us the chain is a long one, and yet, happily, the chain is fastened most securely. The Enemy can go so far and no further. Moreover, his activities are by divine permission. The devil and his angels have strength and influence but they are held in check by a greater power and will.

This twin perspective of a God who not only heals but sends affliction, whether through the Adversary or directly, is shown when Job speaks of the Almighty: 'For he wounds, but he binds up; he smites, but his hands heal' (5:18).

(2) HEALING AND FALLEN HUMANITY

Having established that Yahweh is both healer and afflicter, it is essential that we raise the question of the link, if any, between sickness and sin, and, by implication, between healing and repentance. As we study the Old Testament we can discern two strands in a possible answer.

Firstly, on occasions there is a clear association between individual, or corporate, sin and consequent affliction. The story of Miriam, Moses' sister, in Numbers 12 is a case in point. She and Aaron, perhaps out of resentment towards Moses' 'foreign' wife, Zipporah (Exod. 2:21), complained about their brother's special place in Yahweh's plans. Consequently, she is struck with a disfiguring skin disease. However, through Moses' pleading on her behalf, her illness seems to last only seven days before she is restored within the encampment. Similarly, Psalm 38, one of the so-called 'psychosomatic psalms', demonstrates the linkage between suffering and sin. David cries out to the Lord that 'there is no soundness in my flesh because of thy indignation; there is no health in my bones because of my sin' (v.3). Conversely, in Psalm 32:3–5 we see that repentance and forgiveness lead to healing. The

psalmist recalls that when he declared not his sin, his 'body wasted away'; he goes on to rejoice in the Lord's forgiveness and its consequent blessings.

Secondly, the Old Testament propounds that there is no inevitable connection between sickness and wrongdoing. There is, for example, no intimation that the fatal illness that afflicted the son of the widow of Zarephath was due to personal sin, although the child's mother exclaimed to Elijah, 'What have you against me, O man of God? You have come to me to bring my sin to remembrance, and to cause the death of my son!' (1 Kgs. 17:18). The miraculous healing that followed the prophet's prayers says, it seems, much more about the authentication of Elijah's ministry than any link between family sin and the boy's illness. 'And the woman said to Elijah, "Now I know that you are a man of God, and that the word of the Lord in your mouth is truth" ' (v.24).

Although the Bible reveals that all that spoils the created order, including disease, is a product of humankind's rebellion against the Creator, the story of Job explodes for all time the myth that there is an inexorable connection between personal sin and the individual's sickness. Chapter 1 opens with the declaration that Job 'was blameless and upright, one who feared God, and turned away from evil'; and yet, as we have seen, this same man was afflicted with a foul and suppurating rash which covered and disfigured his entire body. It is not, of course, that Job was sinless but that there was no causal link between any lack of personal worth and his disease. Inevitably, with such a god-fearing man, his illness was a learning experience. Surviving the theological niceties and barbed criticisms of his 'comforters' and the revelation of his holy and righteous God, Job finds a deep repentance, restoration and healing. 'And the Lord restored the fortunes of Job, when he had prayed for his friends; and the Lord gave Job twice as much as he had before' (42:10).

(3) Other healers

As we have already seen, Yahweh is the supreme healer. In Psalm 103:3 David praises the Lord 'who forgives all your iniquity, who heals all your diseases'. The Old Testament does not deny that there are other powers that can produce 'signs and wonders' but any such miracles are deemed inferior to those worked by God. Indeed such miracle-working may be in opposition to Yahweh, as is seen in the confrontation between Moses and Aaron, and Pharaoh. We read in Exodus 7:11 that the magicians of Egypt, when faced by the miraculous power of the Lord God, 'did the same by their secrets'. However, the snakes that they conjured up were promptly swallowed by the superior metamorphosed rod of Aaron.

There is very little in the Old Testament about the healing art of medicine, although there are somewhat incidental mentionings of 'physicians' in Genesis, Job and Jeremiah. In 2 Chronicles 16:12 we read that King Asa of Judah became 'diseased in his feet, and his disease became severe'. The censure that follows seems to be because 'he did not seek the Lord' rather than as the result of seeking 'help from physicians'. His sin was not in attending the doctors but in not attending to the Deity.

The account of King Hezekiah's illness and recovery in 2 Kings 20 is a specific indicator that Yahweh is ultimately the Lord of all true healing—by whatever legitimate means. Facing certain death from septicaemia in an age long before antibiotics, he cries to the Lord with bitter tears. His vehement praying is heard and Isaiah returns to the king with the welcome news that he will be healed and granted a reprieve of fifteen years. Isaiah completes this announcement of divine intervention with the prosaic words, 'Bring a cake of figs. And let them take and lay it on the boil, that he may recover' (v.7). The Lord God the healer restores both miraculously and through the quiet emollient action of a primitive poultice.

Following the Exile, during the intertestamental period, it seems that Judaism built up a most rigid system of beliefs that argued that sickness is invariably the result of individual sin. This unyielding view, as we have seen, is a stranger to biblical teaching and owed a great deal to Greek influences. As Albrecht Oepke has written: 'Judaism . . . can ascribe a particular fault to each sickness, and to each fault a punishment. Ulcers and dropsy are on account of immorality and licentiousness, quinsy on account of neglecting tithes, leprosy on account of blasphemy, bloodshed and perjury, epilepsy and the crippling of children on account of marital infidelity.'[3]

The words of the devout Jew Ben Sira in Ecclesiasticus, written at about 190 BC, may have been aimed as a corrective to such intransigent thinking. His declaration in Chapter 38:1–15 seems not only to be in harmony with the biblical record but is also immensely reassuring to the medical profession! 'Honour the doctor with the honour that is his due in return for his services; for he too has been created by the Lord . . . My son, when you are ill, do not be depressed, but pray to the Lord and he will heal you . . . Then let the doctor take over—the Lord created him too—and do not let him leave you, for you need him.'[4]

(4) CHRIST THE HEALER

As we turn to the pages of the New Testament even the most casual reader is struck by the dominance of Christ the healer. As Morton Kelsey has noted, nearly one-fifth of the Gospel record is taken up with either accounts of the Lord's healings or the reactions and debates arising from them. Kelsey adds that there are forty-one distinct occasions of healings mentioned in the four Gospels.[5]

However, we should appreciate that our Lord's healing work was part and parcel of his overall mission to God's needy world. It is made abundantly clear in the Gospels that Jesus came to reveal the Father by both his words and his actions. As we read in Matthew 4:23: 'And he went about all Galilee, teaching in their synagogues and preaching the gospel of the kingdom and healing every disease and every infirmity among the people.' In Mark 1:35–39 we see that, following a heavy day of teaching and healing in Capernaum, Jesus rose early the next morning and 'went out to a lonely place' to pray. His disciples eventually tracked him down and exclaimed, 'Every one is searching for you.' It appears that the miraculous healings of the previous evening had, not surprisingly, led to a massive search-party on behalf of the afflicted. Our Lord's reply is instructive: 'Let us go on to the next towns, that I may preach there also; for that is why I came out.' Although these words suggest the priority of proclaiming the good news verbally, the account continues, 'And he went throughout all Galilee, preaching in the synagogues and casting out demons.' Jesus' calling was not primarily a great healing crusade, a sort of, 'Make Israel Healthy' campaign, and yet there is no doubt that his preaching and healing were inextricably linked.

Perhaps the nature of the Lord's earthly ministry has its most all-embracing statement in the account in Luke 4:16–21 where we read of Jesus' declaration in the synagogue of Nazareth that Isaiah 61:1,2 has been fulfilled in him. 'He opened the book and found the place where it was written, "The Spirit of the Lord is upon me, because he has anointed me to preach good news to the poor. He has sent me to proclaim release to the captives and recovering of sight to the blind, to set at liberty those who are oppressed, to proclaim the acceptable year of the Lord." ' Although some take these words as purely figurative, the contexts both in Isaiah and here in Luke (and the parallel passages in Matthew and Mark) indicate that the Lord's messianic claim is to deliver humankind from every kind of bondage in every area of life.

This same comprehensiveness is implied in the very name Jesus, the Greek form of the old Testament Jewish name Joshua. Morris

Maddocks quotes Dr. Coggan who has commented on this name: 'Here was an idea whose roots went deep down into Jewish soil. Jesus—Joshua—deliverance *from* and *to* . . . The Name which is above every name is derived from a Hebrew root that denotes "to be spacious" '.[6] One is reminded of those statements in the Old Testament that link Yahweh's deliverance with a new spaciousness in life. For example, Psalm 18:19 rejoices in the 'Lord who rescues' with the words, 'He brought me forth into a broad place; he delivered me, because he delighted in me.' This entering of a broad, or large, place through the Lord's deliverance is evocative of the way Jesus the Saviour can widen our horizons as he fulfils Isaiah's messianic promise. The Kingdom of Heaven is at hand. The new age has begun—and one of the hallmarks of its inauguration is the healing power of Christ made manifest.

Before examining the Lord's healing miracles more closely, let us briefly comment on the main Greek verbs used in the New Testament that are relevant to our theme: *therapeuo, iaomai, hygiaino* and *sozo*.[7]

Therapeuo means to heal or cure; in ancient Greece the word gradually shifted in its meaning from 'to serve a superior', to 'care for another' and so 'to cure, usually by medical means'. The noun 'therapy' is, of course, woven deeply into our modern medical language. *Therapeuo* occurs almost exclusively in the synoptic gospels and Acts, and refers primarily to the miraculous healings of Jesus and his disciples.

Iaomai means to cure or restore, and had both a medical and figurative usage in Greek from Homer's day onwards. Its latter use included freeing from evil as well as psychological healing. The noun *iatros*, physician, is from the same root and gives us the adjective 'iatrogenic' to indicate illness actually caused by the medical profession. In the New Testament the use of *iaomai* is similar to that of *therapeuo*.

Hygiaino means to make well again or cure. Derived from *Hygeia*, the name of the Greek goddess of health, its use was linked with the concept of being healthy, shrewd and of a sound mind. In the Old Testament the Hebrew word, *Shalom*, 'Peace be to you', is generally translated by the noun *hygiaine* in the Septuagint. Morris Maddocks in *The Christian Healing Ministry* emphasizes the importance of the concept of *shalom* in any consideration of healing in that it means 'well-being in the widest sense of the word—prosperity, bodily health, contentedness, good relations between nations and men, salvation'.[8] *Hygiaino*, almost equally distributed between the Gospels and the Pastoral Epistles, has a similarly enlarged meaning and is used in the sense of a profound healing of the whole person. It is the derivative word *hygiainonta* that occurs in the parable of the prodigal son (or, better, as has been pointed out—'the parable of the prodigal father', in that the father's love was prodigal, lavish) when one of the servants replies to the elder son at the wanderer's return: 'Your brother has come, and your father has killed the fatted calf, because he has received him *safe and sound*' (Luke 15:27). Our use of the word 'hygiene' today seems insipid compared with the resplendence of the term's earlier meaning.

Sozo means to save, preserve or rescue, and comes from the same root as *soteria*, salvation, deliverance or preservation. The ancient Greeks regarded their gods as saviours and used *sozo* to refer to divine help in averting life-threatening dangers. It is used sixteen times in the synoptic Gospels of miraculous healing and has the sense of delivering from evil in order to heal the whole being.

(5) The Healing Miracles of Jesus

Before considering the hallmarks of the Lord's healings it is helpful to see these miracles against the background of the healing arts of Greece. As we do so, we need to appreciate that there are, at least, records of miraculous cures outside the Bible and, at the same time, that the healings of Jesus are quite unique.

It is generally held that rational forms of Western medical practice began in ancient Egypt in the third millennium BC although these eventually degenerated into sorcery.[9] Similarly, the ancient Greeks adopted a range of magical incantations and prayers towards their deities for, as Oepke has written, in the Hellenistic mind 'the gods become mediators between Zeus and men, and as such they dispense healing'.[10]

The Greeks looked most of all to the demi-god Aesculapius for the relief of human misery and a number of temples were dedicated to him as sanctuaries of healing. One of these, the temple of Epidauros, was something of an 'ancient Lourdes' whose priests kept records of the god's cures. Needy people would sleep in the temple's colonnades under a form of hypnosis known as 'incubation'. Some of these 'healings' were not particularly eventful; for example:

> Enippos had had for six years the point of a spear in his cheek. As he was sleeping the god extracted the spear-head and gave it to him into his hands. When the day came Enippos departed cured and he held the spear-head in his hands.[11]

Some were spectacular in the extreme as when a woman with a pregnancy said to be of five years' duration was delivered of a four-year-old son! The recorded cures at Epidauros also included the alleviation of gout, sciatica, headaches, parasitic infestations and baldness. In the sixth century BC a more reputable form of medicine emerged around the figure of Hippocrates on the island of Cos. Although this Hippocratic school initiated formal medical study as well as a code of ethics for physicians, strong elements of magic were still interwoven with this more scientific practice.

It is in the context of the more sensational, and sometimes grotesque ingredients in early Greek treatment of illness that the miraculous healings of Jesus stand out in constrasting beauty and simplicity. We can explore their uniqueness under the headings What?, Why? and How?

(a) What?

As we study the content of our Lord's healings we are struck by the chronicity and seriousness of the illnesses of those he restored to health. Their maladies include such organic conditions as blindness, deafness, dumbness, spinal deformity, paralysis, 'leprosy', menorrhagia and 'dropsy', as well as a complexity of mental and spiritual disorder implicit on those occasions when he 'cast out many demons' (see Chapter 7). Moreover, he also dealt with acute disease and trauma as when he healed Simon Peter's mother-in-law who was 'sick with a fever' (Mk. 1:29–31) and restored the severed ear of the high priest's slave (Luke 22:49–51). Profoundest of all, in terms of dealing with 'incurable' conditions, he raised individuals from death on at least three occasions—a widow's only son (Luke 7:11–15), a twelve-year-old girl (Luke 8:41ff.) and a close personal friend (John 11). We see something of the comprehensiveness of Jesus' power over humankind's infirmities in Matthew 4:23: 'And he went about all Galilee, teaching in their synagogues and preaching the gospel of the kingdom and healing every disease and every infirmity among the people.'

This all-encompassing victory over human illness dazzles the eyes when compared with the sometimes crude, sometimes punitive, sometimes suspect healing arts of the ancient Greeks with their tendency to major on the functional rather than on the chronically organic and spiritual.

(b) How?

At the deepest level Jesus healed by the power of God. This perspective comes out succinctly in Luke 5:17 which introduces us to a particularly momentous day in his Galilean ministry: 'and the power of the Lord was with him to heal'. At a secondary, but nevertheless vital, level our Lord used a variety of means to effect healing, including word, touch, certain physical media and the faith of both recipient and onlooker.

Although there were two occasions of healing when Jesus used touch alone and five when he simply spoke a word of command, it was commoner for him to do both.[12] A case in point is the encounter with 'the man full of leprosy' described in Luke 5:12–16. In response to the sick man's plea, 'Lord, if you will, you can make me clean', Jesus 'stretched out his hand, and touched him, saying, "I will; be clean." '

Jesus' acceptance of life in its entirety, including the physical, is shown not only in his healing touch but in his use of saliva, both directly and through the medium of clay. This combination is seen when he heals the man blind from birth (John 9:6, 7). '. . . he spat on the ground and made clay of the spittle and anointed the man's eyes with the clay, saying to him, "Go, wash in the pool Siloam." ' Although the Jews held a certain belief in the medicinal efficacy of saliva, it is probably more appropriate to conclude, with Morton Kelsey, that for Jesus the spittle was a 'carrier of his personality and power'.

Although many today have argued that personal faith is *the* prerequisite for miraculous restoration to health, a significant number of the Lord's healings took place with little or no comment on the receptivity or otherwise of the people to be healed. The all-embracing nature of his healing of whole crowds suggests that his power over disease, and not individual faith, is the arbiter of recovery. However, there is no doubt that the presence (even as little as 'a grain of mustard seen') or absence of faith are crucial factors in the encounter between the needy man or woman and Christ the healer. The efficacy of trust in Jesus' power to heal is seen, for example, in his words to the woman with a twelve years' history of vaginal bleeding: 'Daughter, your faith has made you well; go in peace, and be healed of your disease' (Mark 5:34). Conversely, the limitation imposed on the Lord's ministry by a lack of expectancy was at its most stone-walling in his home town, of which it is written, 'He did not do many mighty works there, because of their unbelief' (Matt. 13:58).

With Jesus, unlike the Greek physicians, there were no spells, conjurations, casting people into the sleep of 'incubation' or miracles of punishment. His healings were in the open and above board, using the simplicity of a word or a touch when appropriate. As we consider how he healed we come back to the primacy of our first point: 'Through him the power of God broke through into the lives of men, and they were made whole. There is little more that one can say.'[13]

(c) Why?

A careful study of the accounts of our Lord's miraculous healings should make us aware that we can answer the question 'why?' on at least two levels. As far as the blind man, the crippled woman and the feverish child were concerned, Jesus healed them out of pure love. We see this aspect in Matthew 14:14 where we read: 'As he went ashore he saw a great throng; and he had compassion on them, and healed their sick'.

There is, however, another perspective—that of the dawning of a new age. As we have seen in Luke's account of Jesus' visit to the synagogue in Nazareth (4:16–22), the Messiah has come and every shade of illness and oppression is open to the saving power of the Mighty One. When the Jews accused Jesus of casting out demons by 'the prince of demons', he proclaimed the inauguration of the gospel era by retorting, 'But if it is by the finger of God that I cast out demons, then the kingdom of God has come upon you' (Luke 11:20). Some theologians refer to this dimension of God's redemptive plan as an 'inaugurated eschatology' in which 'Jesus . . . preached the kingdom of God neither solely as a present reality nor exclusively as a future event.'[14] Eschatology, as the study of the 'last things', presses in upon us here and now. The Lord's casting out of demons predicts the Adversary's final defeat, his raising from the dead is a foretaste of the conquest of death and his healings anticipate the time when there shall be neither 'mourning nor crying nor pain any more' (Rev. 21:4).

This 'inaugurated eschatology' demands a verdict. R. A. Lambourne (who left general practice in order to research the theology of healing) argues this point in his *Community, Church and Healing*. He shows that Jesus' miraculous healings were not only 'effective signs' that demonstrated the kingdom but were also '*public* effective signs' that required a response of trust or disbelief from the onlooker. The healing may be 'in' the individual but those who watched could not stay mere spectators.[15] We see this challenge transmitted for all time to the reader of the gospel record:

> Now Jesus did many other signs in the presence of the disciples, which are not written in this book; but these are written that you may believe that Jesus is the Christ, the Son of God, and that believing you may have life in his name (John 20:30, 31).

(6) Healing in the early church

We now come into an area of more difficult interpretation. That the Church continued to demonstrate God's power to heal miraculously as recorded by Luke in Acts is not under dispute. However, as to whether these 'signs and wonders' were essentially (even exclusively) evidences of the Lord's authentication of the apostolic church, rather than indelible birthmarks of the new age, has been a matter of great controversy among theologians and lay people alike. Let us look briefly at some features in the New Testament account and leave further aspects of the discussion until later.

Each of the Gospels gives witness to the various callings and commissionings that Jesus gave to his followers with respect to their healing ministry. When he first chose the twelve he 'gave them authority over unclean spirits, to cast them out, and to heal every disease and every infirmity' (Matt. 10:1). At the appointing of the seventy, Jesus commanded that, when received into a town, they were to 'heal the sick in it and say to them, "The kingdom of God has come near to you" ' (Luke 10:9). Following Pentecost, we see the power of the risen Lord at work in the church in Jerusalem when we read that the people brought 'the sick and those afflicted with unclean spirits, and they were all healed' (Acts 5:16).

It is important, as with the ministry of Jesus, to appreciate that the witness of the early Christians comprised both word and action. For example, at Iconium, Paul and Barnabas spoke 'boldly for the Lord, who bore witness to the word of his grace, granting signs and wonders to be done by their hands' (Acts 14:3). Further, similarly to their Lord, the miraculous works of the disciples led to opposition and persecution. As a result of the healing of the 'man lame from birth' at the temple gate and the consequent preaching to the crowd, Peter and John were arrested and tried before the high priest (Acts 3 and 4).

Even though we find comparatively little about healing in the Epistles, there are indicators here and there in the letters of teaching that is compatible with Luke's account in the Acts of the Apostles. For instance, in Romans 15:18–19, Paul writes, 'I will not venture to speak of anything except what Christ has wrought through me to win obedience from the Gentiles, by word and deed, by the power of signs and wonders . . . .' Here, once more, is the balance of speech and action, together with the probability that 'signs and wonders', a phrase used in the Gospels a number of times of Jesus' miracles, at least includes healing. Quite specifically, in 2 Corinthians 12:12, Paul declares that these 'signs and wonders' are 'the signs of a true apostle'.

In two places, at least, in the Epistles we have an intimation of a wider view of the Church's calling to heal. In 1 Corinthians 12:9 the inclusion of 'gifts of healing' among the Holy Spirit's gifts to his people, and the passage in James 5, which urges the sick man to 'call for the elders of the church, and let them pray over him, anointing him with oil in the name of the Lord' (v.14), both point to a more widespread and systematic approach to the healing ministry in the early Church.

An Outline of Healing in Church History

During this century there has been a number of assessments of the place of miraculous healing in the life of the church down through the ages, including, on the one hand, works by Evelyn Frost and Morton Kelsey which look favourably on the validity of contemporary documents and, on the other hand, B. B. Warfield's classic book *Counterfeit Miracles*, 1918 (later published as *Miracles: Yesterday and Today, True and False*, 1954) which adopts a highly sceptical view towards post-apostolic miracle. We shall pick up with Warfield's influential position a little later in this chapter. For the moment, let us survey an outline of Christian healing, mainly in conjunction with the scholarship of Frost and Kelsey.

Dr. Evelyn Frost in *Christian Healing* (1940) looks primarily at the writings of the ante-Nicene Church from about 100–250 AD and declares that the patristic literature of this period is 'full of evidence of healing of various degrees of value'.[16] She concedes that some of the material is obscured by legend and that a number of the incidents described as miracles can be explained away in modern terms. However, she argues, the greater bulk of evidences show Christ's healing work continuing through his people. Frost points out that the writings she examined were 'produced as contemporary evidence in legal documents or works that were liable to the same scrutiny as would be required of legal evidence'.[17] Writers evaluated include Justin Martyr of Rome, Tertullian and Cyprian of Carthage, Clement and Origen of Alexandria, and Irenaeus working in Gaul. Irenaeus, writing at about 180 or earlier, reported the witnessing of miracles that used 'the Name of our Lord Jesus Christ', continuing, 'Which Name . . . cures thoroughly and effectively all who anywhere believe in Him'. He stated that the blind received sight, the deaf their hearing, demons were cast out and even the dead were raised 'on account of some necessity'.[18]

Frost further notes that Cyprian, towards the end of the third century, had observed increasing division and moral laxity within the Church, together with a concurrent loss of power in healing. Further deterioration seems to have arisen with the conversion of Constantine early in the fourth century when the Church became an 'organization rather than an organism'.

Morton Kelsey in *Healing and Christianity* (1973) continues the story, pin-pointing the recording of healings throughout the first six centuries. Basil the Great (329–379), for example, had a good knowledge of medicine, founded and maintained a large hospital outside Caesarea and also knew of miraculous healings. Augustine of Hippo (354–430), although arguing in his earlier writings against Christians expecting a continuation of gifts of healing, later (424), having witnessed various miracles of healing, seems to have changed his outlook.[19]

During the sixth and seventh centuries, Western civilization declined and superstitious views of healing began to permeate the Christian Church. Within the twelfth century a series of edicts increasingly divorced the Church from the practice of medicine. One of these (1139) condemned monks who studied and practised as physicians while, in 1163, the Council of Tours prohibited churchmen from working as surgeons because 'the church abhors the shedding of blood'. Within the Church superstition was rife and healing was sought almost entirely through the relics of the 'saints'. The split between Christendom and medical practice was epitomized in 1566 when doctors were required to swear that they would stop seeing a patient if he or she had not confessed their sins by the third day of illness!

During the Reformation, Calvin stated that the gifts of the Spirit, including healing, were only temporary 'to make the preaching of the gospel wonderful'. Luther's position seems to have been similar in his earlier writings although, according to Kelsey, there was a mellowing of his attitude towards miraculous healing when he saw his friend Melanchthon brought back from the point of death as a result of prayer.[20]

In the eighteenth century, John Wesley not only wrote a best-seller on practical medicine, *Primitive Physick* (1747) but also documented a number of miraculous healings in his journals. Among those with an apparent gift of healing in the nineteenth century the German pastor Johann Christoph Blumhardt, who worked in the Black Forest, was outstanding. As a result of his pastoral encounters with a disturbed girl, he is said to have come into a fresh awareness of the Holy Spirit. His congregation was infected by the same renewed life, through which people confessed their sins and experienced dramatic healings.

The Church and Medicine

As we have already hinted, the divergence of ecclesiastical and medical practice with respect to healing continued through the centuries from its origins amid the superstitions and split thinking of the Dark Ages and early medieval period. As has often been pointed out, the Church had become contaminated by the dualistic reasoning of early Greek philosophers. The spirit or soul of an individual was seen as *the* priority for pastoral concern whereas the body (Francis of Assisi's 'poor Brother Ass') was of little consequence. In spite of clear biblical revelation to the contrary, sickness was regarded as inextricably bound up with personal sin. It is not surprising that, although many Christians such as Lister, Simpson and Pasteur were eminent in science and medicine, the streams of scientific enquiry and theological reflection continued to diverge from their common headwaters.

The well-known story of Sir James Simpson's riposte when criticized by the Kirk for his use of chloroform in childbirth is symptomatic of this rift. Many condemned him for contravening the Lord's proclamation to Eve, 'In sorrow thou shalt bring forth children'. The Scottish gynaecologist knew the Scriptures too, and retorted by pointing out God's evident sanctioning of anaesthesia when he 'caused a deep sleep to fall upon Adam' prior to Eve's creation.

An acknowledgement of this cleavage of opinion between the Church and medicine is not to deny the rich legacy of the founding of hospitals, almshouses and other institutions for the relief of the needy by caring Christians throughout history. Nonetheless, ecclesiastical superstition, fostered by Greek dualism, has proved an impossible bed-fellow for the emerging discipline of medicine. The ensuing rationalism of scientific Western medicine has looked back to Hippocrates of Cos for its inspiration rather than to Jesus of Nazareth.

However, towards the end of the last century and, increasingly, within the twentieth century there has been a genuine, if cautious, re-appraisal of questions of healing between theologians and the doctors. This new approximation of our formerly diverging streams was, initially, tentative in the extreme. For example, in 1851 Henry Venn, then secretary to the Church Missionary Society, asked 'whether a missionary does not lose rather than gain influence with the natives by the exercise of medical knowledge'. A year later there were only thirteen European medical missionaries on the books. However, something of a biblical concern for the whole man was beginning to re-emerge and, by 1900, there were 650 in active service.[21]

At the turn of the century perhaps the greatest challenge to the Church's neglect of healing came through the rise of numerous cults and sects which sought to fill the vacuum within orthodox Christian teaching and practice. Among these, Christian Science, founded by Mary Baker Eddy in the States in 1879 and exported to Britain soon after, was particularly influential. This organization sought to solve the dichotomy of 'body versus spirit' by denying the reality of the former and by rejecting the very concept of physical illness. Thousands were ensnared by this latter-day gnosticism.

Within these climates of materialistic medicine and spurious spirituality, the Church began to take note. A number of bodies were formed to encourage dialogue between Christian ministers and the medical profession. These include: the Guild of Health (1904), which is now based at the Edward Wilson House in London and fosters many caring activities, including local prayer groups and hospital visiting; the Divine Healing Mission, originally founded as The Society of Emmanuel in 1905 by the lay-healer, James Moore Hickson and today centred at Crowhurst, Sussex; and the Guild of St. Raphael (1915) with its more sacramental emphasis on anointing with oil and the laying-on of hands. Similar organizations that seek a united front on questions of illness and health include the Divine Healing Fellowship of Scotland, the Healing Prayer Union in both Northern Ireland and Eire, and the Order of St. Luke in the States.[22]

While these societies flourished, a series of Lambeth Conferences within the Church of England explored, in an increasingly confident way, the Church's understanding of the healing ministries. In 1920 the thinking and activity of spiritualism, Christian Science and theosophy were roundly condemned. In 1924 the Committee Report for the 1930 Conference defined 'spiritual healing' as 'that which makes use of (material, psychical, devotional and sacramental) factors in reliance upon God'. In 1930 the 'ministry of healing' was recognized as a fundamental part of orthodox Christianity.

Further ventures by the official churches included the Churches' Council for Health and Healing, initiated by William Temple in 1944 and containing representatives of the Free Churches, and the Archbishops' Commission of 1958, at which clergy and members of the medical and nursing professions met. This latter group presented in an especially clear way the more holistic approach to people's needs which captures something of the biblical imperative. Discarding the partial terms of 'divine', 'spiritual' and 'faith' healing, they argued that the Church's ministry of healing 'is an integral part of the Church's total work by which men and women are to become true sons and daughters of God's kingdom'. The

conferences, production of publications and other activities of bodies like the Institute of Religion and Medicine, the Christian Medical Fellowship and the Guild of Catholic Doctors have contributed greatly to the interchange between doctors and clergy on the subject of healing.

'The new age of the Holy Spirit'

While committees and commissions debated and drew up their reports and recommendations, there were murmurings of strange and wonderful things happening in the market place. James Hickson, the founder of The Society of Emmanuel, first discovered 'his gift of healing at the age of fourteen' when 'he felt moved to lay hands on a cousin suffering from neuralgia and gave her immediate relief'.[23] Later he offered himself to serve the Lord within the worldwide Church as a lay-healer, rejecting Christian Science and accepting the validity of orthodox medicine. In 1924, early in his public healing ministry, he took part in a mission at St. Margaret's, Frizinghall, Bradford whence a 'series of apparently authentic healings' were reported by the Yorkshire papers. Hickson is recorded as saying, 'There is no virtue in my hands as I lay them upon you . . . It is in the name of Jesus Christ that the hands will be laid upon you.'[24] Officialdom reacted adversely. Dean Inge of St. Paul's protested against 'the craze for miracle-mongering' and local doctors made 'sour and sarcastic comments'. In spite of opposition, Hickson's work of healing continued throughout the world until his death in 1933, and a legacy of his ministry has survived in the healing community at Crowhurst.

Another important place of healing has grown up at Burrswood, Kent through the inspiration of Dorothy Kerin. Living at Herne Hill in the south of London, Dorothy Kerin developed tuberculosis during her teen years. This disease progressed inexorably until at the age of twenty-two she was unconscious for long periods and her doctor pronounced that there was no hope of recovery. In February 1912 a 'miraculous intervention' took place watched by 'a group of friends and neighbours who had come in to sit with the family in their daughter's last hours'.[25] To their amazement, the witnesses saw the previously comatosed girl sit up and declare, 'Do you not hear? I am well, I must get up and walk.' Dorothy Kerin has related that she heard her name called three times by an 'Angel of the Lord' who announced: 'Dorothy, your sufferings are over. Get up and walk'. The next day her doctor found her completely recovered, and subsequent X-rays and a six weeks' stay with a Dr. Ash, a specialist in Portman Square, confirmed her dramatic healing.

The healing ministries of James Hickson and Dorothy Kerin, together with the communities that have inherited their vision, may be cited as examples of a much wider, even global, movement of change within which innumerable claims to miraculous healing have been made. Maddocks quotes George Bennett, one of the wardens from Crowhurst who has frequently ministered at healing services at Holy Trinity Church, Brompton, as saying, 'Many of us believe that with this century has begun the new age of the Holy Spirit'. Within Pentecostalism, from the beginning of this century, and in the so-called 'charismatic movement' from the 1950s onwards there have been a great number who have borne witness to a host of miraculous happenings indicative of the Spirit's work—including, in the States, Agnes Sanford, Kathryn Kuhlmann, Graham Pulkingham and Francis MacNutt; and, in the UK, writers such as Michael Harper, David Watson, Reg East and John Gunstone.

Healing Today

When we examined the Scriptures on the subject of healing we saw that God is healer and it is reasonable to conclude that he is the source of all true healing. As Creator of the universe he has constructed living forms with a prodigious capacity to regenerate damaged tissue and combat invading organisms and toxic substances. A person's ability to recover from a lacerated finger, a strained ankle or an attack of influenza is part of this *natural healing*. Further, the animal, vegetable, mineral and elemental resources of the earth, together with human skill in research, experiment, manufacture and operative technique, have contributed to the enormous diversity of *medical healing*. Under this heading we might include the less easily assessable perspective of *psychological healing* in which individuals have found a measure of mental health through a whole range of physical and psychotherapeutic methods. Finally, there is the dimension of *miraculous healing* where a miracle has been defined simply as 'an interference with Nature by supernatural power'.[26] As Mundle has stated, the word miracle etymologically refers 'to the astonishment and amazement created by an unusual or inexplicable event'.[27] Although we have already noted, in the story of Aaron's rod and the Egyptian magicians, that the Enemy can simulate God's mighty acts, this does not detract from the fact that the Lord is *the* healer and worker of miracles. On the other hand, we can surely argue that God's miraculous healing is no more divine than natural, medical and psychological healing; it is simply that the hand of the Lord is more dramatically evident.

This element of miracle may apply to any aspect of an individual's life but is often seen today primarily in terms of physical healing and *inner healing* (a term that can be viewed as synonymous with certain facets of the earlier and vaguer phrase *spiritual healing*). We have already noted the all-embracing nature of biblical healing in restoring the whole person to health, and so we should not be surprised to find the Spirit active in the depths of personality as well as in overcoming organic infirmity. Ruth Carter Stapleton regards inner healing as primarily concerned with emotional health and has defined this form of healing as 'a process of emotional reconstruction experienced under the guidance of the Holy Spirit', adding, 'It is not an attempt to supplant psychiatry or to ignore the wisdom found in secular psychology . . .'[28]

'Inner healing' is a powerfully inclusive term which its practitioners claim embraces the healing of hurtful memories as well as those hidden emotional traumata which reach back to infancy and intra-uterine life. Writers like Agnes Sanford, Catherine Marshall, Ruth Carter Stapleton, Francis MacNutt, Michael Scanlan and Reg East have contributed a great deal to this perspective on healing, while support for this venture into the personal past is given in the research and writings of the late Frank Lake. More controversial is the extension of this pursuit for the healing of our individual histories to the search for genealogical dis-ease, as is put forward in Kenneth McAll's *Healing: the Family Tree*.[29]

The difficulty with all these designations of healing is that many of them imply a view that splits a person into over-defined aspects—physical, psychological, emotional, spiritual, social, historical, etc. The biblical Hebrew perspective on human nature, in contrast, is strongly holistic, stressing that behind every facet of our humanity is found the whole personality. Whatever categories we adopt as a shorthand to ease our thinking, we come back to fundamentals when we declare that *all* restoration to health—natural, medical or miraculous in any or every part of individual or corporate existence—is under the sovereign control of God the healer.

However, it is in the area of the miraculous that contemporary debate and disagreement about healing are at their strongest. Although the range of viewpoints is a wide one it may be most helpful to look, in turn, at two polarizing positions (both of which accept the accuracy of the biblical record on miracles) before attempting a degree of resolution.

(1) 'Dispensationalist'

The 'dispensationalist' perspective on miraculous healing is that

MTB-N

God has dispensed his special gifts on humankind at certain key periods in biblical history. These have been times of extremity for the people of God in which he has demonstrated his power in mighty saving acts and comprise: the Exodus and establishment of the Israelites in Canaan; the period of apostasy and conflict with pagan religion during the days of Elijah and Elisha; the time of Exile within which Daniel challenged the might of Babylon; and the coming of the Messiah and the ensuing apostolic age. This strand of thinking about miracles of healing was held, at least initially, by Augustine and was continued among the Reformers, to some extent in reaction to the superstitious excesses of the Roman Church.

In this century, B. B. Warfield's *Counterfeit Miracles* has become a rallying-point for this form of dispensationalism. He has written of the miracle-working nature of the early Church: 'How long did this state of things continue? It was the characterizing peculiarity of specifically the Apostolic Church, and it belonged therefore exclusively to the Apostolic age . . .'[30] He defends his view that miracles belong 'exclusively to the Apostolic age' both from the New Testament and history, arguing that stories of miraculous healing became 'abundant and precise only in the fourth century' and then continued to increase beyond this period. He sees such accounts as representing 'an infusion of heathen modes of thought into the church' and concludes his historical survey by declaring, 'It seems to be the experience of every one who has made a serious attempt to sift the evidence for miraculous healing that this evidence melts away before his eyes.'[31]

Warfield challenges certain interpretations of those New Testament passages that seem to threaten his position. For example, he regards John 14:12, where Jesus promises, 'He who believes in me will also do the works that I do; and greater works than these will he do . . .', as indicating exclusively 'spiritual works'. Again, he comments that the mentioning of 'gifts of healing' in 1 Corinthians 12 could be referring to their availability for the apostolic age only.[32]

It is within the framework of this 'dispensationalist' view that the pastoral or medical care of the seriously ill can deteriorate into an attitude that dismisses the possibility of miraculous healing, and sees the handling of the situation purely in terms of diagnosis, physical treatment and standard prognosis. This is the stance of, 'Blessed are those who expect nothing for they shall not be disappointed.'

(2) CHARISMATIC

The opposite pole of contemporary views on healing can broadly be labelled 'charismatic' in that the emphasis is on the continuing accessibility of the whole range of the Spirit's gifts to his Church. Here the thesis is that God's people have, for much of their history, lost touch with the Lord in such a way that the gifts of healing have fallen into disuse. Writers like Percy Dearmer, Evelyn Frost, Morton Kelsey and Morris Maddocks have sought to bring to our notice both the continuation of the Spirit's work of healing and the Church's indictable neglect of the same.

The more extreme examples of this view are 'triumphalist' in that they major on the unimpeded availability of the Lord's power to heal in response to the faith of his people. It seems that the releasing factor for this power is a high degree of faith and its only limiting element is a low degre or absence of faith. If certain crucial biblical statements are believed and promises claimed then the power from on high *will* descend to heal. Where no change in the disease in question is observed, then, against all the odds, belief in its healing must be maintained. At times, this approach is at least consistent in refusing medical treatment because, it is argued, such props are no longer needed.

I once had a patient who was a diabetic student and had been persuaded by such Scriptures as 'by his wounds you have been healed' (1 Peter 2:24) to seek healing at the climax of a church service. Her fellow-Christians urged her to stop her insulin as she had prayed the 'prayer of faith'. Three days later I was phoned with a request for an urgent visit. I found her to be in a state of semi-coma and in desperate need of medication. Giving her an injection of life-saving insulin, I suggested that we discuss the theology of the situation when she had recovered physically. This whole episode of 'triumphalism' in action has taken her Christian commitment many years of re-adjustment—years of learning to glorify the Lord as a controlled diabetic.

Just as Warfield's position has difficulty with a handful of biblical texts, so the 'triumphalist' view is much exercised when certain scriptures are raised. Its *bête noir* is Paul's account of his 'thorn in the flesh'. Every effort is made to discredit this passage as a source of comfort to the chronically ill person, who might be helped by the general principle that our sovereign Lord does sometimes reply to our urgent prayer for healing with the words, 'My grace is sufficient for you, for my power is made perfect in weakness' (2 Cor. 12:9). In a situation where, during my own illness with diabetic retinopathy and chronic brucellosis, I was able to discuss the question of God's restoring power with a young woman who exercised a gift of healing, I was taken to task for seeing this Pauline passage as at all applicable to my circumstances. Unless I could claim to have had experiences parallel to Paul's 'visions and revelations of the Lord' (v.1), it was presumptuous of me to seek to assimilate the concept of Christ's power in my weakness.[33]

(3) EVIDENCE FOR HEALING TODAY

Before seeking a measure of resolution within the spread of Christian opinions on healing, let us face the vexed question of the evidence for miracle since the apostolic age. Here we are immediately in difficulty, for we are either needing to evaluate the authenticity of, at best, eye-witness accounts of miraculous healings in the past or we are in the more privileged, though no less daunting, position of assessing claims to miracle today. Even if you or I were present at what appears to be a spectacularly impressive healing, we still have the challenge of careful appraisal. Can we be sure the diagnosis was correct? Is this a condition that is known to have sudden remissions? How can we exclude powerful psychological and emotional factors? What are the tangible evidences for healing? Will there be a relapse in six months, two years, ten years? Can we say anything about the causation of this apparent miracle? Is it in fact a miracle—the result of divine intervention—or shall we play safe and call it an 'inexplicable spontaneous remission'? The exigencies of scientific investigation may make it impossible to confirm or deny miraculous healing. However, we should not, I suggest, be afraid of concluding that there is the strong probability of the Lord's intervention where circumstances, such as a background of prayer, an expectant faith in Christ, the reliability of witnesses, and the durability of the restored condition, all point towards God's hand at work. With these considerations, we can cautiously accept either the findings of an Evelyn Frost as she studies the early Church Fathers and a Morton Kelsey as he surveys records of healings throughout history, or, within this century, the first-hand accounts of a James Moore Hickson or an Agnes Sanford.

The medical profession has rightly been wary about claims of miraculous cure. In 1956, the British Medical Association published the report of an *ad hoc* committee entitled *Divine Healing and Co-operation between Doctors and Clergy*. The strictly medical viewpoint found no evidence of any type of illness 'cured by "spiritual healing" alone which could not have been cured by medical treatment which necessarily includes consideration of environmental factors'. The value of the psychological aspects of 'sound religious ministrations' was acknowledged.'[34]

However, there seems to be a movement of modest proportions

among doctors which is increasingly open to the possibility of God's power to bring dramatic healing. A scholarly contribution within this tendency is the paper written by Rex Gardner and published in the *British Medical Journal* in December 1983. Here he assesses miracles of healing in both Anglo-Celtic Northumbria and in contemporary Britain. Of the latter category, he cites six case studies of apparently miraculous healing, including the story of a young trainee GP, who was admitted in a moribund state to a Welsh hospital in 1975 with meningococcal septicaemia and meningitis. That evening prayer meetings were held on her behalf at four independent localities in North Wales. At 8.30 pm all these groups 'independently but simultaneously believed that their request that she might be healed with no residual disability had been granted'.[35] At the same time there was sudden improvement in her condition. Four days later she regained consciousness and so experienced a complete recovery, confirmed by chest X-ray and ophthalmological changes. It is the latter that were particularly impressive in that the ophthalmologist had observed and photographed deterioration in the left eye caused by intraocular haemorrhage, and had forecast permanent blindness. On scrutinizing her restored fundus, he declared, 'Do you realize you are unique?' In summary, Gardner cautiously makes these comments on his case-studies:

> It is noteworthy that in most cases members of the British medical profession still in practice were actively taking part. No attempt has been made to prove that miracles have occurred, such proof being probably impossible. The adjective 'miraculous' is, however, permissible as a convenient shorthand for an otherwise almost inexplicable healing which occurs after prayer to God and brings honour to the Lord Jesus Christ.

It is likely that this type of honest and circumspect statement is the most explicit that the Christian doctor can reasonably make when faced with the possibility of miraculous healing. The Lord's power to heal is unquestioned. The rigours of scientific enquiry in this or that instance may play their part but, in the last analysis, they have to bow before self-evident restoration and the sort of firm conviction that led the 'man blind from his birth' to exclaim, 'One thing I know, that though I was blind, now I see' (John 9:25).

(4) A MEASURE OF RESOLUTION

It is tragic that the debate between 'charismatic' and Reformed Christians has tended to polarize so strongly. As I have argued in *As Trees Walking*, we can surely state that 'all Christians are charismatic, i.e. gifted by the Spirit "who apportions to each one individually as he wills" (1 Cor. 12:11)'. In spite of this unifying concept, there has been a great deal of misunderstanding, even mud-slinging, between the extreme 'dispensationalist' and the 'triumphalist' camps. Of course, the holding of opposing positions has chequered Church history—Paul v Peter, Arius v anti-Arians, Augustine v Pelagius, Rome v Constantinople, Protestants v Roman Catholics, Arminians v Calvinists, the establishment v 'enthusiasm', believers' baptism v paedo-baptism. At times one extreme or the other has been proved right; frequently the truth has lain in holding a tension between contrary viewpoints. I would commend the second stance in our consideration of healing. Of course the polarized viewpoints cannot *both* be correct. You cannot argue that miraculous healing ceased at the close of the apostolic age and, at the same time, that restoration to health by miracle is freely available today through the prayer of faith. The point of resolution between these opposing camps lies, I suggest, in a fresh affirmation of the sovereignty of God and in an appreciation of the twin biblical themes of both healing and suffering.[36]

As we study the Scriptures we see examples of a range of divine answers to the request, 'Heal me!'. King Hezekiah experienced the response, 'I will—for another fifteen years!'; Job received no immediate reply but, instead, a prolonged and devastating period of darkness before his eventual restoration; Paul's answer was, in effect, 'No—but my grace is sufficient for you in your continuing struggle.' Here, surely, we see God's prerogative to respond to our trust and expectancy, as well as our frustration and anger, in ways that best suit his plans for our lives.

The recent death of David Watson is a case in point. Countless people were moved by his declaration that he believed that God was healing him of inoperable cancer. Not everyone pondered the significance of his honest, and very human, caveat, '—but I may be wrong'. Surely this is the right balance—a profound and confident faith towards Christ the healer coupled with a humble awareness that the Lord knows best. We read of God's rule over the affairs of men and women in Romans 9:15, 16 where the Lord says, 'I will have mercy on whom I have mercy, and I will have compassion on whom I have compassion' and Paul adds, of an individual's destiny, 'So it depends not upon man's will or exertion, but upon God's mercy.' All of us are subject to our mighty God's merciful will—whether we have the international stature, under the Lord, of a David Watson or we are among the least known of Christ's disciples.

On the other hand, can we really explain away Paul's mention of 'gifts of healing' in 1 Corinthians 12 and James's injunction to seek healing in James 5 as purely for the first century? Were the commissionings of Jesus to his followers and the explosion of the Lord's power to heal described in Acts an entirely circumscribed phenomenon for just one generation of believers? Even if Warfield is right to restrict the miraculous to the apostolic age and to dismiss all other historical accounts of healing as spurious, may we not be within another period of God's special intervention, heralding, perhaps, our Lord's return?

And yet, we have to ask, do we really see healings today like those recorded in the Gospels and Acts—healings that were immediate, complete and lasting? Yes, some would answer, we do! Nevertheless, if that is our reply, we still have to compare our limited experience of miracle today with the sheer volume, immediacy, thoroughness, comprehensiveness and durability of Jesus' healing encounters with needy people. The brief account by Michael Harper in a Christian newspaper indicates the gap between our experiences today, however spectacular, and our Lord's earthly ministry in which 'all were healed': 'Together with a team we had prayed for hundreds of people in South Korea, Sri Lanka and India, and seen scores healed, some instantly, others within a few days'.[37] My point is not to deny the validity and wonder of reports like Michael Harper's, but to discourage the pastoral problems that arise out of believing that there should be no difference between the incarnate Lord's face-to-face encounter with the powers of darkness and our work in his name today.

Surely, it is more realistic and in accordance with biblical insight to acknowledge that, although we are living in a new age that was inaugurated most powerfully by the Son of God, nonetheless we still live in an 'in-between' time and the 'best is yet to be'. Though we read in Matthew 8:17 that Jesus 'took our infirmities and bore our diseases' and we know that, in his death, the Lord overcame every work of the Enemy and humanity's rebellion, we still cannot claim final and fullest victory as our new birthright here and now. Just as we experience many triumphs over sin without, in this life, becoming sinless so we enjoy, in a variety of ways, a measure of healing now without, at this stage, knowing complete wholeness.

Although we have the sure and certain hope of 'a new heaven and a new earth', in which the leaves of the tree of life are 'for the healing of the nations' (Rev. 22:2), here today we are still moving towards that joyous completeness. In the meantime, in spite of the messianic promise, people are still imprisoned unjustly, families still suffer crushing poverty, men, women and children still die of malnutrition, countless individuals are still overwhelmed by every form of infirmity. And yet, the Messiah *has* come to bring the dawning of the gospel age, he has overcome the opposing 'strong man' through his death and resurrection, his Spirit is abroad and the Kingdom of God is at hand. You and I are invited to be healers in the here and now, whatever our personal or corporate calling, bringing relief, restoration and redemption to a desperately needy world. We need the Spirit's perception in this awesome ministry as we both acknowledge the Master's sovereign will and, at the same time, reach out in trust knowing that 'whatever you ask in my name, I will do it, that the Father may be glorified in the Son' (John 14:13). With this sensitivity, we shall cry to the Lord for healing both for ourselves and for others; we shall rejoice when his answer is clearly, 'Yes! Be healed', and we shall learn to rejoice when his reply is, 'Not yet' or 'No, I will not remove your affliction; but I will be glorified through it.'

If we hold a large vision of healing, then we are at one with the Lord God the healer. By his Spirit and in the name of his Son we are all called to serve him as we feed the hungry, give drink to the thirsty, welcome the stranger, clothe the naked, visit the sick and imprisoned (Matt. 25:34–40). When we extend a loving hand to the afflicted we should recall the King's words, 'As you did it to one of the least of these my brethren, you did it to me.' As we bring healing, we walk on hallowed ground.

In our representing and serving Christ in the hospital ward, at the bedside of an ill friend, in the home of a family struggling with serious physical or mental handicap, in the counselling of a man whose marriage has broken up or a woman who has recently been bereaved, in the day-to-day relating to a fractious and irritable relative, in the befriending of the lonely or depressed, let us also remember that we are 'all in this together'. Dr. Robert Lambourne, as we have seen, has drawn our attention to the communal element in the gospel healings of Jesus. Although we readily focus on the man or woman who receives healing, the acceptance or rejection of the Lord the healer by the onlookers is also decisive for eternity. As Lambourne writes so eloquently, 'These are moments of judgment. To witness the healing work of Christ is a great and terrible thing because it places the witnesses "on the spot".'[38] Let us remember, in our care of others, that the Lord of glory is the bringer of healing, the sustainer in suffering and the judge of the self-righteous, who say they 'need no physician'.

9

Conscience and Modern Medicine

DOUGLAS M. JACKSON

Direct references in the Bible to the word 'conscience' are limited, but from the opening pages and throughout the book we see conscience at work in the hearts and minds of men and women. It is an inherent attribute and a most valuable gift from man's Creator-God.

The etymology of the Greek word *syneidesis* and its Latin equivalent *conscientia* implies 'knowledge together with something'. It is not simply consciousness or awareness, but consciousness of a moral standard and awareness whether one has lived up to it. In the Greek Old Testament (LXX) the word *syneidesis* occurs only once: 'Curse not the king in thy conscience' (Eccles. 10:20). The Authorised, Revised and Revised Standard Versions have translated it, 'Even in your thought do not curse the king'. In general, Hebrew thinking conceived of the whole person talking to the whole person, and faculties and attributes of the mind were not distinguished.

No great imagination is required to see conscience at work in the accounts of Adam and Eve's disobedience (Gen. 3), the fear of Joseph's brothers after their father died (Gen. 50), the exposure of David's sin by Nathan (2 Sam. 12), and the pronouncement of judgment on Ahab for killing Naboth (1 Kgs. 21). Sometimes the word 'heart' is used in the Old Testament where we might use 'conscience', as in 1 Sam. 24:5 where 'David's heart smote him' after he turned his hand against Saul, the Lord's anointed. And again, the psalmist writes, 'I have laid up thy word in my heart that I might not sin against thee' (Ps. 119:11).

In the Greek New Testament the word *syneidesis* occurs twenty-seven times in the Epistles, chiefly in those of the apostle Paul, twice in Acts, both times in Paul's mouth, and in Hebrews and 1 Peter. It is not found in the words of Jesus although he certainly appealed to the innate moral judgment of ordinary men and women. In contrast to previous Hebrew practice, Greek and New Testament thinking was able to deal with various attributes of the mind and behaviour. Possibly the word *syneidesis* originated in popular Greek thought, and Paul adopted it into Christian thinking.

Our word 'conscience' can refer to the inborn faculty or mechanism of moral appreciation or it can refer to the message, judgment, or verdict which it announces. A 'good conscience' can mean having a sensitive faculty or instrument attuned to God's will, or it can be a favourable judgment that what is contemplated is according to God's moral law.

What is Conscience?

The 'locus classicus' for the Pauline use of '*syneidesis*' is Romans 2:15. Here we read that conscience bears witness to the moral standard we possess within us. Conscience is a faculty by which we apprehend the moral nature of acts, attitudes and motives, and it causes us pain—the pangs of conscience—when we fall short of its demands and pleasure when we satisfy them. This is the language by which conscience communicates. We are born with this faculty and we experience its activity consciously from early childhood. We might speak of it as 'a voice telling us what we ought and ought not to do', but this is loose thinking. In fact, conscience judges only whether an act or attitude is good or bad. Having judged, conscience demands that the good act be done and the evil one abandoned, but it offers no third option. Paul nowhere hints at being governed by God through conscience. The 'imperative' conscience is not found in the New Testament—ie 'Conscience *made* me . . .'

The Bible describes conscience as 'bearing witness' to the moral character of an act, and this it does, partly before the act is committed, and more strongly afterwards. In modern parlance one might describe it as a built-in moral guide, a monitoring device which 'rings a bell' when deviation from the true standard occurs. The fact that we may be rebelling against the standard intellectually, and mustering arguments to reject it, has surprisingly little effect on the clarity and content of the message. Similarly, time may have little effect in dulling the message: the 'bad conscience' may stick in the mind of the one at fault for many years. In some measure conscience is like a railway signal, giving us the red or the green light for some action. However, the individual remains the driver and he can obey or disobey the signal. Conscience is not compulsive like an animal's instinct. Man has free will within his environment, and his conscience is not a homing-device compelling him to hit the target automatically.

Perhaps the most helpful illustration of the nature of conscience is that it is a judgment seat. Indeed, this is more the fact than a metaphor. Hallesby,[1] former principal of the independent free Faculty of Theology of the Church of Norway, in his excellent book entitled *Conscience*, expands this idea. First, a man's conscience is remarkably unbiased in its judgment of him. In other courts we require a judge to be a disinterested party in case he favours or discriminates against the accused; but at the bar of conscience, even though the accused judges himself, the judgment is pronounced without favour or excuse. Furthermore, when conscience has spoken, its verdict cannot be altered (except due to a later change of circumstances). It acts like a supreme court whose verdict cannot be quashed, however much we may try to evade it by enlisting the lower standards and opinions of others. Hodge[2] puts it like this: conscience in its own province is sovereign, and can have no other superior except the revealed word of God. Finally, conscience is no respecter of persons. It speaks regardless of the highest authorities which may confront it, be they governments or public opinion. Peter and John clearly had the support of conscience when they made their courageous reply to the rulers in Jerusalem that they could not but speak of what they had seen and heard (Acts 4:19). Luther was equally explicit when he was ordered before the Emperor Charles V at the Diet of Worms to retract his beliefs. He concluded, 'I cannot submit my faith either to the Pope or to the councils, because it is as clear as the day that they have frequently erred and contradicted each other. Unless, therefore, I am convinced by the testimony of Scripture, or by the clearest reasoning . . . I cannot and will not retract, for it is unsafe for a Christian to speak against his conscience. Here I stand, I can do no other; may God help me. Amen.' Others, like the aged Polycarp of Smyrna, displayed their obedience to conscience and their devotion to Christ by the sacrifice of their lives. When commanded by Statius Quadratus, proconsul, to swear by the godhead of Caesar and blaspheme Christ, he could only reply, 'Eighty and six years have I served Christ, and he has never done me wrong. How can I blaspheme my King who saved me?'

The traditional Christian teaching is that it is a Christian's absolute duty to obey his conscience. This does not mean that conscience is infallibly right. We must take responsibility for our own decisions before God and follow what our moral reason prescribes at the time. We may, of course, decide to give someone else the duty of deciding for us, but that decision itself should be a conscientious one. Even then, if we are ordered to do something against our conscientious judgment, we should disobey.[3]

Conscience and the Moral Law

Natural and revealed law

If conscience judges our actions in relation to a moral standard, we should know what that standard is, together with its origin and reliability. The standard is critical. If the mechanism of conscience could exist without a standard, it would be as useless as a measuring tape without markings.

The Bible tells us that all men know God's requirements; that although the Gentiles have not had a Code of Commandments from God like the Jews, yet what the law requires is written on their hearts, their conscience bearing witness to it (Rom. 2:14, 15) This knowledge is generally called Natural Law.

According to the Bible man was originally made 'in the image of God'. Like God, he was created a person, capable of personal relationships. He was able to love and respond to love. He enjoyed communion with God, and he was aware of God's will and his responsibility to obey it. After the fall of man from his privileged state, this image was defaced; man's original character and attributes were spoiled. The likeness was marred though not completely destroyed; man still retained in his heart a reduced but definite awareness of God and his moral law.

Paul's statements in Romans 1 concerning unregenerate man are perfectly clear:

> 'What can be known about God is plain to them, because God has shown it to them. Ever since the creation of the world his invisible nature, namely, his eternal power and deity, has been clearly perceived in the things that have been made. So they are without excuse; for although they knew God they did not honour him as God or give thanks to him, but they became futile in their thinking and their senseless minds were darkened. Claiming to be wise, they became fools, and exchanged the glory of the immortal God for images

resembling mortal man or birds or animals or reptiles. Therefore God gave them up in the lusts of their hearts to impurity . . . because they exchanged the truth about God for a lie . . . Since they did not see fit to acknowledge God, God gave them up to a base mind . . . Though they know God's decree that those who do such things deserve to die, they not only do them but approve those who practise them' (Rom. 1:19–32).

Paul clearly regarded the knowledge of right and wrong, the capacity to choose between them, and the responsibility for having chosen as all part of human nature and man's original condition before Christian conversion. Man, for Paul, is a moral creature. God has not left himself without witness (Acts 14:15ff), and he has appointed that men should seek and feel after God that they might find him (Acts 17:22ff).

For the Jews, the divine demands were made explicit in the Sinaitic Code, so that they were able to check the moral law in their hearts against God's revealed law, recognized as 'holy, and just and good' (Rom. 7:12).

Since Christ's baptism, when God told Israel in future 'to hear *him*', Christians have had a fuller standard in the life and teaching of Jesus Christ. The aim of the New Covenant was gradually to restore the image of God in man, to write God's moral law once again on the hearts of his children who have received new natures by new birth in Christ. Their growth in obedience requires the inward presence and work of the Holy Spirit regenerating, purifying, and enabling.

Conscience in the Natural and Regenerate Man

The Bible asserts that God has revealed himself to man through his creation, particularly his eternal power and deity (Rom. 1:19, 20). Man's predicament is that his sin and resulting estrangement from God blind him to what is visibly set before his eyes. It is not that he cannot, but he *will not* accept and know the God who so clearly manifests himself to him. He is therefore without excuse.

PURPOSE

The purpose of the law, with conscience bearing witness to it, is to emphasize to man that he is a law-breaker before a holy God. The purpose of the law is to open man's eyes to his guilt, and to close his mouth if he would make excuses (Rom. 3:19). Brunner[4] defined conscience as the consciousness of responsibility: through the law the whole world is held accountable to God. This conviction of sin is no purposeless criticism. It is intended to lead man to repentance, and ultimately to forgiveness and restoration through faith in Christ.

EFFECTIVENESS

What success has conscience in this task? A sensitive conscience is usual in young people. It was so in the case of Josiah, the boy King of Judah who came to the throne at the age of eight. Later, God commended him as a young man because his heart was tender and he humbled himself before the Lord, and God used him as an outstanding reformer. Regrettably, however, the tender conscience of childhood can become the silenced conscience of the man of the world. When a bad conscience produces shame, and a sense of guilt and inferiority, one way of reducing the discomfort is to suppress the hostile accusation in a search for freedom and fulfilment. This may appear to succeed. Sometimes a man whose conscience is asleep may claim—honestly, I believe—that he feels no need for God. The composer of Psalm 73, foolishly fretting at the prosperity of the wicked, observes that they have no pangs at their death. But suppression does not always succeed. There was a recent report in the press that a business man had confessed to the police a fraud he had committed as a young man. It had been on his conscience and ruined his life for thirty years. Others by conscience have been driven to suicide.

AWAKENING

How can a dormant conscience be awakened to God? We have considered the part played by God's law: this is one measure which awakens conscience. But in addition, Jesus told his disciples that it is a work of the Holy Spirit to convince the world of sin, especially the sin of not accepting and believing in Christ (John 16:7–9). The Spirit, using the law and conscience, is a reprover. He can convict of sin in a way that no one else can. We may think this is cold comfort from one who is called Comforter and Helper, but this is God's way; first to convince, and then to comfort; first to lay open the wound, and then to apply the healing remedy. Our conscience may be awakened to recognize the sinfulness of our pride, greed or hypocrisy towards other people, but this cannot compare with the enormity of spurning the death of the Lord Jesus Christ, and of ignoring his sacrifice of himself for our sins on the Cross that we might have forgiveness and eternal life.

Men's consciences towards God were dramatically awakened by the Spirit on the day of Pentecost. As Peter told them, 'Know assuredly, God has made this Jesus, whom you have crucified, both Lord and Christ', their hearts were pricked, their consciences were startled awake by the awful thing that they had done, and they cried out, 'What shall we do?' Some people may be driven into God's kingdom by the fear of God's righteous judgment, but it seems that most people are drawn to Christ by his love. As their guilt and unworthiness is borne in upon them by their consciences, supported by God's word, their hearts are melted and opened by the almost unbelievable and completely undeserved love of the Lord Jesus.

When a man's conscience is awakened by the Spirit in this way, he receives a new awareness of God, and God's will. He is surprised at his past blindness and self-satisfaction and he is shocked by the appreciation that he has been ignoring and opposing God. The awakening is always an intellectual realization of guilt; it may also be an emotional experience of anxiety, sorrow and depression. The sense of guilt is in no way pathological because the guilt is real; it is a proper response to the truth. It is indeed a burden, uncomfortable and oppressive. An awakened conscience is not an end in itself; in fact, it breeds regret and remorse. There is nothing good about it at all except that it is God's appointed gateway to true confession, repentance, forgiveness and eternal life.

Fortunate is the man with an awakened conscience who is presented with the gospel—the good news that Jesus has made a way back to God for all men, and that full and free forgiveness is offered to whoever will turn to God and receive it. There is no cure for an awakened and convicted conscience except the assurance of God's forgiveness. Without that forgiveness a man can only lapse again into suppressing his accusing conscience, or search fruitlessly for relief by earning merit from good works.

The Christian's conscience

Conscience plays a big part in our overall health and well-being. A bad conscience can rob us of peace of mind, joy, confidence and friendships. It is a health factor.

a) The need to develop it

The apostle Paul's attitude to conscience is summed up in a remark in his trial before Felix, the governor: 'I always take pains to have a clear conscience towards God and toward man' (Acts 24:16). This was the practice of his life (see also Acts 23:1, 2 Tim. 1:3).

Paul's conscience after his conversion was no enemy. It was his faithful friend whose opinion he sought in recognizing and obeying God's will. It is up to the Christian to 'let the word of Christ dwell in him richly', to steep himself in it, so that he knows both its teaching and its contemporary application (Col. 3:16). A new Christian may take a little time to incorporate Christian teaching into the standard that his conscience approves. A classic example is the experience of John Newton[5] the slave trader, who described how this was 'a gentleman's profession' in his day, one you could be proud of. After his dramatic conversion in a storm at sea, it took about thirty years before he came to see that 'slaving' was incompatible with his Christian faith. Conscience judges in respect of the standard which a man approves or 'believes in' in his inmost being. It will never condemn what he knows to be right, nor will it approve what he knows to be evil. Hence the importance in having a conscience which springs from a sincere and unfeigned faith in God and his will (1 Tim. 1:5; 4:1).

Paul was brought up a man of conscience, a strict Pharisee. Later in life he was able to say, 'I have lived before God in all good conscience up to this day.' In spite of this, his conscience before his conversion was mistaken. Listen as he speaks before King Agrippa of his pre-conversion days: 'I myself was convinced that I ought to do many things in opposing the name of Jesus of Nazareth. And I did so . . . I not only shut up many of the saints in prison . . . when they were put to death I cast my vote against them . . . I punished them . . . in raging fury against them I persecuted them (Acts 26:9–11). Yet, when he was converted, 'straightaway he preached Christ in the synagogues, that he is the Son of God'. Conscience can be very sure, and yet mistaken. Men have killed each other in good conscience—for an ideology, for a supposed heresy, or for an incurable deformity. Jesus warned his disciples that in the future people would even kill them and think they were doing God's service; and he explained the reason—'they will do this because they have not known the Father or me' (John 16:1–3). That is, because their consciences would not be properly informed, would not be tuned to the character and will of God.

b) The need to guard it

The Christian life is a relationship with God and with other Christians which depends upon maintaining a clear conscience. This is why Paul urges his young friend Timothy to 'wage the good warfare, holding faith and a good conscience'. 'By rejecting conscience', he adds, 'certain persons have made shipwreck of their faith . . . (1 Tim. 1:18; 3:9). The Christian's relationship of love and trust in his heavenly Father, as in a human family, is spoiled by a bad conscience. Hence the importance of 'taking pains' to have a good conscience as Paul tried to do (Acts 23:1; 24:16; 2 Cor. 1:12; 2 Tim. 1:3), and of avoiding wounding the conscience of a weaker, perhaps less well-informed brother (1 Cor. 8:7, 10, 12; 1 Cor. 10; 25, 28, 29; 2 Cor. 4:2). It is evident from Paul's letter that he appealed to his conscience repeatedly in his daily life, as a test. Did it support him in what he was saying (Rom. 9:1) or doing (Heb. 13:18)?

The writer of the letter to the Hebrews deals with the desperate predicament of the man or woman haunted by a guilty conscience. Perhaps a relationship has been spoiled, or the life of another individual ruined by a word or act, committed or withheld. The situation cannot be undone or reversed. How can one be freed from a bad conscience and find peace of heart and mind, especially peace with God? Under the old Covenant, says the writer, animal sacrifices were unable to heal the conscience of the worshipper who wanted to approach and find favour with God (Heb. 9:9). Neither was careful observance of the law, then or today, able to take away consciousness of sin (Heb. 10:2). It is only by trusting in the blood of Christ (Heb. 9:14; 10:22) that we can experience forgiveness and a cleansed conscience. That is, by accepting his blood shed for us for the forgiveness of our sins; or, putting it another way, by accepting Christ who gave his life in our place as the just penalty of our sin. As Hordern[6] puts it, 'Christian faith gives man an uneasy conscience in so far as it convicts him of sin before God. Freedom from this uneasiness is to be found through God's forgiveness rather than through man's own attainments.'

Secular Views of Conscience

In contrast to the Bible's teaching about conscience, there are other views which have sought to explain its origin and activities from a standpoint confined to the natural world and excluding God. Of these, two which are relevant to natural science are those of Sigmund Freud and the evolutionary humanists.

Sigmund Freud 1856–1939

In brief, Freud considered that the super-ego, which was 'the vehicle for conscience', was created in the course of a child's individual development. The super-ego was the successor of the parents and educators who superintended the actions of the individual in the first years of life, and it perpetuated their functions almost without change. Conscience, therefore, was the operation of the judgments we accepted from our parents when we were too young to question them, and these judgments have been introjected into our ego structure and set up in authority as our super-ego. We identify ourselves with these judgments and, whether we rebel against them or submit to them, they represent to us the guiding light, the principle on which we should conduct our lives.[7]

Freud regarded the idea of God and the fact of religious belief as no more than projections of the child's relationship to his father, made in response to the stresses of life. He did not accept conscience as an inherent faculty. It is often part of the object of psychoanalysis to mitigate the distressing effects of conscience.

Freud was aware of weaknesses in his hypothesis although this did not prevent him propounding it. For instance, 'The super-ego seems to have made a one-sided selection, and to have chosen only the harshness and severity of the parents and their preventive and punitive functions, while their loving care is not taken up and continued by it. If the parents have really ruled with a rod of iron, we can easily understand the child developing a severe super-ego, but, contrary to our expectations, experience shows that the super-ego may reflect the same relentless harshness even when the upbringing has been gentle and kind . . .'[8]

Stafford-Clarke[7] makes a valid point when he concludes, 'The ultimate sense of morality, as experienced subjectively in conscience, must be something beyond individual tradition and environment if it is to be meaningful; it cannot be merely the distilled or distorted relics of infantile experience and environment.' By Freud's thesis the problem of the origin of values is shelved rather than solved by attributing the whole of one generation's morality to the conduct of its parents.

EVOLUTIONARY HUMANISM

Evolutionary humanism is a developing system of thought and belief concerned with human activity and destiny. It is not a rigid set of dogmas, but rather an open system capable of indefinite further development. It regards man as a natural phenomenon produced by evolution. Man has responsibility for the future course of evolution, and his aim should be greater fulfilment for human individuals and societies through increased realization of the possibilities.

Waddington[9] points out that whereas in the sub-human world transmission of hereditary 'information' is carried out by genes, in man alone an extra-genetic transmission exists and indeed exceeds the genetic in importance. For instance, man acquired the ability to fly not by any noteworthy change in his store of genes, but by the transmission of information through the cumulative mechanism of social teaching and learning. He has developed a sociogenic or psychosocial mechanism of evolution which overlies, and often overrides, the biological mechanism depending solely on genes.

This psychosocial transmission of accumulated experience in the form of tradition cannot be effective unless the human infant is genetically equipped as an 'authority-acceptor'; he is constructed so as to accept what he is told by his parents as authoritative. This 'proto-ethical mechanism' involves the internalization of external authority in the baby's primitive conscience.

'All this happens before he is old enough to verify his ideas by experience. During his later development he will modify and rectify the content and authoritarianism of what he has accepted, but will generally retain a great deal of both. The aim of the Humanist must be, not to destroy the inner authority of conscience, but to help the growing individual to escape from the shackles of an imposed authority-system into the supporting arms of one freely and consciously built up. And this will involve a thorough reformulation of the ethical aspects of religion'.[9]

Sir Julian Huxley, also writing in *The Humanist Frame*,[10] states, '. . . if I may over-simplify the matter, God appears to be a semantic symbol denoting . . . the various powers felt to be greater than our narrow selves, all bound together in the concept of a personal or super-personal sacred being in some way capable of affecting or guiding or interfering in the course of events. The forces are real enough: what we have done is, quite illegitimately, to project the god concept into them'.

By denying the existence of God, humanism logically rejects absolute moral values. In general, evolutionary humanists believe that the standard by which conscience makes judgments should be freely and consciously modified and built up into what the individual and society regard as their fulfilment. This naturally varies from one individual or society to another. It is basically different from the values and standards of Christian morality which are based on the character and will of God which he has chosen to reveal to us.

Conscience in Some Major Professional Dilemmas

The explosion of new medical knowledge and skill in the last half century has brought individual doctors face to face with some desperate moral decisions which were unasked of their predecessors. Many of these situations focus on a particular ethical conflict involving respect for human life and the compassionate relief of suffering. In the general run of medical practice these incidents are only occasional, but when they arise they cause considerable heart-searching, anxiety and distress to the doctor, and sometimes injustice to the patient. There is no escape from these choices. Vital decision-making is part of the physician's daily duty: to avoid the issue is to choose to do nothing. The varied circumstances in which this conflict arises include abortion on demand, active infanticide and euthanasia. We meet it also in the management of severe spina bifida, Down's Syndrome (mongolism), extensive burns and head injuries, and in clinical research, organ transplantation and *in vitro* fertilization.

Before the twentieth century medical ethics in the western world was virtually the same as Christian ethics. Today, many doctors do not profess to be Christians, though they may still accept the Christian ethic. Many are committed to other faiths, or profess none at all. There will therefore be many shades of opinion, conscientiously held, though fortunately there has been a beneficial unifying influence throughout the profession until now, inspired by the civil law, medical ethical codes, and the advice given by professional bodies such as the British Medical Association and the Medical Research Council. The British Medical Association's Handbook of Medical Ethics,[11] discussing abortion, states, 'If a doctor is uncertain he should always consult other colleagues, follow his own conscience, and act in the best interests of his patient.' But how reliable is conscience as a moral guide in the 'grey' areas of medicine? If one doctor's conscience differs from that of another, which of them is right?

At times doctors speak of following conscience when really they are being led by their own application of utilitarian philosophy, which seeks 'the greatest benefit for the greatest number'. This, is an approach which seeks to estimate the likely foreseeable results of a social situation and aims at bringing the best consequences out of it. It has a valuable place in deciding socio-political problems such as whether to spend limited resources on this or that, but when applied in isolation to clinical medicine the principle may be cruel and unjust. Let us take, for instance, a child with irreversible, but not immediately fatal, brain damage. Utilitarianism would take into account the child's management, the future of the relatives, and such social considerations as depriving other people of hospital nursing care, producing a longer waiting list, and using limited resources uneconomically. The decision reached by this philosophy might not be acceptable to the child or the family; but according to this philosophy, if we have any general 'compassion', why should we not manage this child in a way that will solve everyone's social problem—the greatest good of the greatest number?

Leo Alexander,[12] an American psychiatrist who was Chief of Counsel for War Crimes at the Nuremberg trials in 1946, subsequently wrote a paper on 'Medical Science under Dictatorship'. In it he stated, 'Medical Science in Nazi Germany collaborated with the Hegelian trend (ie. utilitarian philosophy) particularly in the following enterprises: the mass extermination of the chronically sick in the interest of saving 'useless' expenses to the community as a whole, (and) the mass extermination of those considered socially disturbing or racially and ideologically unwanted . . .'.

What is lacking in utilitarianism is absolute respect for the individual. When an act is intrinsically wrong in spite of promoting the common good, its wrongness usually consists of the individuäl being treated as a means and not an end. It was for such a situation that Kant proposed his absolute principle of morality, 'Act in such a way that you always treat humanity, whether in your own person or in the person of another, never simply as a means, but always at the same time as an end'. There is probably no sphere in which this counterbalance is more necessary that in medical ethics. It is the same basic ethical insight as the traditional Christian command to 'love your neighbour as yourself', to accord to every human being the same value as we all automatically accord to ourselves.

So the conscience of a utilitarian philosopher may make demands on his will which are different from those of a Christian who is concerned to obey God.

But now, to illustrate, we must discuss the two conflicting principles in rather more depth and detail.

The Apparent Conflict

We have already mentioned some medico-social situations in which the principles of 'respect for human life' and 'responsibility to care for those who suffer' seem to conflict. We may be tempted to balance them against each other, or to sacrifice one for the other, but this is a false antithesis. Respect for human life is part of God's law (and civil law, too) which sets the bounds within which we are required to live. Within that boundary we are to exercise the greatest compassion and care. As we have already noted, God's law is a restriction for the good of mankind. It instructs our minds and consciences, giving us a standard and limit we might well not come to by our own unaided wisdom. Compassion, on the other hand, is the motive and dynamic of our caring. If we turn this upside-down and make compassion for an individual or group our first rule and guide, we shall inevitably be tempted to solve their problems by sacrificing those who stand in the way. So often these are the weak—the unborn child, the infant, the subnormal and the elderly.

An everyday example of the correct position of law and compassion is seen in a Medical Board or Tribunal. A man who has been injured at work may be entitled to an allowance for his residual disability, provided his case fulfils certain criteria laid down by Parliament. A claimant before the Board may be pitifully poor, severely handicapped and genuinely deserving, and the Board members may want desperately to help him *but*, if he does not come within the scope of that particular allowance or benefit, he cannot have it and must seek help from another source. Parliament makes the laws, and parliament is the authority within whose laws the Board must practise with the greatest understanding and compassion. Some may think that Christians make too much of the sanctity of human life. They have no choice. God has made it clear what they ought to do, and if they love him, they must obey him (John 14:15, 21–23). Our compassion to each other needs to operate within the bounds he has laid down for our good.

THE SANCTITY OF LIFE

Let us now examine the biblical view of the sanctity of human life. It is taught in the following passages:

(a) God as the Author and Giver of life (Gen. 1:2; John 1:3; Col. 1:16)

Like an artistic creation to the artist, man is of inherent worth to his Creator-God. For this reason it is wrong for man to spoil or destroy a human life without a divine mandate. Without such a mandate he should regard human life as sacred and inviolable.

Primitive societies often encouraged abortion and infanticide under pressure from food shortage, and both practices were used in Greek and Roman times for economic reasons, to hide illegitimate conception and to preserve the mother's appearance. When the Hebrew Scriptures first taught the sanctity of human life, other contemporary societies were still considering life in terms of expediency. With the spread of Christianity there has been a slow and intermittent but progressive application of this concept within civilized society.

(b) God's judgment on Cain for the murder of his brother Abel (Gen. 4:1–15)

Here God judges and punishes wanton murder. Even the life of the murderer was not to be taken in the way of personal revenge after the pattern of the murderer's own crime. A family blood-feud was forbidden.

(c) God's judgment on violence in the days of Noah (Gen. 9:1–7)

'. . . of every man's brother I will require the life of man. Whoever sheds the blood of man, by man shall his blood be shed: for God made man in his own image'. Man's being made in the likeness of God was the attribute of man that gave his life sanctity, and this reason stands unchanged today. God made man for fellowship with himself and this is what makes him of such worth in God's sight—this, and Christ's death on the Cross to make a way back to God for rebellious man.

(d) The sixth commandment of the Decalogue 'You shall not kill' (Exod. 20:13)

It was a command that was recognized and applied long before the Law given at Sinai, but it was crystallized in the Mosaic Code. The word translated 'kill' here specifically denotes murder: the Code did not, for instance, prohibit capital punishment for certain offences in the Judaic social law. Moreover, the meaning, limited to murder, is also confirmed by the institution of 'cities of refuge' in Canaan to protect the life of the man who had unwittingly committed manslaughter. These cities were not to afford asylum to those guilty of murder (Num. 35:9–28).

(e) Christ's support for the sixth commandment (Matt. 5: 17–26)

In the Sermon on the Mount, Christ claimed that his teaching was in absolute harmony with the Law. He regarded the moral law, including this commandment, as permanent and unchangeable; and he developed in his teaching the positive way in which it was to be kept.

As Christians study such passages as these which clearly teach the worth of every human life to God, their consciences will become tuned more closely to God's will. This tuned conscience will keep a Christian doctor from taking the life of any innocent human being, even if asked to do so, and from abandoning a handicapped child so that it dies as a result. It does not mean, of course, that a doctor should try to prolong the life of the dying by uncomfortable and useless treatment.

This is no exclusively Christian belief. Thomas Jefferson, a Unitarian, regarded the right to life as self-evident, and most people of good will throughout the world will probably hold the same belief. Certainly, if the right to life is denied, all other rights are irrelevant. Nevertheless, those who hold this principle as having divine authority will give it more weight in their attitudes and decision-making.

COMPASSION FOR THOSE WHO SUFFER

It may seem unnecessary to comment at all on this ethical principle which we all claim to respect, but we need to be on our guard to avoid deceiving ourselves and being merely sentimental. It is pleasing to see ourselves as wanting to reduce the pain and suffering of the world in general, but we may be 'too busy' or 'not the best person' to check on the welfare of the lonely old lady next door. True compassion is not the emotion of a moment, but a steadfast purpose to see a particular needy person or persons helped. To get rid of someone else's problem by getting rid of him, and speak of it as considering his welfare, is black humour. It is a far cry from the compassion and sense of duty which compel doctors to refuse to abandon difficult and hopeless cases which they cannot cure. Some of these cases need years of patient support and personal encouragement. Facing up to and overcoming our personal problems and suffering is the only way we can become mature as godly people. It is striking that the suffering that Jesus went through to save us was in some way of benefit to him as Son of Man: 'he learned obedience through what he suffered' (Heb. 5:8).

If mistaking superficial sentiment for compassion is one danger, another is regarding anything done with a compassionate motive as necessarily beneficial. This is a cardinal error of our so-called compassionate society which tries to be kind before it has learned what is good. We need to give serious thought to the effect of our actions or we may—with the greatest compassion—do harm. Many a son has been given his own way and grown up spoilt and undisciplined. Uninformed 'love' has often allowed a little girl to have her bedtime drink in her nightdress by an unguarded fire, resulting in extensive or fatal burns. A surgeon may be faced with a patient's frightened pleading to postpone a life-saving operation: his yielding to misguided compassion would cost the patient his life. Compassion is a potent motivating force, but is not a guide to what is good.

With these twin callings to respect human life and to care for the sick and helpless, it is no wonder that Christians have always been active in the defence of human values. Whether it is Mother Teresa in the streets of Calcutta, Albert Schweitzer in his hospital in Lambarene in Central Africa or the countless nurses and doctors working in mission hospitals, the story is the same—a loving care for individuals who may outwardly seem of little worth.

The Hippocratic Oath (around 400 BC) was a code of conduct for physicians proposed by an obscure group in Greece called the Pythagoreans. In it the doctor promised to do no harm to his patient, never to prescribe lethal drugs even if asked to do so, and not to give a pessary to a woman to procure an abortion. This oath was adopted by Christian physicians in Europe and was still generally accepted until recently. Indeed, in 1948, it was modernized in the Declaration of Geneva and adopted by the World Health Organization and the British Medical Association. The Declaration includes the sentence, 'I will maintain the utmost respect for human life from the time of conception.'

Early Christians were noted for their high regard for human life. Tertullian wrote in AD 200, 'For us, indeed, homicide having been forbidden once and for all, it is not lawful to destroy even that which is conceived in the womb while the life-blood is still being drawn into a human being.'

Conscience in Everyday Medical Practice

The role of conscience in daily medical practice is less spectacular but no less vital than in major professional dilemmas. We all share a common humanity and experience similar temptations. The doctor in his practice is expected to be especially kind, truthful and discreet, and this is because the doctor-patient relationship is one of trust—trust about the patient's most personal and confidential affairs. The doctor is expected to be available, conscientious and disciplined at all times of day or night, ever ready to respond to the emergency needs of his patients. Rewards, or the lack of them, must never interfere with his judgement or his duty to put his patient's interests first. He is expected to be a loyal colleague, a patient teacher and an inspiring team leader. He should have a good name, and of course never steal the good name of another. How much he lives up to his code of ethics, only the doctor knows—he and his conscience. Except when his failures become public, conscience is his only prompter. How important to his patients that that 'faithful friend' is heard and heeded.

We have seen that something more than an ethical code is needed. A code provides no effective incentive to the individual to obey it, except when there is a likelihood of being exposed and penalized. We all know the quickened pulse when we are exceeding the speed limit and see a police car in the driving mirror. We slow down, only to work up to our previous speed 'when it's safe', making a thousand good excuses! And more is needed, too, than a dulled conscience which can be fobbed off with minimal fulfilment, fulfilment of the letter of the law only, fulfilment sufficient to satisfy appearances.

Surgeon Vice Admiral Sir James Watt[13] has described how a Christian interpretation of ethics has become enshrined in the concept of individual accountability to God for both personal conduct and personal responsibility for others. This is guided, he continues, not by rules, but by a conscience sensitized to right and wrong 'through that absolute and enduring standard of reference —Jesus himself'. Here is the supreme standard for the Christian who is trying to walk in the steps of his Master. Would Jesus have done this? Would he have said that? Perhaps, however, we should not draw too great a distinction between Jesus, the living Word, and the Bible, the written Word. We know the character and attitudes of Jesus only from the Bible. It is significant, too, that when Jesus was so artfully and plausibly tempted by the devil, he turned repeatedly to the Scriptures for guidance and strength, and to counter-attack the tempter.

Conclusions

1. Man's conscience judges him by the moral light he has, and not by the light he does not have. One man's conscience may therefore differ from another's although all start with an awareness of right and wrong and of the natural law. If we follow conscience we may not always be right; but if we act against it we shall surely be wrong, because we are acting against the highest standards we have. Here lies the importance of every man reading the Bible to instruct his conscience in the will of God.
2. As an illustrative example we have considered the fundamental evaluation of the worth of human life, an extremely important and topical subject today. Value is an attribute ascribed by a person. Man's estimate of the worth of a human life is often based on social usefulness: on the other hand, a terrorist may devalue life to being

expendable for political ends. From time to time we are surprised to read in the newspaper of a nameless child being flown half way round the world to receive the latest expensive treatment to save its life. At the same time we can ignore that in over 100 countries 40,000 children are dying every day from malnutrition and related diseases. Jesus was not silent about these fickle assessments. To his friends the rich and influential Dives was worth many leprous beggars in the street, but beyond the grave the assessment was reversed (Luke 16:19–31).

In medical practice today, is it right to terminate human life for convenience, or to solve social problems, or to reduce the suffering of the severely handicapped? Conscience is blunted and the will vacillates when God's view of human worth is ignored. God, too, has his own estimate of the worth of human life. To God, man is of inherent worth because he made man in his own likeness, a unique creation intended for fellowship with his Maker, now and eternally, and God longs to have all men and women reconciled to himself.This is why Jesus came to restore man to himself. Man is not just a superior animal who can justifiably be put down for certain reasons, and that is the end of it. If we are going to use our consciences in medical practice this assessment of human worth cannot be ignored. In fact, it is God's assessment of the worth of human life that is the basis of its sanctity and of our responsibility to respect it.

3. But light—even the light of God's will and character, revealed in the Bible and confirmed by conscience—is not enough to enable man to walk in God's ways. The mind can be full of divine light while the heart is devoid of divine love, and the will remains disobedient. Just as the Old Testament law was powerless to make men follow God's will, so ethical principles and professional codes today give light but cannot ensure compliance. When a man turns from his own way and asks Christ to forgive him and to be his Lord, God does something. God responds by giving him 'a new heart'; that is, new desires and affections. Chief among them are a desire and power to do God's will (Phil. 2:18). This, of course, does not mean that the Christian becomes perfect overnight, but he begins a life process of feeding his new nature and being controlled by God's Spirit while starving his old self-centred nature which in the past made him habitually choose his own way. The dynamic of the Christian life is not devotion to an ideology or a creed, nor allegiance to a party, but a desire to please the Lord Jesus in response to his love in giving his life for us.

4. The Christian never outgrows the need for conscience. In the first place, being subject to temptation, he needs the promptings of

conscience to keep him in the path of duty and obedience to God. Isaiah put it like this: 'your ears shall hear a word behind you, saying, "This is the way, walk in it", when you turn to the right or when you turn to the left' (30:21). When the Christian turns off the highway, he will hear a voice behind him hailing him, like a man calling after a traveller who has taken the wrong road. The caller is behind. The traveller cannot see him, but he can see the traveller. While the traveller is on the right road, he will hear no correction and may be reassured.

Secondly, the Christian needs the assurance of a clear conscience if he is going to enjoy God's promised companionship day by day. Such confidence is possible only as we rest on his promises—for instance, 'if we confess our sins he is faithful and just, and will forgive our sins and cleanse us from all unrighteousness' (1 John 1:9).

Notes and Index

CHAPTER ONE

SELECT BIBLIOGRAPHY

Despite the extent of early written evidence many details remain open to differences of interpretation. In part this may be due to some of the texts having been studied by those without special medical knowledge. However, there are today an increasing number of specialist studies in this field. For Egypt, the text publications of H. Grapow and colleagues, and studies by G. Lefebvre and P. Ghalioungui; for Babylonia the text editions of F. Köcher, R. Labat, and earlier R. C. Thompson and E. Ebeling, are fundamental as are the more recent studies of A. L. Oppenheim, R. D. Biggs, J. V. Kinnier Wilson. Biblical (and Talmudic) medicine still relies largely on the study by Julius Preuss and his recent follower F. Rosner.

Of the major histories of Medicine that by H. Sigerist (1951) is spoilt by the overemphasis on the magical and religious aspects. Good overall presentations are included in some volumes devoted to the history of science (e.g. *History of Science* Vol. 8, Cambridge 1969). The symposia edited by D. Brothwell include excellent and detailed studies of specific aspects.

A. GENERAL

BROTHWELL, 1967. D. Brothwell & A. T. Sandison, *Diseases in Antiquity* (Springfield, Ill. 1967).

EDELSTEIN, 1967. L. Edelstein, *Ancient Medicine* (Baltimore, Johns Hopkins Press, 1967).

SIGERIST, 1951. H. Sigerist, *A History of Medicine 1* (Oxford University Press, 1951).

B. OLD TESTAMENT

General

HARRISON, 1979. R. K. Harrison, 'Disease' in *The International Standard Bible Encyclopedia* 1 (Grand Rapids, Wm. B. Eerdmans, 1979), 953–960.

HUMBERT, 1964. P. Humbert, 'Maladie et médicine dans l'Ancien Testament' *Revue. Hist. et Philosph. religieuses* XLIV (1964), 1–29.

MASTERMAN, 1920. E. W. G. Masterman, *Hygiene and Disease in Palestine in Modern and in Biblical Times* (Palestine Exploration Fund, 1920).

PREUSS, 1978. J. Preuss, *Biblical and Talmudic Medicine*, Translated and Edited by F. Rosner (New York, Sanhedrin Press, 1978; reprint of 1911 with notes).

ROSNER (ROSEN) 1977. F. Rosner, *Medicine in the Bible and the Talmud* (New York, Ktav, 1977).

SUSSMAN, 1967. M. Sussman, 'Diseases in the Bible and Talmud' in Brothwell (1967), 209–221.

TOURNIER, 1954. P. Tournier, *A Doctor's Casebook in the Light of the Bible* (London, SCM Press, 1954).

TRAPNELL, 1980. D. Trapnell, 'Health, Disease and Healing' in *The Illustrated Bible Dictionary* 2 (Leicester, Inter-Varsity Press, 1980), 616–625.

KINNIER WILSON, 1982. 'Medicine in the Land and Times of the Old Testament', in T. Ishida (ed.), *Studies in the Period of David and Solomon and other Essays* (Tokyo, Yamakawa-Shuppansha, 1982), 337–365.

Special studies

BROWNE, 1974. S. G. Browne, *Leprosy in the Bible* (London, Christian Medical Fellowship, 1974).

BROWNE, 1970. S. G. Browne, 'How Old is Leprosy?', *British Medical Journal* (12 Sept. 1970) 3, 640–641.

GREENBLATT, 1977. R. B. Greenblatt, *Search the Scriptures: Modern Medicine and Biblical Personages* (Philadelphia and Toronto, J. B. Lippincott, 1977).

MCMILLEN, 1969. S. I. McMillen, *None of these Diseases* (London, Oliphant, 1969).

RATTRAY, 1903. A. Rattray, *Divine Hygiene* (London, James Nisbett, 1903).

SHORT, 1953. A. Rendle Short, *The Bible and Modern Medicine* (London, Paternoster Press, 1953).

C. EGYPTIAN MEDICINE

GHALIOUNGUI, 1973. P. Ghalioungui, *The House of Life: Magic and Medical Science in Ancient Egypt* (Amsterdam, B. M. Israël, 1973).

GHALIOUNGUI, 1965. P. Ghalioungui & Z. El-Dawakhly, *Health and Healing in Ancient Egypt* (Cairo, Dar el-Maaref, 1965).

GRAPOW. H. Grapow (ed.), *Grundriss der Medizin der alten Ägypter* (Berlin, Akademie-Verlag, 1954–1973) 1 (1954), Anatomie und Physiologie; II von den medizinischen Texten (1955); III Kranker, Krankheiten und Arzt (1956); IV Übersetzung der medizinischen Texte (1958); V Die med. Texte in hieroglyph. Umschreibung autographiert (1958); VI

Wörterbuch der aegypt. Drogennamen (1959); VII (ed. H. von Deines-W. Westendorf) Wörterbuch der mediz. Texte (1961/2); VIII Grammatik der medizin. Texte (1962); IX Ergänzungen (1973).

LEFEBVRE, 1956. G. Lefebvre, *Essai sur la Médecine égyptienne de l'Époque pharaonique* (Paris, PVF, 1956).

Special studies

DAWSON, 1967. W. R. Dawson, 'The Egyptian Medical Papyri', in D. Brothwell (1967), 98–114.

GRAY, 1967. P. H. K. Gray, 'Calcinosis Intervertebralis, with special reference to similar changes found in mummies of Ancient Egypt', in Brothwell (1967), 20–30.

RUFFER, 1967. M. A. Ruffer, 'Note on the presence of "Bilharzia Haemotobia" in Egyptian mummies of the Twentieth Dynasty (1250–1000 BC)' in Brothwell (1967), 177.

MORSE, 1967. D. Morse, 'Tuberculosis' in Brothwell (1967), 249–271.

MORSE, 1967. D. Morse *et al.*, 'Tuberculosis in Ancient Egypt', *American Review of Respiratory Diseases* 90 (1964), 524–541.

ROWLING, 1967. J. T. Rowling, 'Hernia in Egypt' in D. Brothwell (1967), 444–448; 'Respiratory Disease in Egypt' *ibid.*, 489–493; 'Urology in Egypt', *ibid* 532–537.

D. BABYLONIAN MEDICINE

General

BIGGS, 1969. R. D. Biggs, 'Medicine in Ancient Mesopotamia', *History of Science* 8 (Cambridge, Heffer, 1969), 94–105.

KÖCHER, 1963. F. Köcher, *Die Babylonisch-assyrische Medizin in Texten und Untersuchungen I-VI* (Berlin, de Gruyter, 1963–1980).

LABAT, 1951. R. Labat, *Traité akkadien de Diagnostics et Prognostics médicaux* (Leiden, Brill, 1951).

OPPENHEIM, 1962. A. L. Oppenheim, 'Mesopotamian Medicine', *Bulletin History of Medicine* 36 (1962), 97–108.

REINER, 1965. E. Reiner, 'Medicine in Ancient Mesopotamia', *Minerva Med.* 56 (1965), 1465–1468.

THOMPSON, 1923. *Assyrian Medical Texts* (London, British Museum, 1923).

THOMPSON, 1949. R. C. Thompson, *Dictionary of Assyrian Botany*, (London, British Academy, 1949).

WHITE, 1967. W. White, 'Diagnostic Principles of Assyrian Medical Texts', Paper presented at the XVVII International Congress of Orientalists, University of Michigan, Ann Arbor, August 16, 1967.

KINNIER WILSON, 1967. J. V. Kinnier Wilson, 'Organic Diseases of Ancient Mesopotamia', in Brothwell (1967), 191–208.

Specialist studies

EDEL, 1976. E. Edel, *Ägyptische Arzte und ägyptische Medizin am hethitisches Königshof*, 1976.

FINET, 1957. A. Finet, 'Les médicins au royaume de Mari', *Annuaire de l'Institut de Philologie et d'Histoire Orientales et slaves* XIV (Brussels, 1954/7), 123–144.

KINNIER WILSON, 1967. J. V. Kinnier Wilson, 'Mental Diseases of Ancient Mesopotamia' in Brothwell (1967), 723–733.

OPPENHEIM, 1960. 'A Caesarian Section in the second millennium BC', *J. Hist. Med. & Allied Sci.* 15 (1960), 292.

OPPENHEIM, 1962. A. L. Oppenheim, 'On the Observation of the pulse in Mesopotamian medicine', *Orientalia* 21 (Rome, 1962), 27–33.

RADBILL, 1973. S. X. Radbill, 'Mesopotamian pediatrics', *Episteme* 7 (1973), 283–288.

WHITE, 1969. W. White, 'An Assyrian Physician's *Vade mecum*, *Clio Medica* 4 (1969), 159–171.

NOTES

(*This chapter was written in 1983; no reference is made to later literature—D.J.W.*)

1 Ghalioungui, 1973.
2 G. E. Smith, *The Royal Mummies* (1912); R. Daird, *X-Raying the Pharaohs* (London, 1973); K. Manchester, *The Archaeology of Disease* (Bradford, 1983).
3 M. Civil, *Revue d'Assyriologie* 54 (1960), 57–72.
4 White, 1969.
5 Thompson, 1923; Labat, 1951; Köcher, 1963; White, 1967.
6 Jubilees 10, cf. Baba Bathra 16.
7 Ebers, I. 82.
8 Herodotus II. 84.
9 Ghalioungui, 1973; Trapnell, 1980.
10 Kinnier Wilson, 1982, 348.
11 C. J. Gadd in *Cambridge Ancient History* III/2 (1975), 39–40.
12 *Archives royales de Mari* I.115; XIV.3.
13 'The Tale of the Poor Man of Nippur', *Anatolian Studies* 6 (1956), 145–164; *Ur* 4 (1980), 31–34.
14 Herodotus I.197.
15 cf. *Journal of the Royal Asiatic Society* 1926, 689. The precise meaning of the Heb. (*ma'ᵃṣēḇ*) 'place of pain' (Isa. 50:11 AV 'sorrow') is unknown.
16 Herodotus II.77.
17 H. Zimmern, *Beiträge zur Kenntniss der babylonischen Religion* I (Leipzig, 1896), 24, 28–30.
18 E.g. Hebrew names compounded with *šlm* ('to be well, in agreement' etc.): Solomon, Shallum, Meshullam etc. Egyptian names with *snb* ('I possess health').
19 Heb. *ḥāyâ* 'to (re)gain health/life'.
20 E.g. lamashtu-plaques; for illustrations see *Illustrated Bible Dictionary* (Inter-Varsity Press, Tyndale House Publishers, 1980), 619, 621.

21 E.g. Rep̄a'el, 'God heals'; Yirpe'el, 'God will heal', and 'il-rp'i, 'El heals (me)' from Ugarit (13th. cent. BC).
22 W. W. Hallo, 'Individual Prayer in Sumerian: The Continuity of a Tradition', *Journal of the American Oriental Society* 88 (1968), 77.
23 Rosner, 1977, 9.
24 M. I. Hussey, 'Anatomical Nomenclature in an Akkadian Omen Text', *Journal of Cuneiform Studies* 2 (1949), 21ff.
25 Biggs, 1969, 101; Ghalioungui, 1973, 46 states that those who opened dead bodies for the embalmers were considered outcasts because of their sacrilegious work and the danger of contamination by evil spirits.
26 Plinius *Histor. Natur.* 19, 27; Rabbi Ishmael, *Tosefta Nidda* 4:17; Preuss, 1911, 41–42.
27 S. Munter in Rosner, 1977, 10: *gid* (nerve, sinew); '*or* (skin); *šok̠* (thigh); *kis* (scrotum); *šet̠* (buttocks); *ḥeq* (bosom); *pêh* (mouth); *šen* (tooth); *'ap̄* (nose); '*ayin* (eye); *rôš* (head); *gûp̄* (body); *gab̠* (back); *lo'â* (throat); *mē'â* (internal organs); *šad* (breast); *dad* (nipple); *kap̄* (palm); *yad̠* (hand) etc.
28 as in Akkadian *libbu*.
29 E.g. anguish (Jer. 23:9); delight (1 Kgs. 8:66); shame (Ps. 69:21); pleasure (Ps. 16:9); love (Exod. 35:22) etc.
30 G. R. Driver, *Zeitschrift für die alttestamentliche Wissenschaft* 65 (1953), 255; D. D. Luckenbill, *Annals of Sennacherib* (1924), 47, vii 30–31.
31 Oppenheim, 1962; J. V. Kinnier Wilson, *Iraq* 24 (1962), 61.
32 Ghalioungui, 1973, 50.
33 Ebbers, 8555c.
34 Ghalioungui, 1973, 49.
35 Heb. *kābed̠;* Baby. *kabādu*, 'to become heavy, fat'. The Babylonians rarely refer to the *kabattu* (which may mean 'belly, inside' in general) since the liver in extispicy is called *amūtu*.
36 Ghalioungui, 1973, 50, 124–5.
37 *mē'â* (plural only).
38 Gen. 43:30; 1 Kgs. 3:26; Cant. 5:4.
39 Ps. 47:9; Jer. 11:20; 17:10; 20:12 cf. Rev. 2:23.
40 Grapow, 1954, 13; Preuss, 1978, 61.
41 cf. n. 71. Rosner, 1977, 70–74.
42 Ebers, 522.
43 R. Labat, *Journal asiatique* (1954), 213 n. 2.
44 Egyptian *Book of Bandagists;* Babylonian words include *riksu*, *ṣimdu*, *adapu*, *e'alu*, *ulapu*, *agittu* etc.
45 Ebers, 504.
46 For trepanning of skulls see O. Tufnell, *Lachish* III (1963), 63, 405.
47 Oppenheim, 1960, 292; Kinnier Wilson in Brothwell, 1967, 203.
48 G. R. Driver, *The Babylonian Laws I* (1952), 416–420 (§§ 215–225).
49 J. Sasson, 'Circumcision in the Ancient Near East', *Journal of Biblical Literature* 85 (1966), 473–6; Zipporah used a flint knife on her son to save his life (Ex. 4:25) and Joshua a similar instrument (Josh. 5:3). For circumcision among Hittites see *Journal of Cuneiform Studies* 35 (1983), 139.

50 Dioscorides V. 158 ('Memphis marble'); Pliny XXXVI.11.2.
51 Heb. *pi'el;* Baby. *purrusu(m)* e.g. *'iwwer* (blind), *passeaḥ* (lame).
52 D. J. Wiseman, 'Law and Order in Old Testament Times', *Vox Evangelica* VIII (1973), 12.
53 E.g. Jer. 39:6–7; 52:10–11; Sennacherib, Lachish reliefs (British Museum 124907).
54 Short, 1953, 64.
55 Preuss, 1978, 230.
56 Short, 1953, 60.
57 Josh. 15:13; Josephus, *Antiq. Jud.* V 213.
58 Skeletons 3.2 m. tall have been found elsewhere in Syro-Palestine.
59 R. Laird Harris (ed.), *Theological Wordbook of the Old Testament* (Chicago, 1980), 551–2 sub *ng', maggēpâ.*
60 2 Sam. 24:15; 1 Chron. 21:12, 14; cf. Josephus, *Antiq. Jud.* VII.326.
61 Heb. *deber* cf. Arab. *dbr.*
62 v.9, LXX 'swelling of the groin'. For such tumours or swellings (Heb. *'opalîm;* AV 'emerods') see also Deut. 28:27. Megillah 256 takes this wrongly as haemorrhoidal tags.
63 Dioscorides and Poseidonus apud Preuss, 1978, 155.
64 J. F. D. Shrewsbury, *The Plague of the Philistines* (London, 1964), 33–39.
65 Herodotus II.141.
66 P. B. A. Adamson, 'Death from Disease in Ancient Mesopotamia', in B. Alster (ed.), *Death in Mesopotamia* (Copenhagen, 1980), 187. E. V. Hulse, 'Joshua's Curse and the abandonment of Ancient Jericho: Schistosomiasis as a possible medical explanation', *Medical History* 15 (1971), 376–386.
67 *Archives royale de Mari* (*ARM*) X 129–130; Finet, 1957, 123–144; *ARM* III 61; V.87.
68 Kinnier Wilson, 1983, 344–5.
69 D. Morse *et al.*, 'Tuberculosis in Ancient Egypt', *Amer. Per. Respiratory Diseases* 90 (1964), 524.
70 The Egypt. *aat* is more likely to be 'plague'. There is some evidence for malaria in the U. Nile valley in prehistoric times but not later in the Delta despite Herodotus' reference to fishing nets used as a protection from mosquitoes (II. 95). The view that the Shunammite boy died of cerebral malaria (2 Kgs. 4:18–20; Short, 1953, 62) or that the 'burning ague' of Lev:26.16 (AV Heb. *qdḥt*) or the 'inflammation', (Deut. 28:22; Heb. *dlqt,* LXX 'intermittent fever') was 'tertian malaria' remains unproven.
71 Based on the form *pi'ālōn* thus 'madness' (*šiggāyōn*); 'severe stupor' (*šimmāmōn,* Ezek. 4:16; 12:19), 'bewilderment of mind' (*timmāhōn,* Deut. 28:28–29); 'anxious care' (*de'ābōn,* Deut. 28:65); 'depression' (*'iṣṣābōn,* Gen. 3:17). In this lexical group emotion states are included e.g. 'trepidation' (AV), 'overhasty judgment' (*hippāṣōn,* Deut. 16:3; Isa. 52:12); 'outbursts of excessive rage' (*'ibbārōn,* Gen. 49:7), 'fear of impending death' (*killāyōn,* Isa. 10:22) and even 'breaking to pieces' (*šibbārōn;* as affecting the loins [lumbago?] Ezek. 21:11, cf. Jer. 17:18; or more generally from fear, Job. 41:17 cf. Prov. 15:4).

72 There is no reason to believe that his behaviour was in imitation of that of Saul (Masterman, 1920, 43) or was 'hallucination' (Rosen, 1977, 10). 'madness' (*šiggāyōn*) is associated with dismay, terror and blindness (Deut. 28:24, 28) and was the observable reaction to disaster. It describes the way a rider (Zech. 12:4), chariot-driver (Jehu, 1 Kgs. 19:16–17) or even a prophet (Hos. 9:7) could act. The parallel Akkadian *šegû* is used of lions, dogs and argumentative women so I have proposed that it denotes 'excessively aggressive behaviour' or the like (*Vetus Testamentum* 33, 1982, 320–321.)

73 J. V. Kinnier Wilson, *Assyriological Studies* 16 (Chicago, 1965), 289ff; but contra, Biggs, 1969, 102; see also p. 00.

74 Harrison, 1979, 956; *Interpreters Dictionary of the Bible* I (1962), 551.

75 Short, 1953, 65; Preuss, 1978, 311.

76 See D. J. Wiseman, *Nebuchadrezzar and Babylon* (British Academy, London, 1985), 103–105.

77 'Prescription for an Anxiety State', *Anatolian Studies* 30 (1980), 25–26; cf. *ašušṭu, hattu pirittu, huṣ hēpī libbi* etc.

78 The Series *Maqlu* (see n. 73).

79 Status epilepticus, Preuss, 1978, 299.

80 Kinnier Wilson, 1983, 351; Labat, 1951, 80; O. R. Gurney, *The Sultan Tepe Tablets* I (1957), 57 (babies); 91 and unpublished inscriptions in the British Museum.

81 Ghalioungui, 1973, 125–127; Egyptian *Book of the Heart* for psychic and mental symptoms; Ebers, 8, 20–22, 31–33. Strangely they thought that paralysis always occurred on the same side as the cranial lesion.

82 Harrison, 1979, 955.

83 Preuss, 1978, 306.

84 Masterman, 1920, 44; Harrison, 1979, 956.

85 Short, 1953, 61.

86 2 Kgs. 4:19; 1 Chron. 4:8 interpreted as headache in Temurah 16c.

87 R. C. Thompson, 'Assyrian Prescriptions for the Head', *American Journal of Semitic Languages* 54 (1937), 12–25; Babylonian *di'u, ra'ibu, ṣidanu* ('dizziness'). For association with epilepsy see Labat, 1951, 86, 53. For a possible description of malignant hypertension see Brockwell, 1967, 201.

88 Ghalioungui, 1973, 126; cf. Ebers, 623–4, 856.

89 Preuss, 1978, 305.

90 Isa. 5:15; Deut. 7:16; Ezek. 24:16 etc.

91 Gen. 29:17 has been taken as a form of corneal opacity (*dak*) perhaps an inflammation of the eyelids (blepheritis ciliarii). Lev. 15:3–6 may describe opthalmia gonorrhea.

92 Exod. 21:16; *Laws of Hammurapi* §§ 198–9; 215–200 cf. 247.

93 Deut. 27:18; 28:79; Isa. 59:10.

94 Gen. 19:11 (*sanwērîm*), cf. Lev. 22:22 *'brt* (*'awwereṯ*).

95 Ps. 146:8; Isa. 42:7 cf. Job 29:15.

96 Ghalioungui, 1973, 130–1; Heb. *'išôn* (AV, RSV, NIV 'apple' of the eye, Deut. 32:10; Ps. 7:8; Prov. 7:2; Lam. 2:18; Zech. 2:8).

97 Interpreted as staphyloma, styges, mydriasis, seasonal opthalmophlegia or trachoma.
98 Thompson, 1923, 16; *šillurmā* blindness 3 ii 8–9; Kinnier Wilson, 1967, 192.
99 Thompson 1923; Kocher & Oppenheim, 1957. The cornea was the 'guardian of the eye' (*lamassat īni*).
100 G. R. Driver, *op. cit.*, 78–81 refers to another operation also requiring 'a deep incision' (lit. 'a grave wound'), see n. 48, but for contra views Oppenheim, 1962 and Von Soden, 1949. A more recent interpretation suggests the opening of the temple area which affected the eye (*Chicago Assyrian Dictionary* 11/1 (1980), 185 sub *nakkaptu*.
101 Exod. 4:11; Isa. 35:5; Job 33:16 cf. Ps. 119:18.
102 Exod. 4:11; Lev. 19:14; Isa. 29:18 (*ḥereš*) cf. Isa. 6:10; 59:1.
103 Ps. 38:14; 1 Sam. 7:8; Ebers, 854e.; Babylonian *hasikku*.
104 R. C. Thompson, 'Assyrian prescriptions for diseases of the ear', *Journal of the Royal Asiatic Society* (1931), 1–25; tinnitus (Kinnier Wilson, 1967, 199) and suppurative otitis media were known.
105 Gen 2:7; Job 27:3.
106 Exod. 15:8; 2 Sam. 22:10; Ps. 18:15. Food coming out of the nostrils (Num. 11:20) was a part of vomiting.
107 AV 'flat nose', cf. NIV 'disfigured'; Rabbis: 'absence of the bridge of the nose' Mishnah *Bekorot* 7.3.
108 Ebers, 854b; Babylonian *ḥasartu, hihinu*.
109 Labat, 1951, 24, 51, 348; *Archiv für Orientforschungen* II (1936), 223, 30; Thompson, 1923, 105.14.
110 Laws of Eshnunna 42.32; Ezek. 23:25; *Annals of the Kings of Assyria* I 294 i. 117; Middle Assyrian Laws 4–5, 15.
111 Heb. *gārōn;* Babylonian *napištum*.
112 Ps. 69:3; Jer. 2:25; the onomatopaeic English 'gargle' is from Heb. '*irer;* Greek *gargariyo;* Arabic *gargar*.
113 Labat, 1951, 84, 29; 34 n. 163; Kinnier Wilson, 1967, 205.
114 The AV 'stammering' lips (Isa. 28:11) or tongue (33:11) probably refers to the (unintelligible) foreign languages (so NIV Heb. *lā'eg*); Bab. 'lisp' (*hasû*); 'stutter' (*šassā'u*).
115 Lam. 3:16; Ezek. 18:12; Ps. 3:7; 58:6.
116 Lev. 24:20; Deut. 19:21; cf. Exod. 21:27.
117 Job 19:20 NIV margin 'only my gums'; cf. F. J. Anderson, *Job* (Inter Varsity Press 1976), 192. For 'gnashing of teeth' as a sign of anger see Job 16:9; Ps. 35:16; 37:12; 112:10; Lam. 2:16.
118 Ghalioungh, 155.
119 *The Legend of the Worm;* J. B. Pritchard, *Ancient Near Eastern Texts relating to the Old Testament* (1969), 100; Anast. papyrus; Ghalioungi, 117; Ebers, 739–740 & 743. Egypt *ībh* 'he who deals with teeth'. Baby. 'wall of the teeth' = gums (*dūr šinni*).
120 *Journal of Near Eastern studies* 2 (1943), 314; cf. *Iraq* 5 (1938), 82–4. Thompson, 1949, passim.
121 Num. 12:10; 2 Kgs. 5:27; cf. Ghalioungi, 134–5; G. J. Wenham, *Leviticus* (NICOT 1979), 194–7, Browne 1974, 5.

122 Browne, *op. cit.;* M. Sussman in Rosen, 1967, 216 contra Preuss, 1978, 374–390. Lev. 13:11 may be chronic syphilis; v. 18 erysipelas adjacent to a boil; v. 24 infection following a burn; v. 29 ringworm or sycocis of the scalp and beard; v. 36 a pustular dermatitis and v. 42 a favus or desert sore or leishmaniasis.

123 Brothwell, 1967, 206–7 (*saharšubbu, epqu*); E. Reiner, *Bibliotheca Mesopotamia* 2/2 (1981), 44.

124 600 skeletons from Lachish were examined; Biggs, 1969, 102; cf. Browne, *British Medical Journal* (1970–3), 640–1 (dating of leprosy); T. Dzierykray-Rogalski, 'Paleopathology of the Ptolemaic Inhabitants of Dakhleh Oasis (Egypt)', *Journal of Human Evolution* (1980), 9, 71–74.

125 For swellings, AV 'emerods', RSV 'ulcers'; 'festering sores' (NIV) cf. AV 'scab', RSV 'scurvy'. Boils and ulcers affected the knees, legs and whole body (Deut. 28:35; Lev. 13:18–20; Exod. 9:9–11). White spots on the skin may be psoriasis (Lev. 13:38). Festering sores are mentioned with scab or scurf (Lev. 21:20–21; Isa. 3:17).

126 Preuss, 1978, 340; Short, 1953, 53. For ringworm see Lev. 13:29; and scurvy and pellagra, Kinnier Wilson, 1982, 360–361.

127 LXX translated 'rub figs on the *šḥn*'; cf. Short, 1953, 55, Pliny *Nat. Hist.* XXII–7; Ugaritic Texts 55.28; 56.33 (mixture of figs, matured raisins and bean flour, extract injected into horses' nostrils).

128 Isa. 15:2; Jer. 16:6; Ezek. 7:18; 27.31f; Amos 8:10; Mic. 1:6.

129 J. Gray, *I-II Kings* (1970), 480 thinks the baldness was a tonsure but there is no evidence for such so early.

130 Perhaps a case of generalized hypertrichosis (Gen. 25:25; 27:11).

131 Ghalioungui, 1978, 135.

132 Bab. *qubbuhu;* cf. *The Myth of Nergal and Ereshkigal*, iv. 31.

133 Rosen, 1977, 59–60; Preuss, 1978, 168; also Rabbinic writers *Sanhedrin* 48b; cf. Ghalioungui, 637.

134 *NY State J. Med.* 1975, 452; Harrison, 1979, 957.

135 Harrison, 1979, 957. For venereal disease see Kinnier Wilson 1982, 358.

136 Kinnier Wilson, 1982, 357–8.

137 Short, 1953, 63; Harrison, 1979, 957–8.

138 D. J. Wiseman, *The Alalakh Tablets* (1953), Nos. 92–94; I. Mendelsohn, 'On Marriage at Alakakh', *Essays on Jewish Life and Thought* (1959), 351–357.

139 Thompson, 1949, passim. The Egyptians used a type of sea-sponge soaked with lemon juice.

140 A. D. Kilmer, 'The Mesopotamian Concept of Overpopulation', *Orientalia* 41 (1972), 160–177.

141 Ghalioungui, 1973, 112.

142 E.g. Ghalioungui, 1973, 113; Labat, 1951, 200.1; 206.70 (yellowness of mother's face taken as sign it would be a boy and belly pointed as her nose a girl).

143 Bab. *edamukku; Chicago Assyrian Dictionary* 4 (1968), 417a; Ebers, 789–793; bilateral oedema of feet and ankles (Kinnier Wilson, 1967, 295); toxaemia, Labat. 1951, 206–8.

144 Isa. 13:8; 21:3; 27:17; 42:14; 66:7; Jer. 4:31; Hos. 13:13; Mic. 5:3; Sir. 19:11.
145 Judg. 13:14; Preuss, 1978, 385.
146 Exod. 21:22; Laws of Hammurapi §§209–211; The arborted foetus was 'a fall' (Ps. 58:9; Job 3:15); abortion (Bab. *ṣalā'u, ṣilittum, nid libbi*).
147 Thompson, 1949, 159–160, 190.
148 i.e. 'hard uterus' (=small pelvis?); cf. 2 Sam. 6:14, 20, 23; Sanhedrin 21a; Megillah 13a.
149 midwife (Heb. *m^eyalledeṯ;* Gen. 38:27–30; Exod. 11:15–21; Bab. *sasurātum, sabsūtu;* Epic of Atrahasis 61–2, 103; 291–2. Birthstones (Heb. *'abanayîm;* Exod. 1:16; cf. Isa. 37:3; Hos. 13:13 *mašber*; Bab. *aban āladi*); K. A. Kitchen 'midwife' in *Illustrated Bible Dictionary* 1980, 998–9.
150 Gen. 25:24–26; 38:38. Masterman (1920), 29 thinks the delivery may have been accompanied by a ruptured perinaeum. Heb. *srk* 'umbilical cord', AV 'navel' (Ezek. 16:4); Bab. *abunnatu*.
151 Breastfeeding was a picture of blessing (Gen. 49:25 cf. Lam. 4:3; Hos. 1:8. For the use of a wet-nurse Gen. 24:59; 35:8; 2 Kgs. 11:2; Laws of Hammurapi § 194). A child on its mother's knee is illustrated c.2100 BC in D. J. Wiseman, *Cylinder Seals on Western Asia* (1958), 38; cf. 2 Kgs. 4:20.
152 Quoted in Short, 1953, 37.
153 S. Munter in Rosen, 1977, 7.
154 Deut. 23:11; Lev. 14:3, 8; Num. 12:14; Lev. 13:46.
155 E. Neufeld, 'Hygiene Conditions in Ancient Israel (Iron Age)'. *The Biblical Archaeologist* 34 (1971), 42–66.
156 2 Sam. 11:12; Akkadian *namraku*, cf. *bīt ramaki*, 'bathroom (in a house)'.
157 Jer. 2:22; Mal. 3:2 (Heb. *neter*; Gk. *nitron*, natron). A detailed story of the cleaner's techniques c.1850 BC at Ur has survived (*Iraq* 25 (1963), 181–188).
158 Ghalioungui, 1973, 155.
159 M. Bimson, *Iraq* 42 (1980), 75–77 and notes from Dr. P. B. Adamson. Compounds were lead and manganese (black/dark brown), copper chloride (green), malachite, lapis (blue), lead sulphate, ochre (yellow), haematite (red), bone ash (white) or vegetable dyes. For anointing see J. B. Pritchard, *The Ancient Near East in Pictures relating to the Old Testament* (1969), 208–9.
160 J. Soler, 'The Dietary Prohibitions of the Hebrews', *New York Review* June 14 (1975), 24–30; only certain fish, birds and insects (locust) were allowed (Lev. 11:9–23).
161 Gen. 4:4; Lev. 11:2; Deut. 14:3; cf. *Journal Asiatique* 246 (1958), 15.
162 Kinnier Wilson in Brothwell, 1967, 206.
163 *The Wisdom of Ani*.
164 Herodotus II. 78.
165 E.g. Prov. 20:1; 31:3; Isa. 5:11; 28:7 etc.; cf. Rosen, 1977, 61–65 (delirium tremens).
166 Ghalioungui, 1973, 154; Ebers Papyrus 189, 855; Dan. 1:11–15

probably reflects the wish to be distinctive or to eat simply. There is no evidence that food at the king's table had first been offered to idols.

167 R. Ellison, 'Diet in Mesopotamia', *Iraq* 43 (1981), 33–45.

168 W. H. Shea, *Famines in the Early History of Egypt and Syro-Palestine* (1976), 129–235; *Illustrated Bible Dictionary* (1980), 617, 623–4.

169 Lam. 4:5, 8, 14f.; Kinnier Wilson, 1983, 360–1; Rosen, 1977, 55–8 (scurvy in the Talmud).

170 Ghalioungui, 1973, 42; Thompson, 1949; Kocher, 1963, passim.

171 I Sam. 16:14–23; 18:10; 19:9; Preuss, 1978, 163; Rosen, 1977, 41–81.

172 Rosen, 1977, 147; for Babylonian prayers for healing see W. W. Hallo, *Journal of the American Oriental Society* 88 (1968), 75.

173 Isa. 65:20; cf. Eccles. 8:12.

174 Abraham 175 (Gen. 25:7); Isaac 180 (Gen. 35:28); Jacob 147 (Gen. 47:28); Joseph 110 (Gen. 50:22) and Moses 120 (Deut. 34:7).

175 Cf. R. D. Greenblatt, *Search the Scriptures: Modern Medicine and Biblical Personages* (Philadelphia 1977), 111–112.

176 Lev. 19:32; Deut. 30:19–29; Prov. 16:31; 20:21; Job 5:15; cf. Ps. 37:25 and, as an ideal, Zech. 8:14; cf. Isa. 65:20; Rev. 1:14.

177 *Pirqē Aboth* 21.

178 O. R. Gurney, *The Sultan-Tepe Tablets* II (1964), 400:5–7; cf. A. Malamat, 'Longevity; Biblical Concepts and some Ancient Near Eastern Parallels', *Archiv fur Orientforschung* Beiheft 19 (1982), 215–224.

179 A. Heidel, 'Death and the Afterlife in the Old Testament', in *The Gilgamish Epic and Old Testament Parallels* (1949), 195.

180 Ghalioungui, 1973, 159.

181 W. G. Lambert in B. Alster (ed.), *Death in Mesopotamia* (1980), 53–65; A. J. Spencer, *Death in Ancient Egypt* (1982).

182 D. J. Wiseman, 'Murder in Mesopotamia', *Iraq* 36 (1974), 249–260; S. Parpola, 'The Murder of Sennacherib' in Alster, *op. cit.*, 171–182.

183 Rosen, 'Suicide in the Bible and Talmud' (1977), 199–200.

184 Rosen, 1977, 214–216.

CHAPTER TWO

1 Benjamin Lee Gordon, *Medicine throughout Antiquity* (Philadelphia: F. A. Davis, 1949), 449. Gordon's valuable work is often cursory in its secondary citations of ancient texts, biblical or otherwise. I am also much indebted throughout this section to C. J. Singer and A. Wasserstein, 'Medicine', *The Oxford Classical Dictionary* ed. N. G. L. Hammond and H. H. Scullard, 2nd ed. (Oxford, Clarendon Press, 1970), 660–664.
2 In Homer *Iliad* 2.732 Asclepius seems to be a mortal physician. Cf. Celsus, *de Medicina* Prooemium 2–3.
3 Ludwig Edelstein, 'The Hippocratic Oath: Text, Translation and Interpretation', *Ancient Medicine. Selected Papers of Ludwig Edelstein*, ed. Owsei Temkin and C. Lilian Temkin. (Baltimore, The Johns Hopkins Press, 1967), 3–63. Douglas Guthrie, *A History of Medicine* (London, Nelson, 1945) 52 takes the Hippocratic Corpus as largely authentic.
4 Singer and Wasserstein, 661.
5 See generally Edelstein, 'Greek Medicine in its Relation to Religion and Magic', *Ancient Medicine*, 205–246, esp. here 220.
6 Edelstein, 225.
7 Edelstein, 245, citing Diodorus Siculus (not verified).
8 The term was used in varying senses. See M. Wellmann in Pauly-Wissowa 2.464–466.
9 Cf. e.g. *IGRR* 4.1445, a tombstone of Smyrna recording a select bibliography of the deceased, a doctor, medical writer and historian, with 77 medical works to his credit. (cf. Pauly Wissowa 8.877–878, 'Hermogenes No. 23'). Both men are otherwise virtually unknown to us. For *archiatroi* see now G. H. R. Horsley, *New Documents Illustrating Early Christianity*, 2 (North Ryde NSW, Macquarie University, 1982), 10–19.
10 See generally Edelstein, 'The Professional Ethics of the Greek Physician', *Ancient Medicine*, 319–348; cf. 'The Hippocratic Oath', 3–63.
11 Martial, in a brief epigram (8.74), refers sarcastically to an eye-surgeon (*ophthalmicus*) turned gladiator, and performing similarly in both capacities. Cf. Guthrie, 81.
12 See now Horsley, op. cit.
13 I am indebted for this account of surgery to C. J. Singer, 'Surgery', *OCD* 1024–1025.
14 Singer and Wasserstein, *OCD* 663.
15 See chapter on Old Testament, and cf. S. Muntner, 'Medicine in Ancient Israel' in F. Rosner, *Medicine in the Bible and Talmud* (New York, KTAV, 1977), 4–10.
16 Josephus, *Jewish War* 2.8.6.136, transl. H. St. J. Thackeray in the Loeb edition. Gordon, 281, wrongly ascribes the passage to the *Antiquities*.
17 J. B. Lightfoot, *St. Paul's Epistles to the Colossians and to Philemon*, 3rd. ed. (London, Macmillan, 1879), 89–90n., citing Josephus, *Antiquities*, 8.2.5.45–48.
18 E.g. Josephus *War* 2.8.5.129; Damascus Rule 10 (G. Vermes, *The Dead Sea Scrolls in English* (Harmondsworth, Penguin, 1962), 111–112).

19 Gordon, 281, suggests that three views of disease were current popularly, of which this was the most 'advanced', the others being the attribution of its cause to spirit possession and to magic, and that these views derived not from the OT, but from Persian influence. Gordon's treatment of the texts should, however, be regarded with caution.

20 This caution applies in using the classic work of G. F. Moore, *Judaism in the First Centuries of the Christian Era,* 3 vols. (Cambridge, Mass., Harvard University Press, 1927–1930).

21 Rosner 151ff. See also C. D. Spivak in *The Jewish Encyclopedia* 8 (New York and London, Funk and Wagnall, 1 904), 409–414.

22 TB 'Abodah Zarah 25b–28b, in *The Babylonian Talmud,* ed. I. Epstein, 'Seder Neziḳin', Vol. 4 (London, Soncino Press, 1935), 129ff.

23 See the important article by A. T. Kraabel, 'The Roman Diaspora: Six Questionable Assumptions', *Journal of Jewish Studies* 33 (1982), 445–462, though I dissent in part from his treatment of the NT evidence.

24 The examples here are taken from Gerald D. Hart, 'The Diagnosis of Disease from Ancient Coins', *Archaeology* 26 (1973), 123–127. The present non-technical writer is deeply conscious throughout this chapter of the perils of trying to wield medical terms he does not properly understand and is greatly indebted to the Editor's vigilance and guidance.

25 N. Haas, 'Anthropological Observations on the Skeletal Remains from Giv'at ha-Mivtar', *Israel Exploration Journal* 20 (1970), 38–59.

26 A. Rendle Short, *The Bible and Modern Medicine* (London, Paternoster Press, 1953), 48.

27 The text in Luke is however doubtful. If the shorter reading of diverse early MSS and versions be adopted, there is no explicit mention here of payment to doctors.

28 H. van der Loos, *The Miracles of Jesus,* 101–104, tends to do this in his discussion.

29 In Modern Greek it means simply 'to do', a sense evidently deriving from the idea 'to be weary with toil', but this weakening of the word seems to be a quite recent development. (G. P. Shipp, *Modern Greek Evidence for the Ancient Greek Vocabulary* (Sydney UP, 1979), 464–466.

30 *Loukas* (Luke) was a familiar form in Greek of the Latin name *Lucius,* itself *Loukios* in Greek transliteration. This name appears at Acts 13:1; Rom. 16:21, but there is no ground for identifying the persons mentioned there with Luke.

31 Dublin, Hodges, Figgis and Co., and London, Longmans, Green and Co., 1882.

32 *The Style and Literary Method of Luke* (*Harvard Theological Studies* 6) (Cambridge Mass., Harvard U.P., 1920), 39–72, a book based on Cadbury's doctoral thesis. It has been said that Cadbury won his doctorate by taking away Luke's [cf. R. N. Longenecker, 'The Acts of the Apostles', *The Expositor's Bible Commentary,* ed. F. E. Gaebelein, Vol. 9 (Grand Rapids, Zondervan, 1981), 240].

33 Not very convincingly in Hobart, 292–297; W. M. Ramsay, *Luke the Physician and Other Studies in the History of Religion* (London, Hodder,

1908), and elsewhere; cf. A. Harnack, *Luke the Physician*, tr. J. R. Wilkinson (London, Williams and Norgate, 1911).

34 Cf., however, now the important study by Dr. Loveday Alexander in her unpublished D.Phil. thesis, where she argues that the prefaces have close literary affinity to those of contemporary technical rather than historical works (L. C. A. Alexander, *Luke-Acts in its Contemporary Setting, with special reference to the prefaces (Luke 1:1–4 and Acts 1:1)*, Oxford, 1977, cited by F. F. Bruce in *BJRL* 65 (1982–3) 49). This perspective could of course be consonant with 'Luke the physician'. I have not consulted the thesis, but have heard her oral presentation of its substance. See now L. Alexander, 'Luke's Preface in the context of Greek Preface-Writing', *Novum Testamentum* 28 (1986) 48–74.

35 C. J. Hemer, 'Luke the Historian', *BJRL* 60 (1977–8), 28–51, and in further studies in preparation.

36 Cf. the important studies of E. A. Judge, *The Social Pattern of Christian Groups in the First Century* (London, Tyndale Press, 1960); 'St. Paul and Classical Society', *Jahrbuch für Antike und Christentum* 15 (1972), 19–36; *Rank and Status in the World of the Caesars and St. Paul* (Christchurch NZ, University of Canterbury, 1982).

37 On the relation of the New Testament church to classical culture see now E. A. Judge, 'The Reaction against Classical Education in the New Testament', *Journal of Christian Education* 77 (July 1983), 7–14.

38 On the underlying philosophical question of miracle see C. S. Lewis, *Miracles: A Preliminary Study* (London, Geoffrey Bles, 1947). The fullest study of the miracles of the Gospels is H. van der Loos, *The Miracles of Jesus (Novum Testamentum* Supp. 9) (Leiden, Brill, 1965). See also C. F. D. Moule (ed.), *Miracles. Cambridge Studies in their Philosophy and History* (London, A. R. Mowbray, 1965); I. T. Ramsey *et al.*, *The Miracles and the Resurrection* (London, SPCK, 1964); C. Brown, *Miracles and the Critical Mind* (Grand Rapids, Eerdmans and Exeter, Paternoster, 1984).

39 For discussion of this kind of explanation see especially van der Loos, 104–113.

40 See below p.00.

41 This view has been developed recently in D. E. Nineham, *The Use and Abuse of the Bible* (London, Macmillan, 1976); cf. 'The Strangeness of the New Testament World', *Theology* 85 (1982), 171–177 and 247–255. Nineham greatly overplays the cultural alienness of the pre-Enlightenment world. See the reply by R. H. Preston, 'Need Dr. Nineham be so Negative?' *ExpT* 90 (1978–9), 275–280.

42 Miracle is of course prominent in the Lukan writings, and I am not denying this. My point is rather to stress the reserve with which he treats the subject, notably so where he was closest to the events. But he certainly believed the miracles both of Jesus and the apostles and saw great significance in them.

43 J. G. Machen, *The Virgin Birth of Christ* (London and Edinburgh, Marshall, Morgan and Scott, 1930), 217. Cf. J. Wilkinson, 'Apologetic Aspects of the Virgin Birth of Jesus Christ', *Scottish Journal of Theology* 17 (1964), 159–181, esp. 176–177, 180–181.

44 Machen, 390.

45 A. Rendle Short, 'The Virgin Birth of Our Lord and Saviour Jesus Christ', *Evangelical Quarterly* 1 (1929), 147–155, esp. 147–149. Cf. more recently R. G. Gromacki, *The Virgin Birth. Doctrine of Deity* (Grand Rapids, Baker Book House, 1974), 95–99.

46 E. L. Kessel, 'A Proposed Biological Interpretation of the Virgin Birth'. *Journal of the American Scientific Affiliation* 35.3 (Sept. 1983), 129–136.

47 Important discussions from the medical viewpoint are contained in A. R. Short, *The Bible and Modern Medicine,* 95–100; J. Wilkinson, 'The Physical Cause of the Death of Christ', *ExpT*, 83 (1971–2), 104–107 and 'The Incident of the Blood and Water in John 19:34', *Scottish Journal of Theology* 28 (1975), 149–172; also from a sceptical viewpoint, denying that Jesus died at all, in W. B. Primrose, 'A Surgeon looks at the Crucifixion', *Hibbert Journal* 47 (1948–9), 382–388.

48 Haas, *IEJ* 20 (1970) 38–59; cf. the accounts of the archaeological and epigraphical aspects of the finds, by V. Tsaferis, ibid. 18–32 and J. Naveh, 33–37; and Y. Yadin, 'Epigraphy and Crucifixion' *IEJ* 23 (1973), 18–22.

49 See M. Hengel, *Crucifixion,* transl. J. Bowden (London, SCM Press, 1977), 24–29.

50 I do not accept the textual variant which introduces the spear-thrust into Matt. 27:49 *before* the death: thus S. Pennells 'The Spear Thrust (Matt. 27:49b, *v.l.*/John 19:34)', *JSNT* 19 (1983), 99–115.

51 I am further indebted here to Dr. Robert Sibbald, who has shown me also R. Bruce-Chwatt, 'Death on the Cross', *World Medicine* 19.14 (21 April 1984), 17–19, which confirms this point. Dr. Sibbald would diagnose death in such a case by immobility, where the victim was no longer able, even under stimulus (as of the spear-thrust) to make the instinctive reaction of raising himself to breathe.

52 *ExpT* 83 (1971–2), 104–107. A special difficulty in this subject is the prevalence of assumptions, where ancient evidence has been repeatedly read in the light of pious traditions and then has seemed to corroborate practices for which no evidence exists independently. Thus the *suppedaneum* (actually 'foot-rest'), mentioned by Bruce-Chwatt 19, was, according to Wilkinson 106n, an invention of medieval art. The earliest occurrence I have found of the word (in a quite different connection) is in Lactantius (4th cent.). Even the two earlier references to breaking the legs as a punishment (Plautus *Poenulus* 886 and Cicero *Philippics* 13.12.27), neither using the word *crurifragium,* may have had the crucifixion setting arbitrarily read into them in view of John 19:31. A stronger confirmation is the fact that the crucifixion victim buried at Giv'at ha-Mivtar had had his legs deliberately broken (Haas 42), and the supposition that this was common practice in Judaea is supported by the Jewish requirement of compliance with Deuteronomy 21:23, even at times other than the Passover Sabbath.

If this discussion seems to focus unduly upon Wilkinson, it is because he has set out the options in a form accessible to the non-specialist and is at home with the exegetical, no less than with the medical, aspects of the problem. It may then become too easy to follow him in his hesitations also, where the caution of ignorance may be masked by undue dependence on his knowledgeable caution. The fact remains that it is legitimate to seek the physical cause of death, and that differing positive views are vigorously maintained.

53 R. O. Ball, 'Physical Cause of the Death of Jesus: (1) A Theological Comment', *ExpT* 83 (1971–2), 248, in response to Wilkinson.

54 K. Leese, 'Physical Cause of the Death of Jesus: (2) A Medical Opinion', ibid. 248. While we should stress the appalling cruelty and horror of crucifixion, it is not clear that loss of blood would be so large a factor at this stage, for the nails would be carefully placed in a natural anatomical tunnel, the open mesocarpal space of Destot, according to Bruce-Chwatt 17, but in the actual remains from Giv'at ha-Mivtar in the forearm, in the interosseous space between the radius and the ulna (Haas 58).

55 Leese, loc. cit.

56 Wilkinson, *SJT* 28 (1975), 149–172, citing here 161; *ExpT* 83 (1971–2), 105.

57 See Wilkinson's discussion, *SJT*, 158–169.

58 Wilkinson, *ExpT*, 106.

59 'Watery fluid from the stomach, and blood from the heart and great vessels of the thorax', A. Rendle Short, *The Bible and Modern Medicine*, 96.

60 There is a logical flaw in Wilkinson's third criterion for an acceptable solution (*SJT* 166). It need not necessarily be applicable to either side of the body: a correct solution might even permit discrimination as to which side, a question in dispute since the time of the early church. In practice this adjustment of formulation would not affect the likely range of options, for it touches only the Cameron-Rendle Short view, to which there are other, more substantial, objections.

61 Primrose, *Hibbert Journal* 47 (1948–9), 382–388.

62 Cf. further Josephus, *Life* 75. 420–421, cited against Paulus by Strauss, 737n. Josephus recognized at Tekoa three of his acquaintances among a batch of crucified prisoners, and told Titus Caesar, who had them taken down and given the most careful medical treatment. Two of them died but one survived. Josephus does not say how long they had been on the cross, presumably not long.

63 J. P. Kane, *Palestine Exploration Quarterly* 103 (1971), 103–108. It should be noticed that each of these two ossuaries also bears a charcoal graffito of an upright cross. But the Hebrew letter *tau* was a Jewish motif and it is unproven that the cross was a symbol of Christianity at a date nearly as early as this.

64 This kind of conclusion is often unacceptable today on *a priori* grounds to those who hold a world-view which denies the possibility of the supra-natural events implied here. Most modern scientific and other disciplines have been heavily, if sometimes unconsciously, influenced by the presuppositions of the *Aufklärung* (Enlightenment) of eighteenth-century Germany. The history of the influence of this movement upon certain schools of NT interpretation is especially instructive, but cannot

be pursued here. Its effect is commonly seen in the strong tendency to reconstruct and reinterpret texts to a supposedly rational theology acceptable to the critic. This engenders only an uneasy sceptical synthesis propped on a multiple compounding of special pleading. The appeal to the evidence of the text must carry a willingness to take it seriously at its ostensible value, with all due allowance for the proper qualifications of genre and context. The divine element is inseparable from the straightforward reading of the text, and there is no question about what the original writers believed and meant about it. Modern man may of course reject their view, but he should be clear when he is doing that, and not resort to the kind of gratuitous rewriting of evidence which disguises a cavalier disregard of it.

65 See especially J. M. C. Toynbee, *Death and Burial in the Roman World* (London, Thames and Hudson, 1971), 39–42. Tacitus (*Annals* 16.6) describes the elaborate embalming of Nero's empress Poppaea as a strange foreign extravagance alien to 'Roman custom' of cremation.

66 The identification embodied in the Church of the Holy Sepulchre may be traced back ultimately to the second century, and its locality, even if not the actual spot, must be conceded the strongest claim. Subsequent structure of the central shrine leaves no visible or accessible trace of the character or period of the original tomb it covers. For a good recent discussion see J. P. Kane, 'Palestinian Archaeology and the New Testament', *Religion* 2 (1972), 57–75, esp. 59–69.

67 See further C. J. Hemer, 'Bury, Grave, Tomb', *The New International Dictionary of New Testament Theology*, ed. C. Brown, Vol. 1 (Exeter, Paternoster, 1975), 263–266.

68 See E. M. Blaiklock, *Out of the Earth* (London, Paternoster, 1957), 32–39, for a clear account accepting this view of the Nazareth Decree, following Momigliano, who later thought better of his former view; cf. *Buried History* 9 (1973), 41–46.

69 See I. Wilson, *The Turin Shroud* (London, Gollancz, 1978); V. Bortin, 'Science and the Shroud of Turin', *Biblical Archaeologist* 43 (1980), 109–117.

70 I am indebted for many thoughts here to past conversations with Dr. J. P. Kane of Manchester, who has made some considerable study of the Shroud as an archaeological problem, and has a healthy, open-minded scepticism towards its claims on grounds of method. He points out for instance that the evidence of pollen from plants of Palestine and Asia Minor is presented in general terms, with no controlled mapping of the limits of distribution of the plants concerned, if indeed the evidence were recoverable for the specific periods involved.

It is curious that Primrose receives the evidence of the Shroud when denying that Jesus died.

For discussion of the evidence for the resurrection see J. N. D. Anderson, *The Evidence for the Resurrection* (London, Inter-Varsity Fellowship, 1950); *Christianity: The Witness of History* (London, Tyndale Press, 1969). A new swoon-resuscitation theory has recently been put forward by another oriental lawyer/NT scholar, J. D. M. Derrett, *The*

Anastasis: The Resurrection of Jesus as an Historical Event (Shipston-on-Stour, P. Drinkwater, 1982).

71 R. E. D. Clark, 'Men as Trees Walking', *Faith and Thought* 93 (1963), 88–94.

72 W. H. S. Jones, *Malaria and Greek History* (Manchester, U.P., 1909).

73 See the valuable discussion in E. N. Borza, 'Some Observations on Malaria and the Ecology of Central Macedonia in Antiquity', *American Journal of Ancient History* 4 (1979), 102–124. The Greek lexica render *pyretos* by the general term 'fever' as they render *lepra* by the inaccurate 'leprosy'.

74 According to Herodotus 3.33 the Persian king Cambyses suffered from the 'sacred disease'.

75 J. Wilkinson, 'The Case of the Epileptic Boy', *ExpT* 79 (1967–8), 39–42.

76 It is interesting to note that modern styles in scepticism, here as in many other areas, were already present and debated among keener intellects in the ancient world.

77 Wilkinson, 'The Case of the Bent Woman in Luke 13:10–17' *EQ* 49 (1977), 195–205.

78 Luke 13:11. The Greek might be taken as 'altogether unable . . .' (AV, RV, Moffatt, Phillips, NEB, NIV) or 'unable to straighten altogether' (RSV, Knox).

79 P. M. Shepherd however favours senile kyphosis (*The English Bible: Its Contribution to the Art and Science of Medicine,* M.D. Thesis, Glasgow, 1924). I have not seen this work, and am indebted to Dr. D. Johnson for the tabulation of Shepherd's results. We have no means of knowing the woman's age.

80 Thus L. D. Weatherhead, *Psychology, Religion and Healing* (London, Hodder and Stoughton, 1951), 60.

81 E. M. Merrins, 'The Deaths of Antiochus IV, Herod the Great, and Herod Agrippa I', *Bibliotheca Sacra* 61 (1904), 548–562.

82 Cf. Merrins, 'Biblical Epidemics of Bubonic Plague', *Bibliotheca Sacra* 61 (1904), 292–304.

83 Thus F. N. Hepper in *IBD* 3, 1238.

84 J. Barr, *The Semantics of Biblical Language* (Oxford UP, 1961), offers a sharp corrective to the popular tendency to over-interpret by accumulating connotations.

85 *Holoklēria* (wholeness, soundness) is used to express the idea in Acts 3:16. Possibly *hygieia* was avoided, as often personified as a goddess.

86 Thus Ignatius, *Ephesians* 20:2 (of c. 115 AD) calls the Eucharist a '*pharmakon* of immortality'. Whatever be thought of his forced language or of his theology, he means the word in a positive way, and this type of usage may be paralleled elsewhere.

87 J. Wilkinson, *Health and Healing. Studies in New Testament Principles and Practice* (Edinburgh, Handsel Press, 1980), 120. I am much indebted here to Wilkinson's discussion of this question (Chapter 11, 112–142).

88 Perhaps as early as c. 32, if the crucifixion and resurrection are placed in 30. In the various calculations note that the ancients usually reckoned incomplete years inclusively.

89 Among those suggestions which Wilkinson mentions in various categories of physical defect or disease are stammering, deafness, wounds from attempted crucifixion, toothache, gout, sciatica, rheumatism, recurrent renal colic, migraine, a small acute brain haemorrhage, conjunctivitis, trachoma, infestation by lice, smallpox, leprosy and brucellosis (Malta fever). Most are wholly unsupported speculations, or at most prompted by doubtful connections with passages elsewhere.

90 W. M. Ramsay, *The Church in the Roman Empire before* AD *170* (London, Hodder and Stoughton, 1893), 62–66.

91 Pisidian Antioch and the other cities mentioned lay in the southward extension of the Roman province of Galatia, though not in the original Celtic homeland of the north. In any case this is the point of arrival in territory called 'Galatia'. See F. F. Bruce, 'Galatian Problems. 2. North or South Galatians?', *BJRL* 52 (1969–70), 243–266; C. J. Hemer, 'Acts and Galatians Reconsidered', *Themelios* n.s. 2 (1976–7), 81–88. Ramsay's pioneer work on this question was a most fruitful breakthrough, and offers ground for a natural and far-reaching harmonization of the biographical evidence of Acts and Epistles.

92 M. Wellmann, 'Demosthenes No. 11', in Pauly-Wissowa-Kroll, *Realencyclopädie,* and in *Hermes* 38 (1903), 546–566. I have made a fuller study of the present topic in my book *The Letters to the Seven Churches of Asia in their Local Setting* (Sheffield: JSOT Press, 1986), 196–199. See also *Buried History* 11 (1975), 183–184.

93 The Galen passage is known to me only in the very old edition of the Greek text in C. G. Kühn, *Medicorum Graecorum Opera Quae Exstant* (Leipzig, 1823), Vol. 6, 439.

94 See now H. Nielsen, *Ancient Ophthalmological Agents. A pharmaco-historical study of the collyria and seals for collyria used during Roman antiquity, as well as the most frequent components of the collyria* (Odense University Press, 1974), to which I am indebted for much of the following account.

95 The texts of these stamps are collected in the *Corpus Inscriptionum Latinarum,* Vol. 13, Part 1, Fasc. 1, 559–610, Nos. 10021. 1–231. I cite No. 10021.60.

96 Wilkinson, *Health and Healing,* chapter 12, 143–158. The commentaries are sometimes disappointing here. See especially J. B. Mayor and R. V. G. Tasker.

97 There is a question whether the participle *energoumenē* should be construed actively, 'effectively working' (most translations), or passively, 'effectually exerted'.

98 See further Alan Cameron, 'The Exposure of Children and Greek Ethics', *Classical Review* 46 (1932), 105–114; D. Engels, 'The Problem of Female Infanticide in the Greco-Roman World', *Classical Philology* 75 (1980), 112–120; E. Eyben, 'Family Planning in Graeco-Roman Antiquity', *Ancient Society* (Louvain) 11–12 (1980), 5–82.

99 B. P. Grenfell and A. S. Hunt, *The Oxyrhynchus Papyri* 4, No. 744, accessible in A. Deissmann, *Light from the Ancient East,* tr. L. R. M. Strachan (London, Hodder, 1927), 167–170.

CHAPTER THREE

1 Alexander Rattray, *Divine Hygiene: Sanitary Science and Sanitarians of the Sacred Scriptures and Mosaic Code*, 2 Vols. (London, James Nisbet, 1903).
2 Gerhard Venzmer, *500 Years of Medicine* (London, Macdonald, 1972).
3 Fred Rosner, *Medicine in the Bible and the Talmud* (New York, KTAV Publishing House; Yeshiva University Press), 1977.
4 Fielding H. Garrison, *History of Medicine* (Philadelphia and London, W. B. Saunders Company, 4th Edn., 1929), 68.
5 Gordon Wenham, 'Leviticus', *The New International Commentary on the Old Testament* (Grand Rapids, W. B. Eerdmans, 1979).

CHAPTER FOUR

1 Sir Risdon Bennett, *The Diseases of the Bible* (London, Religious Tract Society, 3rd Ed. 1896).
2 J. F. A. Sawyer, *Vetus Testamentum* 26 (1976), 16.
3 Derek Browne, *The Stigma of Leprosy—a Reproach and a Challenge* (St. Bartholomew's Hospital, J. 1963), 135 (*see J.Amer.med.Ass.* 186, 1963, 67).
4 D. C. Danielssen and W. Boeck, *Traité de la spedalsked ou éléphantiasis des grecs* (Paris, 1848). (Translated from Norwegian original; Christiana, 1847).
5 G. A. Hansen, *Undersoegelser angaende spedailskhedens arsager, tildels udfoerte sammen med forstander Hartwig* (1874). English translation in *Brit. for med.chir.Rev.* 55 (1875), 459; and *Int. J.Leprosy* 23 (1955), 307.
6 Sir Godfrey Driver, personal communication (1970).
7 N. H. Snaith, *The New Century Bible, Leviticus and Numbers* (London, Nelson, 1967).
8 J. Wilkinson, 'Leprosy and Leviticus: the problem of description and identification' *Scot. J. Theology* 31 (1978), 153.
9 Hastings 'Leprosy'. *Dictionary of the Bible* (One Vol.). 2nd Ed. (Edinburgh, T. & T. Clark, 1963).
10 I. Jacobvits, personal communication (1978).
11 J. Wilkinson, 'Leprosy and Leviticus: a problem of semantics and translation' *Scot. J. Theology* 30 (1977), 153.
12 H. Danby, *Mishneh* (London, Oxford University Press, 1933).
13 L. I. Rabinowitz, 'Leprosy in the Second Temple' *Encyclopaedia Judaica* (Jerusalem, Keter Publishing House, 1971).
14 S. G. Browne, 'Leprosy: The Christian Attitude' *Expository Times* 73 (1962), 242. Reprinted in *Int.J.Leprosy* 31 (1963), 229.
15 Leprosy Review 'Editorial' 9 (1938), 48.
16 R. K. Harrison, 'Leprosy' Interpreter's Dictionary of the Bible (Nashville, Tennessee, Abingdon Press, 1962).
17 L. R. Oppenheim, quoted in O. F. Skinses, *Leprosy Review* 35 (1964), 115.
18 J. V. Kinnier Wilson, 'Leprosy in Ancient Mesopotamia' *Revue d'Assyriologie et d'Archéologie Orientale* 60 (1966), 47.
19 M. Yeoli, 'A "Facies Leontia" of Leprosy on an Ancient Canaanite Jar' *J.Hist. Med.* 10 (1955), 331. Reprinted in *Int. J. Leprosy* 30 (1962), 211.
20 J. Lowe, 'Comments on the history of Leprosy' *Indian med. Gaz.* 77 (1942), 180. Reprinted in *Leprosy Rev.* 18 (1947), 54.
21 Browne (1963).
22 Johs G. Andersen, 'Studies in the Mediaeval Diagnosis of Leprosy in Denmark' *Danish Med. Bull.* 16, Suppl.IX (1969), 1.
23 V. Moeller-Christensen, *Bone Changes in Leprosy* (Copenhagen, Munksgaard; Bristol, John Wright, 1961).
24 V. Moeller-Christensen, 'Diseases of Ancient Man' *British Medical Journal* 1 (1962), 852.

25 T. Dzierzykray-Rogalski, 'Paleopathology of the Ptolemaic inhabitants of Dahkleh Oasis (Egypt)' *Journal of Human Evolution* 9 (1980), 71–74.
26 G. Elliott Smitth and W. R. Dawson, *Egyptian Mummies* (London, 1924).
27 J. L. Rowling, 'Pathological Changes in Mummies' *Proc. Roy. Soc. Med.* 54 (1961), 409.
28 J. Thorwald, *Science and Secrets of Early Medicine* (London, Thames and Hudson, 1962).
29 V. Moeller-Christensen, 'The History of Syphilis and Leprosy—an osteo-archaeological approach' *Abbotemps,* Book 1 (1969), 20.
30 R. Edwards, 'The Challenge of Leprosy' *Middlesex Hosp. J.* 63 (1963), 61, 72.
31 O. F. Skinses, 'Leprosy in Society' *Leprosy Rev.* 35 (1964). 21, Leprosy has appeared on the face; 105, The pattern of concept and reaction of leprosy in oriental antiquity; 175, The relationship of the social to the medical pathology of leprosy.
32 F. C. Lendrum, 'The Name "Leprosy" ' *Amer. J.trop.Med.Hyg.* 1 (1952), 999.
33 R. G. Cochrane, *Biblical Leprosy—a Suggested Interpretation* (London, Tyndale Press, 1961).
34 E. V. Hulse, 'The Nature of Biblical Leprosy and the use of alternative medical terms in modern translations of the Bible' *Palestine Exploration Quarterly* 107 (1975), 87.
35 J. Tas, 'On the leprosy of the Bible'. *Actes de 7e Congrès intern.d'Histoire des Sciences, à Jerusalem* (1955), 583.
36 W. MacArthur, 'Mediaeval "Leprosy" in the British Isles' *Leprosy Rev.* 24 (1953), 8.
37 S. G. Browne, 'Some Aspects of the History of Leprosy: The Leprosie of Yesterday' *Proc. Roy. Soc. Medicine* 68 (1975), 485.
38 J. M. Kerr, 'Social factors operating against effective leprosy control in the Highlands of Papua New Guinea', *Papua New Guinea Med.J.* 16 (1975), 118.
39 K. P. C. A. Gramberg, 'Leprosy and the Bible', *Trop. Geogr. Medicine* 11 (1959), 127. Reprinted in *The Bible Translator* (1960), 11.
40 Matt. 8:2–4; 10:8; 26:6; Mark 1:40–45; 14:13; Luke 4:27; 5:12–15; 7:22; 17:11–19.
41 Sir Godfrey Driver, personal communication (1974).

CHAPTER FIVE

All biblical references are taken from the *New International Version* (except where stated).

1 R. F. R. Gardner, *Abortion, the personal dilemma* (Exeter, Paternoster Press, 1972).
2 Aldous Huxley, *Brave New World* (1932).
3 M. Warnock, *Report of the Committee of Inquiry into Human Fertilization and Embryology* (HMSO, 1984).
4 D. M. Mackay, 'The Beginnings of Personal Life' . . . *'In the Service of Medicine' Journal of Christian Medical Fellowship*. Vol. 30, 2 (No. 118) (1984), 9.
5 'The Beginning of Life' Editorial Commentary. *'In the Service of Medicine' Journal of the Christian Medical Fellowship*. Vol. 29:3, No. 115 (1983), 2.
6 F. A. Schaeffer and C. C. Koop, *Whatever Happened to the Human Race?* (London, Marshall, Morgan and Scott, 1978).
6a F. A. Schaeffer and C. C. Koop (Supplement to above book dealing with recorded public discussion).
7 G. Wenham, 'A Biblical Theologian Looks at Abortion' *Third Way* (July/Aug. 1984) Reprinted by CARE Trust 1983.
8 G. R. Dunstan, *Dictionary of Medical Ethics* (Darton, Longman and Todd, 1981), 7.
9 D. J. Wiseman, Cross Reference in 'Bible and Medicine' (1986).
10 V. Turnbull, 'Abortion how early, how late, how legal?' *British Medical Journal* (1979), ii 253.
11 Supreme Court of U.S., 23.1.73 (Roe v. Wade and Doe v. Bolton).
12 G. Stirrat, *Legalised Abortion—the continuing dilemma* (London, Christian Medical Fellowship, 1979).
13 D. W. Vere, 'Working out Salvation: Is there a Christian Ethic?' *'In the Service of Medicine' Journal of the Christian Medical Fellowship*. Vol. 30:1. No. 117 (1984), 13.

Other Relevant Reading

Christian Medical Fellowship (1984) 'Respect for Life'—a Symposium.
O. O'Donovan, *The Christian and the Unborn Child* (Grove Booklet on Ethics No. 1, 1973).
B. N. Nathanson, *Aborting America* (Toronto, Life Cycle Books, 1979).
C. G. Scorer, *Life in our Hands* (England, IVP, 1978).
C. G. Scorer and A. Wing (Eds.), *Decision Making in Medicine* (London, Arnold, 1979).
D. Shoemaker, *Abortion, the Bible and the Christian* (Michigan, Baker, 1976).
H. S. Smyth, *The Value of Human Life* (London, C.M.F., 1979).
R. Winter, 'Abortion, The Continuing Ambivalence', *Third Way* (July/Aug, 1982). Reprinted by CARE Trust 1983.

CHAPTER SIX

1 F. E. Kenyon, 'Homosexuality—Male and Female', *Teach-In* (August 1974).
2 A. W. Steinbeck, 'Of Homosexuality: The Current State of Knowledge' in D. J. Atkinson, *Homosexuals in the Christian Fellowship, Latimer Studies 5/6* (Latimer House, 1979).
3 Peter Coleman, *Christian Attitudes to Homosexuality* (SPCK, 1980), 116.
4 Tertullian, *De Pudicitia* (T. & T. Clark), 64.
5 D. J. Atkinson, *Homosexuals in the Christian Fellowship, Latimer Studies 5/6* (Latimer House, 1979), 12.
6 H. Thielicke, *The Ethics of Sex* (James Clarke, ET 1964), 282.
7 Quoted in Peter Coleman, *Christian Attitudes to Homosexuality*, 138.
8 Peter Coleman, op. cit., 142.
9 Quoted in Peter Coleman, op. cit., 140.
10 A. C. Kinsey *et al.*, *Sexual Behaviour in the Human Male* (W. B. Saunders, 1948).
11 'Psychiatry and the Homosexual: A Brief Analysis of Oppression' (Gay Information 1973).
12 H. Ruitenbeck, *Homosexuality: A Changing Picture* (Souvenir Press, 1973), 13.
13 From the tape recording of the meeting. Quoted by D. J. Atkinson, op. cit., 7.
14 'A Christian Understanding of Human Sexuality'. *Methodist Report* (1979).
15 'Homosexual Relationships'. *Report of a special working party of the Church of England Board of Social Responsibility* (October 1979).
16 *The Nottingham Statement* (Falcon Books, 1977), Section R3.
17 H. Kimball Jones, *Towards a Christian Understanding of the Homosexual* (Association Press, N.Y., 1966), 108. Quoted in D. J. Atkinson, op. cit., 18.
18 Norman Pittenger, *Time for Consent* (SCM Revised Edition, 1976), 75.
19 From the literature of the Gay Christian Movement.
20 D. Sherwin Bailey, *Homosexuality and the Western Christian Tradition* (Longmans, 1955).
21 Letha Scanzoni and Virginia R. Mollenkott, *Is the Homosexual My Neighbour?* (S.C.M., 1978), 61.
22 Richard F. Lovelace, *Homosexuality and the Church* (The Lamp Press, 1978), 94.
23 D. J. Atkinson, *Homosexuals in the Christian Fellowship*, 93.
24 Ibid.
25 John Green, David Miller, 'Male homosexuality and sexual problems' *Brit. J. Hosp. Med.* (June 1985), 353.
26 A. W. Steinbeck, op. cit., 38, 41.
27 Elizabeth Moberly, 'Homosexuality: Structure & Evaluation', *Theology* (May 1980).
28 Irving Bieber *et al.*, *Homosexuality: a psychoanalytic study* (New York, Basic Books Inc., 1962).

29 J. Money, quoted in *New Zealand Listener* March, 15, 1986.
30 Alan Bell, Martin Weinberg and Sue Hammersmith, *Sexual Preference* (Indiana University Press, 1981), 218, 219.
31 E. Mansell Pattison and Myrna Loy Pattison, 'Ex-Gays': Religiously Mediated Change in Homosexuals' *Am. J. Psychiatry* 137 (12 December, 1980), 1562.
32 Ibid., 1558–1559.
33 W. H. Masters & V. E. Johnson, *Homosexuality in Perspective* (Boston, Little, Brown & Co., 1979).
34 A. C. Kinsey *et al.*, op cit.
35 J. Bancroft, *Deviant Sexual Behaviour: Modification & Assessment* (New York, Oxford University Press, 1974).
36 Richard F. Lovelace, op. cit., 65–86. Leanne Payne, an American counsellor, who has helped many people with sexual identity problems, gives very helpful insights into the root causes and psychodynamics of homosexuality in her books *Crisis in Masculinity* and *The Broken Image* (Crossway Books, USA). She writes very helpfully but I believe a little over-optimistically about the speed of change and healing.

CHAPTER SEVEN

Biblical references and quotations are taken from the New International Version.

I am grateful to Dr. Alexander Cooper, Dr. Ruth Sims and Dr. Charles Sims for their helpful comments.

1 G. Zilboorg and G. W. Henry, *A History of Medical Psychology* (New York, W. W. Norton & Co., 1941).
2 King James I *Daemonologie, in form of a dialogue* (Edinburgh, Waldegrave, 1597), cited in R. Hunter and I. Macalpine, *Three Hundred Years of Psychiatry, 1535–1860* (London, Oxford University Press, 1963).
3 H. Falret, 'On the construction and organization of establishments for the insane' *American Journal of Insanity* 10, (1854), 218–267.
4 A. Huxley, *The Devils of Loudun* (Harmondsworth, Penguin Books Ltd., 1952).
5 I. Veith, *Hysteria: The History of a Disease* (University of Chicago Press, 1965).
6 S. Freud, *Three Contributions to the Theory of Sex.*
7 B. W. Tuchman, *A Distant Mirror* (Alfred A. Knopf, USA, 1978).
8 N. Cohn, *Europe's Inner Demons* (Sussex University Press, 1975).
9 J. W. Goethe, *Fauste* (1832), trs. P. Wayne (Harmondsworth, Penguin Books Ltd., 1949).
10 K. Jaspers, *General Psychopathology* (1962), trs. from the German 7th Edition by J. Hoenig and M. W. Hamilton (University Press, Manchester).
11 C. S. Lewis, *The Last Battle* (London, Bodley Head, 1956).
12 A. C. P. Sims, *Neurosis in Society* (Basingstoke, Macmillan, 1983).
13 World Health Organization, *International Statistical Classification of Diseases, Injuries and Causes of Death;* 9th Revision (Geneva, W.H.O., 1977).
14 Daily Telegraph, 'Unbalanced judge beat "devil" wife' (Friday, October 29, 1982), 3.
15 J. P. Watson, 'Aspects of personal meaning in schizophrenia' in *Personal Meanings,* E. Shepherd and J. P. Watson (eds.) (Chichester, John Wiley & Sons, 1982).
16 A. F. Cooper, 'Possession and exorcism' *The Scottish Baptist Magazine* (November 1975), 10–11.
17 W. Sargent, *The Mind Possessed* (London, Heinemann, 1973).
18 W. H. Trethowan, 'Exorcism: A psychiatric viewpoint', *Journal of Medical Ethics* 2 (1976), 127–137.
19 J. C. Barker, *Scared to Death* (London, Muller, 1968).

CHAPTER EIGHT

Select Bibliography

Donald Bridge and David Phypers, *Spiritual Gifts and the Church* (Leicester, IVP, 1973).
Jones D. Caradog, *Spiritual Healing: an objective study of a perennial grace* (London, Longmans, Green & Co., 1955).
James H. Casson, *Dying: the greatest adventure of my life* (London, CMF, 1980).
Joni E. Eareckson, *Joni* (Glasgow, Pickering & Inglis, 1978).
Reginald East, *Heal the Sick* (London, Hodder, 1977).
V. Edmunds and Gordon C. Scorer (eds.), *Some Thoughts on Faith Healing* 3rd Edn. (London, CMF, 1979).
Ann England (ed.), *We Believe in Healing* (Basingstoke, Marshall, Morgan & Scott, 1982).
Evelyn Frost, *Christian Healing* (London, Mowbrays, 1940).
Henry Frost, *Miraculous Healing* (London, Marshall, Morgan & Scott, 1961).
Monica Furlong, *Burrswood—Focus of Healing* (London, Hodder, 1978).
Phyllis L. Garlick, *Man's Search for Health: a study in the inter-relation of religion and medicine* (Highway Press, 1952).
Charles W. Gusmer, *The Ministry of Healing in the Church of England: an ecumenical-liturgical study*. (Mayhew-McCrimmon, 1974).
Roger F. Hurding, As Trees Walking (Exeter, The Paternoster Press, 1982).
Morton Kelsey, *Healing & Christianity: in ancient thought and modern times* (London, SCM, 1973).
R. A. Lambourne, *Community, Church and Healing* (London, Darton, Longman & Todd, 1963).
Roy Lawrence, *Invitation to Healing* (Eastbourne, Kingsway, 1979).
C. S. Lewis, *Miracles* (London, Collins, 1947).,
Francis MacNutt, *Healing* (Ave Maria Press, 1974; Bantam, 1977).
Francis MacNutt, *The Power to Heal* (Ave Maria Press, 1977).
Morris Maddocks, *The Christian Healing Ministry* (London, SPCK, 1981).
Bernard Martin, *The Healing Ministry in the Church* (London, Lutterworth Press, 1960).
W. J. Sheils (ed.), *The Church and Healing: papers read at Meetings of the Ecclesiastical History Society* (Oxford, Blackwell, 1982).
Benjamin B. Warfield, *Miracles: Yesterday and Today, True and False* (Grand Rapids, Eerdmans ed., 1965).
Michael Wilson, *The Church is Healing* (London, SCM Press, 1966).
Michael Wilson, *Health is for People* (London, Darton, Longman & Todd, 1975).

NOTES

1 Morris Maddocks, *The Christian Healing Ministry* (London, SPCK, 1981), 7.

2 Michael Wilson, *The Church is Healing* (London, SCM Press, 1966), 18.
3 Albrecht Oepke in Kittel (ed.), *Theological Dictionary of the New Testament* Vol. III (Grand Rapids, Eerdmans, 1965), 201.
4 The Jerusalem Bible.
5 Morton Kelsey, *Healing and Christianity* (London, SCM Press, 1973), Chapter 4.
6 Donald Coggan, *Convictions* (London, Hodder, 1975), 272 quoted in Maddocks op. cit., 9.
7 See, in particular, Colin Brown, *The New International Dictionary of New Testament Theology* (Exeter, The Paternoster Press, 1976), Vol. 2, 163ff., Vol. 3, 205ff.
8 Maddocks, op. cit., 10.
9 For a helpful comparison between Ancient Medicine and Jesus' healing ministry, see: Oepke in Kittel (ed.), op. cit., 195–215.
10 op. cit., 198.
11 Kenneth Walker, *The Story of Medicine* (The Anchor Press, 1959), 38.
12 Kelsey, op. cit. Chapter 5 lists these as: touch only—Mark 6:5; Luke 22:51; word only—Mark 5:8; Luke 17:14; John 4:50; 5:8; 11:43.
13 op. cit., 87.
14 Bertold Klappert in Brown (ed.), op. cit., Vol. 2, 384.
15 R. A. Lambourne, *Community, Church and Healing* (London, Darton, Longman and Todd, 1963), 35–43.
16 Evelyn Frost, *Christian Healing* (London, Mowbrays, 1940), 50.
17 op. cit., 120.
18 op. cit., 66.
19 Kelsey, op. cit., 185–7.
20 Martin Luther, *Letters of Spiritual Counsel* (ed. 1955), 51f. quoted in Kelsey, op. cit., Chapter 9.
21 Peter C. Williams, 'Healing and Evangelism: The Place of Medicine in later Victorian Protestant Missionary Thinking' in W. J. Sheils (ed.), *The Church and Healing: Papers read at Meetings of the Ecclesiastical History Society* (Oxford, Blackwell, 1982), 272.
22 For a fuller account of initiatives on healing, see Maddocks, op. cit., 103–111.
23 Charles W. Gusmer, *The Ministry of Healing in the Church of England* (Mayhew-McCrimmon, 1974), 12.
24 Stuart Mews, 'The Revival of Spiritual Healing in the Church of England 1920–26', in Sheils (ed.) op. cit., 304–331.
25 Monica Furlong, *Burrswood—Focus of Healing* (London, Hodder, 1978), 29, 30.
26 C. S. Lewis, *Miracles* (London, Bles, 1947), 9.
27 Wilhelm Mundle in Brown (ed.), op. cit., Vol. 2, 620–1.
28 Ruth Carter Stapleton, *The Experience of Inner Healing* (London, Hodder, 1978), Introduction.
29 Kenneth McAll, *Healing The Family Tree* (Sheldon Press, 1982).
30 Benjamin B. Warfield, *Miracles: Yesterday and Today, True and False* (Grand Rapids, Eerdmans, edn. 1965), 5, 6.
31 op. cit., 191.

32 op. cit., 157ff.
33 See Roger F. Hurding, *As Trees Walking* (Exeter, The Paternoster Press, 1982), 208–215 for a fuller consideration of this 'triumphalism' in approaches to healing.
34 Gusmer, op. cit., 21ff.
35 Rex Gardner, 'Miracles of Healing in Anglo-Celtic Northumbria as recorded by the Venerable Bede and his contemporaries: a reappraisal in the light of twentieth century experience' *British Medical Journal* 24–31 (Dec. 1983, Vol. 287), 1927–1933.
36 See Hurding op. cit. (particularly 208–236) where the double theme of healing and suffering is explored.
37 Michael Harper, *Church of England Newspaper* (March 9, 1984), 14.
38 Lambourne, op. cit., 60.

CHAPTER NINE

1 O. Hallesby, *Conscience* (London, Hodder and Stoughton, 1939).
2 A. A. Hodge, *Outlines of Theology* (Grand Rapids, Eerdmans, 1928), 283.
3 R. H. Preston, *A Dictionary of Christian Ethics*, ed. J. Macquarrie (London, SCM Press, 1967).
4 E. Brunner, *Nature and Grace* (London, Geoffrey Bles, 1946), 25.
5 J. Newton, *Thoughts Upon the African Slave Trade* (London, 1788).
6 W. Hordern, *A Dictionary of Christian Theology*, ed. A. Richardson (London, SCM Press, 1969), 71.
7 D. Stafford Clarke, *What Freud really said* (London, Macdonald, 1965), 202–204.
8 S. Freud, *New Introductory Lectures on Psychoanalysis* (London, Hogarth Press), 80ff.
9 C. H. Waddington, *The Humanist Frame*, ed. J. Huxley (London, George Allen and Unwin, 1961), 72–73.
10 J. Huxley, op. cit., 44–45.
11 British Medical Association, *Handbook of Medical Ethics* (London, British Medical Association, 1981).
12 L. Alexander, 'Medical Science under Dictatorship' *New Eng. J. Med.* 241 (1947), 39–47.
13 J Watt, 'Conscience and Responsibility' *Brit. Med. J.* Vol. 281 (1980), 1687–1688.

Index